# Community in Contemporary British Fiction

# Community in Contemporary British Fiction

*From Blair to Brexit*

Edited by
Sara Upstone and Peter Ely

BLOOMSBURY ACADEMIC
LONDON • NEW YORK • OXFORD • NEW DELHI • SYDNEY

BLOOMSBURY ACADEMIC
Bloomsbury Publishing Plc
50 Bedford Square, London, WC1B 3DP, UK
1385 Broadway, New York, NY 10018, USA
29 Earlsfort Terrace, Dublin 2, Ireland

BLOOMSBURY, BLOOMSBURY ACADEMIC and the Diana logo are trademarks of Bloomsbury Publishing Plc

First published in Great Britain 2023
Paperback edition published 2024

Copyright © Sara Upstone, Peter Ely and contributors, 2023, 2024

The editors and contributors have asserted their right under the Copyright, Designs and Patents Act, 1988, to be identified as Authors of this work.

For legal purposes the Acknowledgements on p. ix constitute an extension of this copyright page.

Cover design by Eleanor Rose
Cover image: Time Forms, Anna Lytridou, 2020, acrylic, coloured pencils and pastel on paper.

All rights reserved. No part of this publication may be reproduced or transmitted in any form or by any means, electronic or mechanical, including photocopying, recording, or any information storage or retrieval system, without prior permission in writing from the publishers.

Bloomsbury Publishing Plc does not have any control over, or responsibility for, any third-party websites referred to or in this book. All internet addresses given in this book were correct at the time of going to press. The author and publisher regret any inconvenience caused if addresses have changed or sites have ceased to exist, but can accept no responsibility for any such changes.

A catalogue record for this book is available from the British Library.

A catalog record for this book is available from the Library of Congress.

ISBN: HB: 978-1-3502-4402-3
PB: 978-1-3502-4406-1
ePDF: 978-1-3502-4403-0
eBook: 978-1-3502-4404-7

Typeset by Newgen KnowledgeWorks Pvt. Ltd., Chennai, India

To find out more about our authors and books visit www.bloomsbury.com and sign up for our newsletters.

*For Sheila Mirchandani (PE) and Daniel Tong (SU)*

# Contents

Acknowledgements ix
List of Contributors x

Introduction: Rewriting community in an age of crisis and nostalgia 1
   *Peter Ely and Sara Upstone*

Part 1   National Community

1   'The little links are broke': Ethnocentrism, Englishness and loneliness in contemporary political science, political theory and contemporary British fiction 25
   *Robert Eaglestone*
2   'Our uneasy mixed community': Cross-community romance, magic realism and Northern Ireland 45
   *Alison Garden*
3   Incomers and settlers: Nomadism and entanglement in contemporary Scottish fiction 67
   *Timothy C. Baker*

Part 2   Speculative Community

4   Beyond the multicultural: Queer community in Jackie Kay's *Trumpet* 89
   *Peter Ely*
5   Community versus commodity: Neoliberalism and (sub)urban identities in twenty-first-century London novels 111
   *Caroline Lusin*
6   Writing othered Asian British skins: Interrogating racism in fictional Asian British communities 131
   *Devon Campbell-Hall*

Part 3  Precarious Community

7   Performing the nation: A disunited kingdom in Jonathan Coe's *Middle England*  155
    Kristian Shaw
8   'Why would you play a game like that?': Community and the pandemic in Kazuo Ishiguro's *Klara and the Sun*  177
    Emily Horton
9   Even the ghosts: Community in the wake  199
    Sara Upstone

Index  221

# Acknowledgements

Acknowledgements sections are where our academic, literary and familial communities can be found, even where we sign a text largely with a single name. They remind us that every writer contains multitudes.

Our sincere thanks to our excellent editors at Bloomsbury, who have been so supportive and encouraging throughout the project. We are grateful to our esteemed contributors, who have entered into dialogue about the project with a generosity that embodies many of the very best features of community that this book endeavours to support. Community is a concept that provokes a wide range of thoughts and subject matters, and we are thankful for the stimulating array of political, philosophical and social subjects as well as the diverse range of literary texts it has brought together in this book.

Much of the work in this collection is very new, responding to contemporary events as they appear now with striking regularity. Nonetheless, some of the ideas presented have been brewing for a long time, and we thank Kingston University for supporting much of this research, as well as Goldsmiths, University of London, Warwick University and Loughborough University, BACLS and Writers' Kingston (amongst many others) for hosting conferences and events where these ideas have been discussed and developed.

Crucial collaborators have been found in Fidelma Murphy, Kate Scott, Steven Fowler, Evangeline Upstone-Tong, Daniel Tong, Sofi Shall, Isabell Dahms, Alva Gotby and Iain Campbell, who have offered insight, inspiration and correction.

# Contributors

**Timothy C. Baker** is Personal Chair in Scottish and Contemporary Literature at the University of Aberdeen. He is the author of five books, most recently *New Forms of Environmental Writing: Gleaning and Fragmentation* and *Reading My Mother Back: A Memoir in Childhood Animal Stories* (both 2022).

**Devon Campbell-Hall** is the Course Leader for the English degrees at Solent University, Southampton, and genuinely enjoys research-led teaching and helping students reach their potential. She is widely published in the area of postcolonial literature, particularly on the works of Monica Ali, Chitra Banerjee Divakaruni, Cauvery Madhavan, Michael Ondaatje, Ravinder Randhawa, Arundhati Roy, Kamila Shamsie, Meera Syal and Zadie Smith. Devon is an experienced PhD supervisor and examiner who has presented her research in India, Turkey, Malta, Spain, the United States and the UK.

**Robert Eaglestone** is Professor of Contemporary Literature and Thought at Royal Holloway, University of London. He is the author of seven books, including *The Broken Voice: Reading Post-Holocaust Literature* (2017), and the editor or co-editor of ten more, including *Brexit and Literature* (2018) and *The Routledge Companion to Twenty First Century Literary Fiction* (2019). His work has been translated into six languages.

**Peter Ely** is a postdoctoral researcher at Kingston University in London. His research works at the intersection of philosophy, critical theory and literature to examine the political potential of 'community' in contemporary British society. He is currently converting his PhD into a monograph entitled *The Politics of Community in Contemporary British Literature*.

**Alison Garden** is a UKRI Future Leaders Fellow at Queen's University Belfast, in the School of Arts English and Languages, where she is currently writing her second book on 'Love across the Divide' during the Northern Ireland Troubles. Alison's research explores the complicated entanglements between love, sexuality and politics in Britain and Ireland. Her first book, *The Literary Afterlives of Roger Casement 1899–2016*, was published in 2020.

**Emily Horton** is Senior Lecturer in English Literature at Brunel University, London. She is the author of *Contemporary Crisis Fictions* (2014) and editor of *The 1980s: A Decade of Contemporary British Fiction* (2014) and *Ali Smith* (with Monica Germanà, 2013).

**Caroline Lusin** holds the Chair of English Literary and Cultural Studies at the University of Mannheim. Her research focuses on contemporary British and Irish fiction and comparative literary studies. She has published monographs on Virginia Woolf and Anton Chekhov and on Anglo-Indian life-writing; her (co-) edited collections of essays includes *Community, Seriality and the State of the Nation: British and Irish Television Series in the 21st Century* (2019).

**Kristian Shaw** is Senior Lecturer in English Literature at the University of Lincoln. He released his first monograph, *Cosmopolitanism in Twenty-First Century Fiction*, in 2017. His research was funded by the Arts and Humanities Research Council. Shaw's second monograph is entitled *Brexlit: British Literature and the European Project* (2021) – a term he coined in 2016 to describe cultural responses to Brexit. He is co-editor of two collections: *Kazuo Ishiguro* (with Peter Sloane, 2022) and *Hari Kunzru* (with Sara Upstone, 2022), and serves as the co-editor for Twenty-First Century Perspectives series for Manchester University Press.

**Sara Upstone** is Professor of Contemporary Literature and Faculty Director of Postgraduate Research at Kingston School of Art, Kingston University. Her publications include *Rethinking Race and Identity in Contemporary British Fiction* (2017), *British Asian Fiction: Twenty-First-Century Voices* (2011) and *Spatial Politics in the Postcolonial Novel* (2010). She is the co-editor of *Postmodern Literature and Race* (2015), *Researching and Representing Mobilities: Transdisciplinary Encounters* (2014), *Postcolonial Spaces: The Politics of Place in Contemporary Culture* (2011) and the forthcoming *Hari Kunzru* (with Kristian Shaw, 2022). She serves as the co-editor for the Twenty-First Century Perspectives series for Manchester University Press.

# Introduction: Rewriting community in an age of crisis and nostalgia

Peter Ely and Sara Upstone

In a pivotal speech to the 1994 Labour Party Conference in Blackpool, the newly elected party leader Tony Blair sought the approval of his party for a radically new direction for politics in Britain. Taking the podium just three months after his election as leader, Blair laid out a starkly different branding for the party as 'New Labour' that would come to define his premiership from 1997 to 2007. In the second section of his speech entitled 'Rebuilding Community', Blair argued community would be the foundational ethical and political basis for a fresh vision for politics, stating his deep belief in 'society, working together, solidarity, cooperation, [and] partnership' (Blair 1996: 38). Community would prove vital for his rethinking of the Socialist principles upon which his party had thus far been founded, allowing for a redefinition of Socialism itself:

> It is not the socialism of Marx or state control. It is rooted in a straightforward view of society: in the understanding that the individual does best in a strong and decent community of people, with principles and standards and common aims and values. It is social-ism. We are the party of the individual because we are the party of community. (38–9)

In seeking to revalorize 'community' Blair clearly had in mind the figure of Margaret Thatcher, whose influence still loomed large over British politics. Thatcher encapsulated her political project through the claim that 'there is no such thing as society', locating the realm of political right solely in the space of the 'individual' and their 'families' and denying any other positionality or communality as a legitimate political actor. Despite Blair's enduring commitment to a broadly Thatcherite, globalized, laissez-faire and market-driven economy, he sought to distance himself from Thatcher's atomistic political perspective by proposing community as a new ethical basis upon which this economic project could develop. In so doing, Blair set in motion an influential model for understanding British society, combining an investment in market capitalism with a progressive relation to culture which was to be reimagined as diverse and dynamic, just like the new neoliberal market logic that underpinned it. Writing in the Labour-aligned think tank *Demos*, Mark Leonard's influential report 'Britain™: Renewing Our Identity' (1997), a rebranding exercise for the nation, proposed the figure of 'Cool Britannia' as a new model of national identity. For Leonard, Britain had always been 'a hybrid nation' encompassing a great number of stories and communities: '[t]ogether', these 'add up to a new vision of Britain as a global island, uniquely well placed to thrive in the more interconnected world of the next century' (3).

This vision of community from Blair and his policy advisors, despite its apparent departure from Thatcherism, nonetheless maintained strong investments in the figure of the 'individual' as well as a unified, national community. A rhetoric of community allowed for such figures themselves to be reinvented through the lens of culture, which, for then secretary of state for culture Chris Smith, 'gives us a sense of identity both as individuals and as a nation' and is therefore something that 'lies at the very heart of [the] mission of the new government' (Bewes and Gilbert 2000: 7–8). During this period, philosopher Gillian Rose observed that the development of this new politics meant that 'political identity is no longer formed by class interests and allegiance' but is increasingly located within community 'interest group[s]' defined through discrete categories of ethnicity, race, religion, language or gender (1996: 3–4). For Rose, this turn to the communitarian coincides with decreasing awareness of 'actualities of structure and authority', where communities increasingly cannot imagine a political society that goes beyond its current configuration, rather simply attempting to find recognition within it. Following Blair's vision of community, which allows for 'a more rational idea of self-interest ... recognizing that people need to cooperate as well as compete' (1996: 218), community was acknowledged at the same time as subordinated to a neoliberal economic logic which it was ultimately unable to effectively challenge.

This book's subtitle, 'From Blair to Brexit', demarcates a periodization which has been defined by these competing logics – on the one hand, a departure from Thatcherite principles in favour of a revitalized commitment to community at both local and national levels but, on the other, a 'conclusive and irrefutable [neoliberal] hegemonisation' (Bewes and Gilbert 2000: 1) that has placed such commitment increasingly under erasure. For many critics, New Labour advocated a progressive future based in a new articulation of a politics of aspiration but nonetheless did 'not reduce ... inequality [or] social exclusion' (Levitas 2005: 229). Likewise, it advocated a pluralized, diverse and multicultural society but repeatedly invested in a vision in relation to both domestic and global politics that would undermine the possibility of an inclusive sense of either national or local community.

In domestic politics, these tensions solidified in the summer of 2001, when riots broke out in parts of northern England, led by predominantly young Asian men from the deprived towns of Oldham, Bradford and Burnley. For Ash Amin writing in 2003, the riots were a sign that Labour's creation of a society ostensibly 'repelled by racially motivated violence and harassment, institutional racism, and discrimination' was giving way to a mood 'disturbingly reminiscent of the Thatcher years, when it was only the strangeness of the stranger that was noted' (460). The riots, however, were not just about racism but also about the inflection of that racism through a lens of growing austerity, the dual forces of 'deprivation and desperation' (461). Just a year earlier the Trussell Trust established the first UK food bank when Paddy Trussell started his own emergency food supply service for the local people of Salisbury from his garage. A striking indictment of the lack of government action over economic disadvantage, the location of food banks in local areas asked the public to contribute directly to the welfare of those most in need in the streets surrounding them, described in Trussell publicity as 'grassroots, community organisations aimed at supporting people who cannot afford the essentials in life'. By 2020, there were more than twelve hundred food banks in operation across the UK within the Trussell Network alone (which accounts for two-thirds of all UK food banks), distributing around 1.6 million emergency food supply packages. There were twenty-eight thousand volunteers working in these local centres.

If food banks were a sign of local community filling the void left by government neglect, then the political response to the 2001 riots led to a new government approach in 'community cohesion'. Defined in opposition to ethnic association and in favour of a collective commitment to shared values and a way of life, it was presented by the government as the solution to social discord in the resurrection of local and national bonds of allegiance. While the term quickly gained traction and became the subject of multiple government reports and initiatives, it was also the subject of intense criticism from many academics and civil rights organizations (Cantle 2001; Denham 2002; Pilkington 2008). Community cohesion, these voices argued, was a shorthand for assimilation – legitimizing through the positive connotations attached to community a policy designed to demand that minorities modify their behaviours and values to appease a white, middle-class majority (Rhodes 2009).

On a global scale, this tension was felt most starkly in the declaration of war against Iraq in 2003, following military action against Afghanistan in response to the attacks on the World Trade Center on 11 September 2001. The fallout of the terrorist attacks in the United States consisted in a sharp rise in Islamophobia and a return of the racist rhetoric associated, in Britain at least, with the 1980s under Thatcher's Conservative government. A decision which has haunted the legacy of the New Labour administration, military intervention in Iraq has been seen as a failure to address the corrosive racial politics that had emerged, ushering in a period associated not only with Islamophobia but also with the demonization of asylum seekers and the erosion of religious and ethnic tolerance (Moosavi 2015). At the same time, the national feeling against the war created a new sense of both global and grassroots community. On the weekend of 15 and 16 February 2003, protesters in London made up approximately one million of what is estimated to have been between six and ten million protesters across the world marching against the proposed military action.

If Blair was to advocate a multicultural vision which saw Britain's diverse communities and cultures as part of its global brand, the Conservative-Liberal coalition government which followed in 2010 only intensified the strategic use of community for the furtherance of neoliberal principles through its policy of 'Big Society'. Initially the flagship policy of David Cameron's election campaign, 'Big Society' was adopted by the coalition and centred around increased emphasis on local decision-making, community volunteering and citizenship. Yet the policy came in the context of cuts to public spending, leading to criticisms that it was designed not to empower communities but rather to reduce its commitment to state welfare. In 2015, an audit by the Civil Exchange think tank reported that 'The Big Society has not reached those who need it most. We are more divided than before' (Slocock 2015: 4).

As many commentators have recognized, this context makes the result of the 2016 European referendum in many ways unsurprising; rather than a sharp break from the past, the resurgent nationalist sentiment surrounding the vote can be seen as the last vestiges of a desire for collective identification violently eroded by its strategic usage in the service of neoliberal politics. By 2015, the UK OECD ranking on income inequality placed it twenty-eighth out of thirty-four countries, far closer to the United States (who ranked thirty-first) than its European neighbours (Slocock 2015: 47), and these rankings were a prescient indicator of an evolving national mood that would have more in common with the turn to fundamentalism in US politics than to identification with Europe. The failure to construct meaningful, anti-austerity politics and a genuine commitment to inclusive social welfare led to what Robert Eaglestone (2019) terms a cruel nostalgia in which the void of the recent past was eschewed by the general public in favour of an idealized imagining of a historic Britain to which departure from the European Union became irredeemably attached.

The referendum result is thus symptomatic rather than causative; as Lisa McKenzie (2017) has argued, it is indelibly linked to a class politics which transcends left and right, where the working classes since Blair have been universally socially excluded. We mark it here as the explicit realization of a political ambivalence implicit in the construction of community for so long but also as a useful limit point for a trajectory in which there has been an increasingly intensified and normalized concern with 'the ostensible problems of immigration, multiculturalism, and ethnic diversity' across much of political discourse (Valluvan and Kalra 2019: 2394). An increasing body of analysis has sought to define the current era as one largely characterized by revamped and growing nationalist sentiment, where feelings of collective belonging and national community have been resuscitated through the 'exclusionary politics of Othering' (2394). Such nationalist investments are not restricted to a small minority or traditionally illiberal constituencies within British society; rather they are part of a 'methodological nationalism' present within all sectors of society, where inadequate attention to 'the imperial and colonial histories that shape most current Western national polities' has led to an especial failure in the English and British context to 'reckon with the long-standing injustices that increasingly bear down upon us' (Bhambra 2017: S227).

Neoliberal subjectivity has imposed individualism and competitiveness at every level of social life such that community has become an often-distant proposition amongst rising feelings of atomization, alienation and loneliness (Gilbert 2013). The British and Northern Irish context in this respect plays host to one of the first and most influential experiments in neoliberal statecraft, where it arguably extended a cultural and political hegemony into the deepest strata of state and public institutions. By focusing on the British and Northern Irish landscape, there is therefore a special and vital need for ways of thinking community beyond its dominant depiction and understanding since the cultural and political transformations of the 1980s. Regional and national variations are significant here – devolved government in Scotland and Wales, and the complex positioning of Northern Ireland as a nation within the United Kingdom but not formally part of 'Britain' – and have led to radically different thinking on community. This is particularly evident in terms of national identity, as evidenced in the very different referendum results in each constituent nation (with both Scotland and Northern Ireland voting in the majority to remain within the EU), and in the continued independence movement within Scotland in particular. Positioned as a 'choice between two unions' (McEwen 2018), the preference for Europe over allegiance to the UK can be read not only as a recurrence of a postcolonial politics but also as a statement in favour of devolved communal identifications. This includes a markedly different attitude to community – 'Big Society' was never a domestic policy in the devolved nations, for example; instead Scotland and Wales retained a model of 'community planning partnerships' which preceded English reform, while Northern Ireland introduced these partnerships in 2015. Such policies have retained a focus on bringing together government bodies, community groups and local businesses to work together on localized solutions without the economic drivers implicit in Big Society. While they have not been without tensions, they nevertheless indicate a 'clear dichotomy' (Pemberton 2017: 188) between England and the rest of the UK in terms of community planning, and thus the potential for alternative models of collective allegiance within the UK.

Within this context of emerging counter-discourses, there are many examples of localized community which can be cited as possible alternatives to a top-down mobilization of localized affiliation, including the tradition of local ethnic and religious communities (Ritchie 2019). To think community in these terms, the book recognizes, is to deal with a shifting signifier that is never synonymous with a particular scale or form of allegiance. Perhaps most notably, the growth of environmental activist movements such as Extinction Rebellion have offered a space for collective action that is not determined by racial group, ethnicity, wealth, gender or even political affiliation. They mark, instead, what Ted K. Bradshaw (2009) has defined as 'post-place community': the construction of networks based not on geographical location but rather on shared allegiance and a connected sense of identity. With the rise in virtual communication, such ties complicate the idea that community is where you are, with the suggestion that it might also be what you believe.

Such conceptual meeting spaces are no less susceptible, however, to co-option and manipulation. As the furore over Facebook algorithms and the role of Twitter in the growth of the Alt-Right in the United States indicate, any notion of a 'pure' grassroots movement is problematized by the ways in which online platforms manipulate user experience and how indeed they can be purposively manipulated. Equally, social reproduction theorist Sara Farris (2017) has framed evolving neoliberal uses of nationalism in the growth of care and domestic sector jobs in the neoliberal economy, where migrant and racialized women increasingly play a major role in the reproductive sphere. Focusing on how neoliberalism induces specific and novel forms of nationalism to suit its own context and goals, Farris details the rise of a 'femonationalism' that has developed the distinctive feature of combining a 'mobilization of women's rights within xenophobic campaigns' (14). These have had the effect of stigmatizing 'Muslim men' as national enemies, at the same time as framing the increasing use of Muslim women as domestic workers within a framework of 'saving' them from 'Islam as a quintessentially misogynistic religion and culture' (4). In this way, the recent 'electoral achievements' of 'far-right' nationalist parties across many countries in Europe have in part been able to repurpose feminist rhetoric and imaginaries of the liberal state in order to legitimize new forms of violent border control, xenophobia and specifically anti-Islam forms of state chauvinism and exclusion (1).

In 2020, the emergence of the Covid-19 pandemic dramatically altered again the British and Northern Irish public's relationship to questions of community. The mass support for NHS workers, exemplified in a weekly Thursday evening 'clap for the NHS' and support for those shielding by local community groups, indicates belonging at both local and national scales, typified by a shared commitment to public sector workers and to the most vulnerable, a nascent collectivism interrogative of neoliberal values and individualism. At the same time, however, the crisis has also revealed the vast injustices in British and Northern Irish society. The disproportionate level of infection in BAME populations, the scandal surrounding treatment of elderly in care homes and DNR orders for disabled patients, and the crippling financial burden on the self-employed and those forced to self-isolate all reveal the limits of diverse community in the wake of continued and deep-rooted structural injustice. At the time of writing this introduction in late 2021, the end of lockdown and the removal of most protective measures have resulted in the increased marginalization of those deemed clinically vulnerable, with little protection either in law or in daily life. Such social exclusion makes it again difficult to conceive of an inclusive sense of community and equally difficult not to see the barriers to such inclusion as intimately interwoven with questions of neoliberal politics.

## Writing community

Brexit revealed the success of nostalgically (and colonially) inflected calls to 'take back control', resonant not only with international political developments – Trump's rhetoric to 'Make America Great Again' – but also with Thatcher's similar call to 'Make Britain Great Again' in the 1970s. In this respect the vote demonstrated a *long durée* attachment of authoritarian and socially conservative politics to nationalist sentiment but also the mobilization of an imagined community particularly relevant to the concerns of this book. National community is, we often forget, a relatively recent 'invention' and 'myth' of Modernity and has a special tenacity and importance for understanding the overall political complexion of British and Northern Irish society (Hobsbawm 1990). As scholars such as Benedict Anderson and Eric Hobsbawm have made clear, the development of the nation-state coincides with the evolution of the novel as a literary form capable of encapsulating the nation in its 'simultaneity' in 'homogenous, empty time' (Anderson 1983: 25). This was a technology capable of creating and disseminating a cultural conception of the political body bound to the increasingly centralized and rationalized power of the state, which required the building of a cultural consciousness and national tradition to justify its own existence. In the current context of insurgent and novel forms of nationalism, turning to the novel and fiction more widely as a cultural form with deep resonance and affinity with the nation-state, both as an ally and as a critic, is of clear importance for the study of literature and community.

A context of globalization has induced an evolving function in fiction to provide a capacious space which can formally mirror the increasingly complex networks of capital, migration, data and commodities. For Caroline Edwards, the 'disparate' temporal and 'spatial' coordinates of contemporary life are 'interconnected at the level of narrative structure, as well as being thematically interlaced' in the 'network novel' (2018: 15) found in David Mitchell's *Cloud Atlas* (2004), Michael Cunningham's *The Hours* (1998) and Hari Kunzru's *Gods without Men* (2011) (15). Likewise, cosmopolitan perspectives have located the function of the contemporary novel in its capacity to capture the experience of our 'globalised condition' as an 'interconnected planetary community' (Shaw 2017: xiii). Such experiences can be found not only in the imaginative world-fictions of Kunzru and Mitchell but also in multicultural localities in Zadie Smith and Nadeem Aslam, where atomized contemporary life can produce a 'form of community that moves beyond merely ethnic or territorial concerns'

(22). Nick Bentley has also identified a growing concern with geographical regionality and locality in contemporary literature's exploration of community, where the 'interrogation of the concepts of Irishness, Welshness, Englishness and Scottishness has' enriched our 'cultural discourses of national identity' (2008: 260).

The twenty-first century has seen the return of the writer as public intellectual and social commentator and, in an era of systemic crisis, writers have been moved by global events to find a renewed public voice. As insurgent nationalisms, sustained economic crises, waning political and ideological hegemonies and viral contagions have laid bare the deep inequalities, precarities and violence which inhere in the relational fabric of our lives together, many writers have found community to be a valuable repository for affective and political investment. So it is that we can look to writers, in particular, to comment on the existing state of community and its future possibilities, as literature reimagines our shared lives and heterogeneous communities through creative gestures beyond the restraints of the present. Since 2008, austerity politics have been a major economic but also cultural force in British and Northern Irish life and have therefore impacted deeply on contemporary fiction, constituting the setting through which its depiction of urban life and interactions take place and providing a near inescapable context for its narratives and social evocations (Marcus 2013). Equally, as collections such as *Brexit and Literature* (2019) and Kristian Shaw's monograph *Brexlit* (2021) evidence, the challenge of Brexit has offered authors the opportunity to counter the prevailing Leave discourse with alternative possible solidarities that evidence the values of cross-cultural dialogue, while at the same time exploring the reasons for the vote through narratives that examine the erosion of global community in the wake of economic underinvestment, regional inequality and the collapse of the welfare state. Finally, an emerging discourse around Covid-19 sees authors reflecting on the meanings revealed by the virus, with Ian McEwan (2020) predictably leading the literary intervention as he did after 9/11. For Ali Smith, the connection to community around the pandemic is already evident – she recounts hearing someone say 'We're all in the same boat now' only to ask, 'Weren't we "always" in the same boat'? (Smith 2020b: n.p.).

Authors in this regard can be seen to present community in Britain and Northern Ireland within the context of a cultural moment which is yet to be defined with any clear consensus. Variously described as post-postmodernist, metamodernist, transglossic or renewalist, amongst others, the current cultural moment proceeds from an ethical turn which began in the 1990s and has been shaped in the twentieth century by concepts such as new sincerity and reality hunger which mark a sustained attention on issues of authenticity and affective connection. In keeping with community, such theories are concerned with creating meaningful connections – with the possibility of solidarity, mutual understanding and the appreciation of difference. For Peter Boxall, 'after the decline of postmodernism', the novel exhibits 'an emergent cultural imaginary – an imagined community' which nonetheless 'remains … difficult to conceive or codify' (2019: 8).

For critics such as Martin Eve (2012), this moment is not a departure from preceding postmodern cultures so much as a revelation of their underlying complexity in defiance of popular simplifications. Indeed, the representation of community in contemporary fiction includes much that resonates with the seminal philosophical texts of the late twentieth century. These texts equally oscillate between an expression of pessimistic grief at the apparent loss of communal structures and an enduring philosophical commitment to the possibility of new and genuinely inclusive community. Such positioning can be seen, for example, in Jacques Derrida's writings on democracy, hospitality and friendship; in Giorgio Agamben's *The Coming Community* (1990) and in Jean-Luc Nancy's *The Inoperative Community* (1991). Nancy's landmark work begins with the dispiritingly resonant observation that 'community' has been experienced largely through a sense of loss in the period termed Modernity. This broad historical marker, beginning with the growth of capitalism in early-twentieth-century Europe and extending to the global economic and political configurations of the present day, is said to have its 'gravest and most painful testimony' in the 'dissolution, the dislocation, or the conflagration of community' (Nancy 1991: 1). Nancy argues that to experience community through a sense of lack is also to question whether it is something that ever truly, or at least straightforwardly, existed. In this respect, Nancy's work exemplifies a response to community common in much late-twentieth-century thinking that asks whether our experiences of loss are not in fact instead a heightened awareness of a previously obscured unreality.

At the initial moment of publication of Nancy's text, thinking on community was easily aligned with postmodern ideas regarding the death of the grand narrative and the deconstruction of concepts such as authenticity and truth. Yet in the post-postmodern cultural moment, these ideas have been resurrected with the emphasis not so much on the absence they signify but on the future possibilities they potentially offer in the promise of a community, in some way 'to come'. An idea of a community yet to come, which might arise in the wake of the hybrid politics of contemporary culture, is one which emphasizes the value which comes in diversity, and which emerges in the collective voices of those marginalized in conventional top-down politics. Powerful examples of this new imagining come in texts such as David Hollinger's *Postethnic America* (1995) and Elena Kiesling's *Aesthetics of Coalition and Protest: The Imagined Queer Community* (2015). To return to community in these terms is to evoke commonality not in the denial of the lessons of postmodernism but rather in recognition of them: a post-postmodern quest for collectivity which is riven by an understanding of internal difference and the provisional and strategic nature of much affiliation. In such a way, to think of community is to radically challenge a conservative discourse of nostalgia which associates community with closed groupings and narrow or absolute concepts of identity.

Bringing together a wide and diverse range of perspectives and texts, this book seeks to demonstrate what the study of contemporary British and Northern Irish fiction can bring to our collective understanding of community. The collection investigates the deep social, political and philosophical implications community convokes, exploring how literature responds to crises of community in the current era, whilst also gesturing to the fragile but vital ways these may be overcome. Straddling various sociological foci, the voices in this book work between the field of literature as a distinct sphere of artistic activity and the important social and political implications that literary experiments and representations can have for the real world. Covering a wide range of contexts and positions, and addressing crucial issues of nationality, race, regionality, gender and global pandemics, this text can nonetheless hardly do justice to the sprawling fields of contemporary fiction production and literary criticism. The title of the collection in itself presents tensions in the categorization and naming of national and literary communities, extending in the word 'British' a focus on Northern Irish literature which is outside of its immediate orbit. Northern Irish literature is in many ways aligned in influence with British literatures but also writes into and draws on a specifically *Irish* canon firmly outside, and sometimes against, the cultural and political significance of Britishness. Especially in the Brexit context, the cultural and national focus on this collection is designed precisely to attend to the importance of marginal, peripheral and regional communities, exposing internal and external borders and exclusions within the British context as well as pushing beyond its borders to the vital relationships it shares with Ireland, Europe and the rest of the world. By assembling important names in contemporary British and Northern Irish literary criticism and by extending its gaze to some of the most prescient texts and issues for community today, this book aims to offer a valuable overview of the stakes and crucial interventions that literary criticism can make in our collective understanding of community. Through analysing and closely reading contemporary fictions, and putting them in dialogue with crucial debates in theory, philosophy and politics, we hope to make a timely intervention in the strange and disorienting times in which this collection is written.

In placing its exploration of contemporary fiction in relation to political, social and philosophical questions of community, the essays in this volume offer heterogeneous perspectives on some of the crucial challenges, exclusions and political possibilities held within the sphere of community as a zone of relationality, interdependence and collective struggle. Like the literature explored in the collection, the contributors have not shied away from tackling the prescient events and crises of the contemporary moment or assumed a literary autonomy or lofty distance from the various pressures, contingencies and political and ethical demands of our social landscape. Instead they have taken literary criticism as an active field of study, charged with its own kinds of critical and socially informed interventions. From the philosophical thinking of Hannah Arendt, Jean-Luc Nancy, Zygmunt Bauman and Jacques Derrida, to political theorists and sociologists such as Anne Applebaum, Paul Gilroy, Stuart Hall and Michael Silk, this collection demonstrates the multiple methodological overlaps that any adequate thinking of community requires. Combining such perspectives with a close hermeneutical focus on contemporary British literature, these essays embrace the multiple registers of community as both a geographically located and conceptual form, and take as their general themes the expanding influence of nationalism as a cultural and political force, Covid-19, gendered and racialized exclusions across categories of citizenship, the vexed category of Britishness, and regional and class-based discrepancies in representation in Britain today. Drawing on various literary explorations of such obstacles for contemporary community, the collection's analysis of texts also moves beyond immediate empirical concerns towards more futural investments in post-pandemic possibilities, post-national imaginaries and 'counter-communities', all within a broadly shared orientation towards a 'democracy to come' (Derrida 2005).

The socially minded literary criticism of this collection may be said to mirror a turn in recent literature towards more explicitly politically committed and engaged forms of narrative, with Brexit forming a potent example of an event that has inspired concerted literary responses from a number of important British novelists. Nowhere are the complexities of the literary engagement with community better evidenced than in the recent work of Ali Smith's seasonal quartet – four novels beginning with *Autumn* (2016) and *Winter* (2017) and concluding with *Spring* (2019) and *Summer* (2020a). In an interview, Smith has spoken of her motivation behind the novels as being driven by a desire to produce fiction that would speak to political happenings really close to the event, a 'keeping the novel novel project' (Armistead 2019: n.p.). The endeavour expresses in the very relentlessness and speed of its publication a concerted investment in producing a politically engaged literature with the capacity to influence and even intervene in current events. Smith's argument that '[f]iction and lies are the opposite of each other' (n.p.) exemplifies a metamodern/ transglossic positioning of the author as public intellectual, and the novel as a force for social good against the post-truth society identified with Donald Trump's period as US president and its aftermath.

It is in this context that the quartet explicitly acknowledges the crumbling of national community and the barriers to its resurrection in contemporary Britain. The closeness to political events creates fiction with a palpable emotional, temporal intimacy and immediacy, generating an energy in Smith's prose that is designed to challenge the strongest political rhetoric, but which also refuses to shield the reader from the harsh realities of contemporary Britain. Each novel is haunted by a social or political catastrophe which can be read as indicative of the erosion of care for others – the murder of Jo Cox, the referendum result, the Grenfell fire, Trump's presidency, the refugee and detention centre crises, the murder of George Floyd and finally the Covid-19 pandemic. *Autumn* begins the quartet with the picture of a bleak neo-Dickensian Britain in the 'worst of times' and 'split into pieces' (Smith 2016: 3, 61), the legacy of neoliberalism gestured towards in the statement that 'the haves and the have nots have stayed the same' (61). By the publication of *Spring* in 2019 in the wake of the Windrush scandal, the tone is one of stark despair:

> Common wealth, she said. What a lie. Why hasn't there been an outcry the size of this so-called United Kingdom? Those things would've brought down a government at any other time in my life. What's happened to all the good people of this country?
>
> Compassion fatigue, Richard said.
>
> Fuck compassion fatigue, she said. That's people walking about with dead souls. (66)

Yet despite the stark consciousness of this atomized reality, the quartet maintains to the final instalment a concomitant sense of optimism. The connections between each book, the recurring presence across the quartet of characters such as Daniel, the almost stream of consciousness prose that connects ideas via associative processes, are strategies that affirm Smith's affinity for form itself as meaning (see Smith 2012), while embedding at the level of structure a commitment to interconnection, closeness and cross-fertilization. Repeatedly, resonantly and in layer upon layer, the quartet celebrates hybrid, cross-cultural dialogue; as Justine Jordan writes in her review of *Spring* a quartet novel is one which 'contains multitudes' (2019: n.p.). This dialogue is central not only to artistry but also (and because of artistry, it can be seen) to social justice. If there is to be a transformation and an end to the 'bleak times', this will come not via defensiveness or fear of the new, but rather through radical openness. So it is that in *Autumn* Daniel speaks of collage as 'an institute of education where all the rules can be thrown into the air … and because of this everything you think you know gets made into something new' (Smith 2016: 72–3). In the final novel of the quartet, *Summer*, it is fittingly Daniel who returns to these ideas in a conversation with his dead sister, Hannah. Brought magically together across time and space (and with Hannah in the guise of a boy), Hannah evokes Einstein's critique of separation to tell her brother that the notion is an illusion, that the fluidity of matter 'makes you and I more than just you or I … It makes us us' (197).

The hopes represented in *Summer*, written at the beginning of the pandemic, seem wildly optimistic given the situation in 2021: the awakening Smith's characters look towards in which the disease has led to the realization that 'we have to stop being poisonous to each other' (247) seems further away than ever. In this respect, however, they form an even more crucial counter-discourse, representative of the potential of contemporary literature to provide translatable, indefinable scenarios which might communicate the more abstract concepts of philosophical thinking on community. When Daniel directs Elisabeth as to the power of narrative he speaks at the same time to a new responsibility of the contemporary author. Yet he is also speaking of Derrida's hospitality, of Nancy's being-in-common; he is speaking of Levinas's encounter with the other, and of Benedict Anderson's imagined communities:

> And whoever makes up the story makes up the world, Daniel said. So always try to welcome people into the home of your story. That's my suggestion …
> 
> And always give them a choice – even those characters like a person with nothing but a tree costume between him or her and a man with a gun. By which I mean characters who seem to have no choice at all. Always give them a home. (120)

In the midst of seemingly insurmountable ideological differences, Smith's quartet announces the possibility for reconciliation in a humanized and intimate politics of encounter and empathy: the belief expressed in *Winter* that '[t]he human will always surface' (2017: 318) or the call on the final page of *Spring* for 'the great connective ... new life already at work' (2019: 336). This emerges, in the spirit of the 'to come', as an answer to the anticlimax of the narrative proper: a response to the colon in the preceding chapter with its final words 'Story over. Well almost:' (333). At the centre of these possibilities are ebullient young women (Elisabeth in *Autumn*, Lux in *Winter*, Florence in *Spring*, Sacha in *Summer*) striking out for new modes of connection with unexpected visitors: a consistent trope of Smith's oeuvre. These young people are always in dialogue with a host of others – often older – who are reminders that there is an enduring history which shapes the present, containing cautionary lessons, but also vital knowledge and inspiration. *Winter*, for example, reveals this message in its intertextual references to *A Christmas Carol*; the younger woman Lux, a migrant visitor, brings a strident call for change which jars against the Leave politics of her host, Sophia. Yet Sophia's sister, Iris, still protesting in her seventies, carries with her a history of communal protest traced back to the 1970s – a warning against conservative nostalgia conterminous with a reminder of the importance of remembrance. These unexpected, multigenerational relationships lead to protests, demands for truth and detention centre breakouts, but also to small moments of togetherness such as Sophia and Lux singing a song together in German: flashes of understanding which suggest the hope of connection even in the midst of the most vitriolic political oppositions. The communities these conjunctions represent are not local or even national but international – small, grassroots movements of unlikely conspirators brought together by their sensitivity to the brutalities of the contemporary world and their burning desire to find alternatives, their declaration that '[w]e've got to come up with a better answer' (Smith 2017: 206).

Smith is not alone in such future-thinking: indeed in this respect British writers are part of a globalized community also represented, for example, in the environmentalist communities of Richard Powers's *The Overstory* (2018) and Imbolo Mbue's *How Beautiful We Were* (2021), or the smaller scale, personalized elevations of intimacy in Hanya Yanagihara's *A Little Life* (2015). These works affirm how contemporary fiction is interested not only in documenting the failures of current attempts to forge connection but also in shaping the conversation around what joining together might mean in a yet to be written future. While there has been much discussion recently about the redundancy of the novel form (see, for example, Self 2014), fiction remains a vital site of the 'community to come'; a potent cultural force for thinking through the question of what it means, in the aftermath of five years of economic, political and health crises, to truly live with a commitment to one another.

## Chapters

Given the recurring significance of the imagined nation as a source of communal belonging, Part 1 of the book, entitled 'National Community', examines the ways in which contemporary fiction has responded to the crisis of Britishness through complex imaginaries of its constituent nations. It opens with Robert Eaglestone's provocative examination of post-Brexit Englishness, '"The Little Links Are Broke": Ethnocentrism, Englishness and Loneliness in Contemporary Political Science, Political Theory and Contemporary British Fiction', which extends Eaglestone's earlier influential work on cruel nostalgia to ask questions about the enduring loneliness of English identity in the wake of the unravelling of Britain's relationship with Europe. Constructed around an innovative conversation among social science, literary fiction, comic books and genre fiction, the chapter reveals with desperate honesty the disillusionment and alienation at the centre of ideas of community in contemporary England, at times challenged by authors but in other moments reinforced.

The diversity of Eaglestone's reference points draws attention to a politics of form in which texts which exceed the boundaries of realist representation are offering vital interventions into questions of communal belonging, a position that is shared with the next essay in the section, Alison Garden's '"Our Uneasy Mixed Community": Cross-Community Romance, Magic Realism and Northern Ireland'. Garden's chapter reframes the question of British community and literature from a crucial but understudied periphery, demonstrating how Northern Ireland and its literature operate on a significant border and limit of the British nation-state and its fiction. Although Northern Irish literature can in some cases take 'Britishness' as an identity it can subscribe to, the question of community is nonetheless crucially altered in this context, with internal tensions between two 'putative communities' and a colonial past inflecting deeply on its social fabric. Focusing on recent short stories, Garden examines how the 'magical' offers optimistic gestures of intercommunity relations that promise to exceed the limits of post-Brexit tensions. Such gestures, which have the potential to both unsettle and reshape communities, provide evidence of what Paul Gilroy (2004) has termed a 'convivial future', a resistance at the level of Britain's constituent national identities that interrogates the wider state of the nation.

This simultaneous unsettling and reshaping is the central focus of the final chapter in this section, Timothy Baker's 'Incomers and Settlers: Nomadism and Entanglement in Contemporary Scottish Fiction'. Reading the representation of rural Scottish communities in Malachy Tallack's *The Valley at the Centre of the World* (2018) and Linda Cracknell's *The Call of the Undertow* (2013) alongside the cosmopolitan concerns of Leila Aboulela's story collection *Elsewhere, Home* (2018) and Sarah Moss's *Summerwater* (2020), Baker suggests that community is imagined as both fragile and open to renewal in works that explore questions of belonging, exclusion, movement and settlement. Eschewing overt concerns with national community, such texts instead examine via localized communal concerns the underlying principles that may have shaped Scotland's unique perspective – simultaneously made up of micro-communities of care that may in part explain Scotland's Remain majority in the 2016 European Referendum and a postcolonial protectionism which is not always welcoming of outsiders and which is contextualized by Scotland's ever-evolving independence movement.

The second section of the book, entitled 'Speculative Community', follows from Baker's concern for localized identity to ask how writers have explored regional, ethnic and identity-based communal identification as a radical counterpoint to hegemonic national discourses. The essays in this section are thus united by their sense of alternative modes of communal identification, which offer the potential for, if not always the realization of, future substitutions to tired and discordant national belonging. In the first essay in this section, entitled 'Beyond the Multicultural: Queer Community in Jackie Kay's *Trumpet*', Peter Ely examines how Kay's novel, as an evolution and solidification of ideas expressed in her poetry, posits trans identity as an alternative to the institutional community of the nation-state. The latter, for Ely, is intimately bound with a reductive politics of multiculturalism associated with the political climate that has shaped Kay's career, most notably the Blairite Labour administration of the late 1990s. Seeing Kay's recent poetic reflections on Brexit as bearing the legacy of her earlier writings, the chapter thus comes to encapsulate the movement between the late 1990s and current communal feeling indicated by the collection's title.

For Ely, the potential of Kay's text is that it offers, via comparison to Blanchot and Bataille, a vision of the 'community of lovers' whose personal interactions might serve as a model for a twenty-first-century community. Such community aligns itself not with capitalist pragmatics but rather with Marxist impulses, a gesture towards the fictional drive for political transformation that is also emphasized in Caroline Lusin's paper. Entitled 'Community versus commodity: Neoliberalism and (sub)urban identities in twenty-first-century London novels', Lusin's chapter reads two crucial but understudied novels, Kae Tempest's *Let Them Eat Chaos* (2016) and Fiona Mozley's *Hot Stew* (2021), seeing in each a critical account of neoliberalism and its influence on metropolitan community. Working within a tradition of novels that focus on micro-communities within London, Lusin argues that these most recent texts bring into sharp relief the role of capitalism in eroding communal feeling, the barrier to connection 'in a world in which everyone is fending for themselves'. Nevertheless, within such strictures they also offer models of resistance that – like Kay's queer community – centre around the value an individual places on another: discourses of empathy that imagine the tentative beginnings of new modes of association and connection.

The final essay in this section is Devon Campbell-Hall's 'Writing Othered Asian British Skins: Interrogating Racism in Fictional Asian British Communities', an analysis of the complexities of British Asian community, which draws attention to how contemporary writing has concerned itself with the materiality of imagined communities. Like Lusin, Campbell-Hall reads the fictional text in this sense as drawing attention both to existing barriers to inclusion and to a tangible politics from which resistance may emerge. Focused on questions of skin colour in Raman Mundair's *Lovers, Liars, Conjurers and Thieves* (2003), Zadie Smith's *White Teeth* (2000) and Meera Syal's *Anita and Me* (1996), and contextualized by Ravinder Randhawa's groundbreaking *A Wicked Old Woman* (1987), Campbell-Hall argues that contemporary writers have used community as a space within which counter-discourses to racism within Britain might emerge, and yet these ethnic communities are often at odds with idealistic social discourse on multicultural community. In this sense, fiction does not easily align itself with the optimism of thinkers such as Tariq Modood or Yasmin Alibhai-Brown, for whom multiculturalism is now an entrenched part of the national imaginary.

Campbell-Hall's measured conclusion naturally leads into the final section of the book – 'Precarious Community'. Here, the undercurrents of neoliberalism and racism which haunt previous chapters are thrown into relief by the twin pressures of Brexit and the Covid-19 pandemic. This discussion begins with Kristian Shaw's chapter, 'Performing the Nation: A Disunited Kingdom in Jonathan Coe's *Middle England*'. Drilling down into the issues which preoccupy his recent monograph *Brexlit* (2021), Shaw reads Coe's novel as a powerful examination of the events that would foreshadow the 2016 European Referendum result. The novel's representation of the 2012 Olympics opening ceremony in London suggests that the divisions exposed by the vote were already entrenched and visible in the national spectacle, and Shaw reads such awareness as a powerful indicator of the need to admit to the myths and fictions upon which national community has conventionally relied.

For Shaw, echoing Eaglestone's chapter, such myths are problematically woven into the novel itself as much as exposed by its form, and this power of cultural myth is picked up by Emily Horton in her essay '"Why Would You Play a Game Like That?": Community and the Pandemic in Kazuo Ishiguro's *Klara and the Sun*'. Reading the novel as an example of an early pandemic fiction, Horton examines how Ishiguro's concern for the uniqueness of the human offers a tragic reading of the sacrifice of the vulnerable to the needs of a humanist discourse which celebrates individuality at the expense of the collective. As responses to Covid-19 in Britain have exposed the fault-lines in an already fragile sense of shared experience, so Horton exposes how Ishiguro's futuristic narrative is in fact not so far from the present.

It is the question of past and future precarity that preoccupies Sara Upstone in the final chapter of the book. 'Even the ghosts: Community in the wake' is a creative critical piece. Embracing the idea that creative critical writing is that which 'seeks to do justice to what can happen ... when we are *with* an artwork' (Benson and Connors 2014: 5, emphasis added), it aims to realize the transglossic form that Upstone has recently recognized in fictional writings in a literary critical context (Shaw and Upstone 2021), a 'speaking across' which is inherently directed towards notions of collectivism. Built around readings of Niall Griffith's *Broken Ghosts* (2019), Jon McGregor's *Even the Dogs* (2010) and Max Porter's *Lanny* (2019), Upstone's lyrical prose asks how it is that we might salvage some communal feeling from a space in which the pandemic has emerged as a limit point of earlier violences against the sacredness of life. Both a commentary and a plea, the essay captures the ongoing desire for connection that every chapter in the collection recognizes, a defiant spirit which believes that fiction, still, might offer us some model for how not only to imagine but also realize the possibility of meaningful and inclusive community.

# References

Agamben, Giorgio (1990), *The Coming Community*, Minnesota: University of Minnesota Press.
Amin, Ash (2003), 'Unruly Strangers? The 2001 Urban Riots in Britain', *International Journal of Urban and Regional Research*, 27 (2): 460–3.
Anderson, Benedict (1983), *Imagined Communities*, London: Verso.
Armistead, Claire (2019), 'Ali Smith: "This Young Generation Is Showing Us We Need to Change and We Can"', *Guardian*, 23 March, https://www.theguardian.com/books/2019/mar/23/ali-smith-spring-young-generation-brexit-future.
Benson, Stephen, and Clare Connors (2014), 'Introduction', in Stephen Benson and Clare Connors (eds), *Creative Criticism: An Anthology and Guide*, 1–47, Edinburgh: Edinburgh University Press.
Bentley, Nick (2008), *Contemporary British Fiction*, Edinburgh: Edinburgh University Press.
Bewes, Timothy, and Jeremy Gilbert (eds) (2000), *Cultural Capitalism: Politics after New Labour*, London: Lawrence & Wishart.
Bhambra, Gurminder K. (2017), 'Brexit, Trump, and "Methodological Whiteness": On the Misrecognition of Race and Class', *British Journal of Sociology*, 68: S214–232.
Blair, Tony (1996), *New Britain: My Vision of a Young Country*, London: Fourth Estate.
Boxall, Peter (ed.) (2019), *The Cambridge Companion to British Fiction, 1980*, Cambridge: Cambridge University Press.
Bradshaw, Ted K. (2009), 'The Post-Place Community: Contributions to the Debate about the Definition of Community', *Community Development*, 39 (1): 5–16.
Cantle, Ted (2001), *Community Cohesion: A Report of the Independent Review Team*, London: Home Office.
Cunningham, Michael (1998), *The Hours*, New York: Farrar, Straus and Giroux.
Denham, Lord (2002), *Building Cohesive Communities: A Report of the Ministerial Group on Public Order and Community Cohesion*, London: Home Office.
Derrida, Jacques (2005), *Rogues: Two Essays on Reason*, trans. Pascale-Anne Brault and Michael Naas, Stanford: Stanford University Press.
Eaglestone, Robert (2019a), 'Cruel Nostalgia and the Second World War', in Robert Eaglestone (ed.), *Brexit and Literature: Critical and Cultural Responses*, 92–104, London: Routledge.
Eaglestone, Robert (ed.) (2019b), *Brexit and Literature: Critical and Cultural Responses*, London: Routledge.
Edwards, Caroline (2018), 'The Networked Novel', in Robert Eaglestone and Daniel O'Gorman (eds), *The Routledge Companion to Twenty-First Century Literary Fiction*, 13–24, London: Routledge.
Eve, Martin Paul (2012), 'Thomas Pynchon, David Foster Wallace and the Problems of Metamodernism: Post-Millennial Post-Postmodernism?', *C21 Literature: Journal of 21st-Century Writings*, 1: 7–25.

Farris, Sara R. (2017), *In the Name of Women's Rights: The Rise of Femonationalism*, Durham, NC: Duke University Press.

Gilbert, Jeremy (2013), *Common Ground: Democracy and Collectivity in an Age of Individualism*, London: Pluto.

Gilroy, Paul (2004), *After Empire: Melancholia or Convivial Culture?*, London: Routledge.

Hobsbawm, Eric (1990), *Nations and Nationalism since 1780: Programme, Myth, Reality*, Cambridge: Cambridge University Press.

Hollinger, David (1995), *Postethnic America: Beyond Multiculturalism*, New York: Basic.

Jordan, Justine (2019), 'Spring by Ali Smith Review – a Beautiful Piece of Synchronicity', *Guardian*, 30 March, https://www.theguardian.com/books/2019/mar/30/spring-by-ali-smith-review.

Kiesling, Elena (2015), *Aesthetics of Coalition and Protest: The Imagined Queer Community*, Heidelburg: Universitätsverlag Winter.

Kunzru, Hari (2011), *Gods Without Men*, London: Penguin.

Leonard, Mark (1997), 'Britain™: Renewing Our Identity', *Demos*, London, https://www.demos.co.uk/files/britaintm.pdf.

Levitas, Ruth (2005), *The Inclusive Society? Social Exclusion and New Labour*, Basingstoke: Palgrave Macmillan.

Marcus, David (2013), 'Post-Hysterics: Zadie Smith and the Fiction of Austerity', *Dissent Magazine*, https://www.dissentmagazine.org/article/post-hysterics-zadie-smith-and-the-fiction-of-austerity.

Mbue, Imbolo (2021), *How Beautiful We Were*, New York: Random House.

McEwan, Ian (2020), 'Ian McEwan: The Strange Vocabulary of Coronavirus', *Spectator*, 25 April, https://www.spectator.co.uk/article/ian-mcewan-the-strange-vocabulary-of-coronavirus.

McEwen, Nicola (2018), 'Brexit and Scotland: Between Two Unions', *British Politics*, 13 (1): 65–78.

McKenzie, Lisa (2017), 'The Class Politics of Prejudice: Brexit and the Land of No-Hope and Glory', *British Journal of Sociology*, 68 (S1): S265–80.

Mitchell, David (2004), *Cloud Atlas*, London: Sceptre.

Moosavi, Leon (2015), 'Orientalism at Home: Islamophobia in the Representations of Islam and Muslims by the New Labour Government', *Ethnicities*, 15 (5): 652–74.

Nancy, Jean-Luc (1991), *The Inoperative Community*, ed. Peter Connor, trans. Peter Connor, Lisa Garbus, Michael Holland and Simona Sawhney, Minneapolis: University of Minnesota Press.

Pemberton, Simon (2017), 'Community-Based Planning and Localism in the Devolved UK', in Sue Brownhill and Quintin Bradley (eds), *Localism and Neighbourhood: Planning Power to the People?*, 183–99, Bristol: Policy.

Pilkington, Andrew (2008), 'From Institutional Racism to Community Cohesion: The Changing Nature of Racial Discourse in Britain', *Sociological Research Online*, 13 (3), http://www.socresonline.org.uk/13/3/6.html.

Powers, Richard (2018), *The Overstory*, New York: W. W. Norton.

Rau, Petra (2019), 'Autumn after Brexit', in Robert Eaglestone (ed.), *Brexit and Literature: Critical and Cultural Responses*, 31–43, London: Routledge.

Rhodes, James (2009), 'Revisiting the 2001 Riots: New Labour and the Rise of "Colour Blind Racism"', *Sociological Research Online*, 14 (5): 1–10.

Ritchie, Angus (2019), *Inclusive Populism: Creating Citizens in Global Age*, Notre Dame: University of Notre Dame Press.

Rose, Gillian (1996), *Mourning Becomes the Law: Philosophy and Representation*, Cambridge: Cambridge University Press.

Self, Will (2014), 'The Novel Is Dead (This Time It's for Real)', *Guardian*, 2 May, https://www.theguardian.com/books/2014/may/02/will-self-novel-dead-literary-fiction.

Shaw, Kristian (2017), *Cosmopolitanism in Twenty-First Century Fiction*, London: Palgrave Macmillan.

Shaw, Kristian (2021), *Brexlit: British Literature and the European Project*, London: Bloomsbury.

Shaw, Kristian, and Sara Upstone (2021), 'The Transglossic: Contemporary Fiction and the Limitations of the Modern', *English Studies*, 102 (5): 573–600.

Slocock, Caroline (2015), 'Whose Society? The Final Big Society Audit', *Civil Exchange*, London: Civil Exchange.

Smith, Ali (2012), 'Style versus Content: How Should Authors Approach the Task of Writing a Novel Today?', *Edinburgh World Writers' Conference*, 18 August, https://www.youtube.com/watch?v=bHOSXziim9A.

Smith, Ali (2016), *Autumn*, London: Hamish Hamilton.

Smith, Ali (2017), *Winter*, London: Hamish Hamilton.

Smith, Ali (2019), *Spring*, London: Hamish Hamilton.

Smith, Ali (2020a), *Summer*, London: Hamish Hamilton.

Smith, Ali (2020b), 'The Litmus: An Update from Ali Smith', *Trinity College Cambridge News*, 17 April, https://www.trin.cam.ac.uk/news/the-litmus-an-update-from-ali-smith/.

Valluvan, Sivamohan, and Virinder S. Kalra (2019), 'Racial Nationalisms: Brexit, Borders and Little Englander Contradictions', *Ethnic and Racial Studies*, 42 (142): 2393–412.

Yanagihara, Hanya (2015), *A Little Life*, New York: Doubleday.

# Part 1
# National Community

1

# 'The little links are broke': Ethnocentrism, Englishness and loneliness in contemporary political science, political theory and contemporary British fiction

Robert Eaglestone

Something is rotten in the state of England. Observers of all sorts seem aware that England in the late 2010s and early 2020s seems unhappy, angry, uncertain or too certain, above and beyond the damages caused or exposed by Covid-19. I argue that one significant aspect of this is the complex conjunction between a rising English (not British) ethnocentrism and an economically, culturally and politically induced loneliness.

This is, in the phrase of Raymond Williams, a contemporary 'structure of feeling' (1954: 21) to which fiction gives us access: but it is not that alone. It is visible in other, more methodologically positivist ways too. So I propose an experiment in method. I will contrast three different ways of understanding contemporary British communal life: interpretive accounts based on quantitative political science; an account drawing on Arendtian political theory; and accounts developed from three contemporary novels. I do not believe that any one of these approaches offers a full picture or that 'adding them up' creates one. I do believe that, interwoven, these complementary threads illuminate each other and tell us something important about England today.

## Political science: Divided and lonely

Despite its title, *Brexitland*, by political scientists Maria Sobolewska and Robert Ford, argues that the EU referendum was not so much a moment of creation but rather a moment of awakening ... when the social and political processes long underway finally became obvious and the different groups of voters finally recognised themselves as two distinct and opposed camps. (2020: 2)

Their account draws on extensive quantitative research and frames the profound divides in contemporary community in Britain in three overlapping timescales: long-term demographic change and its impact; the past twenty years; and the EU referendum campaign itself. In this way, their work expands the chronological range and depth of other quantitative research about the referendum (see, for example, Clarke, Goodwin and Whiteley 2017). Sobolewska and Ford identify two long-term changes: 'educational expansion and ethnic diversification' (2020: 22). Waves of university expansion since the 1960s have changed the UK's demography: in 1987, 8 per cent of voters were graduates; by 2017, the rate had risen to 24 per cent. Similarly, 'within a single lifetime', the UK has changed from 'a nearly all-white society to a racially diverse one' (27). But the different waves of migrants have had different impacts. While Commonwealth migrants and their descendants 'could use the power of the ballot box', more recent EU migrants could not, which 'skews the political debates towards those threatened by their arrival' (32). However, Sobolewska and Ford's key conclusion, and the core of this chapter, concerns the consequence of these changes: ethnocentrism.

People's ethnocentric views – that the world is 'us versus them' (36) – are profound and stable: those who express them 'reliably express similar views if you ask them again years or even decades later' (39). The social changes Sobolewska and Ford analyse have led to conflict between 'those who embrace an ethnocentric worldview' (34) and those who reject it (although, one might note that this is already a fairly 'them and us' view of politics). Ethnocentrism, while often quiescent, can be easily 'activated when ethnocentric voters perceive a threat' (40) and is both 'uniquely capable of shifting white vote choices' (35) and shaping the voting decisions of those 'influenced by their experience of white hostility' (35). A subtle but powerful literary illustration of this activation from quiescence occurs in Jonathan Coe's 'state of the nation' novel, *Middle England* (2018). Grete, a Polish woman, is attacked in a shop for speaking Polish on her phone. Her formerly friendly and supportive employer, the English Mrs Coleman, is a witness, but when asked to retell the story to the police, instead says to Grete, 'I think, on the whole, it would be better if you and your husband went home' (383), not only refusing solidarity but also taking the side of the aggressor. Another character says of Mrs Coleman's son Ian that 'his basic model for relationships comes down to antagonism and competition, not cooperation' (327).

However, ethnocentric views vary by education level and ethnic identity. This is the driver for the increasing radical division of the British polity and the key idea in *Brexitland*. Sobolewska and Ford identify three broad groups. The first group is *conviction liberals*: mostly younger, graduates, cosmopolitan, pro-migration and embracing diversity, and so opposing ethnocentrism as a matter of belief. Second, *necessity liberals*: ethnic minorities for whom 'anti-racism and pro-diversity stances are not a matter of personal values but of necessity' (Sobolewska and Ford 2020: 5). Third, *identity conservatives*: formerly the unquestioned dominant group in Britain whose ethnocentric views 'defined the mainstream' (46):

> From their point of view, it is society that changed and left them behind ... It is therefore no surprise that such voters tend to adopt a conservative stance ... Change is perceived as a loss for ethnocentric voters: a loss of their dominant position, and a loss of the cultural conformity and continuity which they value. (46)

Sobolewska and Ford argue that this group's 'decline has been dramatic, and the experience of this decline has been disorienting and disillusioning for them' (6). Their view of losing position and power is not 'irrational' because 'as this group shrinks, so the political incentive to respond to it also declines, particularly when its concerns conflict with the concerns of rapidly rising identity liberal groups' (6). These groups have even come to live in different spaces, in a UK version of 'white flight'. Identity conservatives are in general ethnocentric voters and have 'a distinctive political agenda' (60) based on the conflict between in- and out-groups: migration, equal opportunities, devolution and constitutional reform. Indeed, framing any issue as a conflict between groups is the source of the culture war rhetoric.

*Brexitland* explores issues of immigration in some detail and shows similarities in responses to the two surges of migration to the UK (the 'post Imperial' wave of the 1950s and 1960s, and the wave of migrants from post-Communist EU countries). In both cases, the elite was more liberal than the rest of the population, and the numbers 'activated ethnocentric hostilities in the native electorate who perceived the new migrants as a threatening outgroup' (88). In turn these perceptions of identity conservatives were stirred up by extreme right political actors (Enoch Powell in the 1960s, United Kingdom Independence

Party in the 2010); and, in turn again, there was an identity liberal pushback (Labour's race relations legislation it the 1960s; perhaps, more speculatively, the slow growth of post-referendum opposition to the 'hostile environment' developed by the Home office in the 2010s and 2020s). Sobolewska and Ford are also interesting about issues of race, over which there has been considerable social change across all three groups, and they use a social science experiment about racism to demonstrate their point. They suggest there is a consensus that racism is 'a personal failing and a social evil' (72) but disagreement about 'what constitutes racist and thus unacceptable behaviour' (73): identity liberals seek to 'apply more expansive definitions of racism in order to expunge prejudice from society' while identity conservatives push back, feeling that these 'definitions … inhibit free expression of legitimate views and groups attachments, and stigmatise them unfairly' (73). They offer a reading of the (clichéd) phrase 'I'm not racist but …' which, they argue, while

> widely perceived as being a prelude to saying something that is in fact racist, actually reflects invocation of a shared recognition that racism is unacceptable. It is an attempt to reach out to those on the other side of the conversation, seeking common ground and trying to neutralise an anticipated hostile response to views that the speaker worries may be seen as contentious. Yet it usually has the opposite effect … The roots of this social tension lie in an ongoing struggle to settle the boundaries separating beliefs and behaviour that should be stigmatised as racist from more benign expressions of group attachment and judgment about others. (76)

*Brexitland* reveals a polarized nation, dominated by ethnocentric identity conservatives.

This 'activated' ethnocentrism is illuminated by another major quantitative and interpretive study, Alisa Henderson and Richard Wyn Jones's *Englishness: The Political Force Transforming Britain* (2021). This draws on more than a decade's worth of data and traces the growth, content and consequences of a specifically English ethnocentric nationalism. Exploring the range of distinctions between British and English identities (respondents describe themselves as 'English not British', 'More English than British', 'equally English and British', 'more British than English', 'British not English'), Henderson and Jones uncover a relatively stable sense of interwoven identity. However, they also trace, during the 2010s, an increasing English grievance that England is 'unfairly treated both financially and politically within the union' (58): they call this 'devo-anxiety' (59). Moreover, those who felt more 'English not British' or 'more English than British' were more profoundly Eurosceptic over a range of issues and significantly more hostile to migration. This 'English response' they note is 'often fundamentally at odds with what had been – until June 2016, at least – the geopolitical trajectory of the UK state' (97).

Henderson and Jones present an 'English world view'. 'Englishness' is demonstrated by beliefs such as, for example, 'English culture is not as valued as other cultures', 'St George's day should be a holiday' and 'English values are different'; Englishness is shaped by grievances, is profoundly Eurosceptic, resents devolution and believes that the devolved nations get 'more than their fair share'. Henderson and Jones correlate these views to what they call 'efficacy', by which they mean the ability to influence political and communal decisions. Very strikingly, they find that

> the lower one's sense of efficacy, the more one scores highly on the 'Englishness' dimension of the world view ... The less one believes in an ability to influence politics – the less voice one feels one has – the greater the appeal of this particular vision of England as a political community. (129)

The authors show how this vision of England is tied into a sense of the past: the 'veneration of the past, and a desire to preserve the past through institutions ... have long featured in English political culture', and the 'politicised English identity' is a 'direct continuation of this' (133). Moreover, those who 'identify as English' are 'hankering for a time in which it was felt that they (or people like them) actually mattered: a time in which the English felt valued in England and Britain, and an England-dominated Britain knew its proper (elevated) place in the world – and naturally, the rest of the world knew it too' (133). This is a powerful nostalgia.

To these analyses of ethnocentrism and its impact and of Englishness, we can add one more: loneliness. Noreena Hertz's study *The Lonely Century* (2020) offers a more extensive understanding of loneliness in England than, for example, the Campaign to End Loneliness or the Jo Cox Foundation: for her, loneliness is 'an internal state and an existential one – personal, societal, economic and political' (9). It is inspired by Robert Putnam's famous *Bowling Alone* (2000) and like Putnam's book aimed at the general reader, Hertz draws on many academic studies to argue that neoliberal capitalism has led to people feeling 'isolated and alienated, disconnected both from their fellow citizens and from national governments who, they feel have not been listening to them or looking out for their interests' (2020: 35). She shows the impact of economic insecurity, 'negative politeness cultures' (60), hostile social environments and the collapse of social institutions (in 'the UK, a third of youth clubs and nearly 800 public libraries have shut down since the 2008 financial crisis' (81), along with 41% of adult day centres). This destruction of the social bonds creates loneliness and destroys self-esteem. Populists offer 'belonging' (48) as a panacea, which in the UK is defined in terms of race, the 'them and us' ethnocentrism by which Ford and Sobolewska analyse.

All these studies (and the work they draw on) offer a pretty grim picture of community in contemporary Britain. The English ethnocentric majority of identity conservatives are easily 'activated' by right or far-fight politicians and have a profound sense of grievance towards Europe, the other nations of the UK and the liberal elites. They feel unheard and politically inefficacious and venerate the English past as a time when they mattered. Moreover, with communities destroyed by neoliberal policies, they feel lonely, isolated and disconnected from each other and the state and, again, are very open to the idea of 'belonging'. In contrast, a smaller number of conviction and identity liberals are located mostly in cities. Between these two polarized sides there is friction and conflict over migration, racism, national identity, devolution and the sharing of national wealth. The actors in the contemporary 'culture wars' both draw on and intentionally inflame these divisions.

## Political theory: Arendt, loneliness and tribal nationalism

The studies I have looked at above are interpretative and evidence-based political science which demonstrate both the growing ethnocentrism and the increasing loneliness in England. It is the more theoretical work of Hannah Arendt – indeed, she described herself as a 'political theorist' – that helps us see these in conjunction. She specifically discusses exactly this in *The Origins of Totalitarianism* (1958). To turn to this work is not to say that the UK is becoming a totalitarian or ethnocentric state (although Henderson and Jones's rather bald assertion that 'it would be politically ill-advised and analytically nonsense to seek to understand English Nationalism as a species of fascism' (2021: 202) seems inaccurate to me because English nationalism does, in fact, share some fascist characteristics). However, it is to take Arendt seriously when she writes, in the 1950s, that 'totalitarian solutions may survive the fall of totalitarian regimes' (459) if we 'continue to think of our world in utilitarian terms' (459).

Arendt identified loneliness as a key factor in the rise of totalitarianism. Like many ideas in Arendt, loneliness is tied into a much larger philosophical matrix (which I can only touch on here). Regimes run on terror need isolation, which prevents people working together: 'political contacts between men are severed ... and the human capacity for action and power are frustrated' (Arendt 1958: 474). Isolation is a step towards loneliness: in isolation, people can still shape their world, make things, even if they cannot act together. Loneliness is more extreme. It comes from uprootedness and being made superfluous. These are 'the curse of modern masses since the beginning of the industrial revolution', made acute by 'the rise of imperialism' (475) and 'the break-down of political institutions and social traditions in our own time' (475). She goes on: 'To be uprooted means to have no place in the world, recognised and guaranteed by others; to be superfluous means not to belong to the world at all' (475). Loneliness is 'at the same time contrary to the basic requirement of the human condition and one of the fundamental experiences of every human life' (475). She means that we live with people and so share a 'common sense' but also that, in the end, we will die and leave the shared world and show ourselves to be superfluous to it and others.

This loneliness used to apply only to outcasts or those in 'old age' (478), but, Arendt argues, the modern age has expanded it into an 'everyday experience of the ever-growing masses of our century' (478). Loneliness became a mass experience when the 'class system' broke down 'and carried with it the whole visible and invisible threads which bound the people to the body politic' (314). (By class system, Arendt seems to mean more than a simply Marxist analysis of class and implies the whole panoply of a social order.) The masses, she writes,

> grew out of the fragments of a highly atomized society whose competitive structure and concomitant loneliness of the individual had been held in check only through membership in a class. The chief characteristic of the mass man is not brutality and backwardness but his isolation and lack of normal social relationships. Coming from the class-ridden society of the nation-state, whose cracks had been cemented with nationalistic sentiment, it is only natural that these masses, in the first helplessness of their new experience, have tended towards an especially violent nationalism, to which mass leaders have yielded against their own instincts and purposes for purely demagogic reasons (317).

While she is discussing the early part of the twentieth century, this holds true for much of the present in the UK too: the decay of the party system (as Ford and Sobolewska show) is at the same time a result of the shift and change in the social order.

The crucial consequence of this loneliness that I want to draw out here lies in what Arendt calls 'tribal nationalism', which is instantiated in contemporary ethnocentric English nationalism. She argues that the huge Pan-German and Pan-Slav movements at the end of the nineteenth century created a new kind of 'tribal nationalism' from those fissured, 'rootless' and 'atomised' societies which led to the ruin of the nation-state system (and this historical account runs parallel to that of Miroslav Hroch, which in turn shaped Henderson and Jones's understanding of English nationalism).

Arendt argues that there is a tension between the state, which stands for the universal rule of law and the defence of human rights, and the more nebulous sense of a nation, 'a people' in which a specific national identity is important. For the state, I am a human; for the nation, English, Scottish and so on. The state is about equality and law; the nation about affect and feeling, belonging, or not. Nationalism, in more normal times, is the cement that holds the imagined community of the nation-state together. However, as society becomes increasingly fractured and polarized, nationalism becomes increasingly important, and more 'tribal nationalism' emerges as the nation outgrows the state. Indeed, tribal nationalism is hostile to the state precisely because the state is set in contrast to (or even against) the nation or tribe. Crucially, 'tribal nationalism' is opposed to the state system of government itself, to parties and to the 'old' system which it seeks to sweep away. This hostility to the state is apparent in England: to the EU obviously, which Brexiteers see as a state (and so opposed to the 'tribe'); but also to the UK state and its institutions, including the judiciary, as 'enemies of the people', the BBC and the media, the universities and Parliament. This hostility arises regardless of what these institutions may actually do. This is precisely the strange situation where the ruling English ethnocentric Conservative Party often sounds as if it is in opposition to the state, as opposed to ruling it. It leads as well to the mythical idea of a 'deep state', beloved of conspiracy theorists.

There are other characteristics of tribal nationalism which illumine the present. Tribal nationalism is interested in the past only as chthonic myth in order to bind a nation together. It offers a glorious past (for example, the memory of the Second World War; Eaglestone 2018); the present is seen as a time of crisis and decline; a wonderful future awaits (the 'Empire 2.0' and 'global Britain'; Mitchell 2021; Sanghera 2021) if the nation is allowed to take over the state. Tribal nationalists are not interested in specific policies or in social questions but in a form of general exhortation. They are not aligned, either, with specific interests, including those of capital (emblematically, Johnson is supposed to have said: 'Fuck business' (BBC News, 26 June 2018)). Membership of the tribe exceeds the state boundaries: this is the source of the idea of the

Anglosphere (see Wellings 2017) and explains the expats who feel themselves to be straightforwardly English despite not living within the territory.

Tribal nationalism also changes the relationship within the human species. As Arendt writes, to them, 'a Russian appears as different from a German as a wolf is from a fox' (1958: 234). This is why many leading English ethnocentric nationalists have no interest in the ecological crisis (or deny it is even occurring). The idea of a common humanity, which this form of nationalism denies, implies a common sharing of responsibility, including – we can add to Arendt here – a common responsibility for the survival of life on this planet. Tribalism is a way of escaping this 'planetary' and species-wide responsibility. Moreover, tribalism is premised on a form of racism in which other 'tribes' are understood as other races.

Finally, and significantly, tribal nationalists do not claim to be a party but a movement, embodying 'the will of the people'. Parties (used to) represent conflicting interests and competing ideologies within the state and develop philosophies to justify these interests. By contrast, a tribal nationalist movement does not seek to take over the state but to consume and destroy it. It suborns the institutions of the state to itself. It does not need a social programme: rather, it makes a mass appeal to a 'mood'. Lacking specific policies and opposed to the state in principle, tribalism continues to attack the state even when in power.

In Arendt's very positive and frankly rose-tinted view of the British two-party system, she offers an explanation of why totalitarianism never arose in the UK: she argues that our alternating parties have always been internal coalitions, and these coalitions have been held together by a desire to hold power in the national interest. However, this is no longer really the case. The long-awaited end of the two-party system is de facto here, as *Brexitland* shows, and following Arendt's approach, the state itself is in jeopardy.

## Contemporary fiction: The despair of present

Recent work in political science has uncovered the dominant English ethnocentrism, motivated by grievance and a painful nostalgia, set in a profound political conflict. Arendt's account of loneliness and one of its consequences, tribal nationalism, reveals a threat to the state. How are these expressed in the contemporary literary imaginary? I have chosen, not at random, three novels from a sociocultural range: one is literary fiction from the establishment 'home of new writing' *Granta*, Sarah Moss's *Ghost Wall* (2018); the second is also literary fiction but from the non-established Wrecking Ball Press, and from the pages of popular monthly comic *Viz*, Barney Farmer's *Drunken Baker* (2018); the third is firmly a genre novel from a highly commercial publisher, HarperCollins, a historical adventure, from the bestselling series by Bernard Cornwell, *Warlord* (2020). In each of these very different contemporary fictions, the theses of this chapter emerge.

Sarah Moss's short 2018 novel *Ghost Wall* begins with a short account of an Iron Age ritual sacrifice of a young woman, focalized through the victim: a foreshadowing to suggest, perhaps, the imagined chthonic roots and violence of contemporary tribalism. Most of the novel is told by Silvie and is set over a few summer days. Silvie, her mother and her father, a bus driver, are with university archaeologist Professor Slade and his students Pete, Dan and Molly, all undertaking an 'experiential archaeology' (6) experiment, trying to live as Iron Age people: her father calls them 'Ancient British' (6). They forage for food, wear tunics, cook over a firepit, collect water, excrete outside and sleep (mostly) in a roundhouse. Of course, there are unavoidable anachronisms (Iron Age people probably did not have sheep, but the experimenters use sheep skins; they hunt rabbits, introduced to the country by the Romans, and so on).

The novel tells two interlocking stories. The first is Silvie's increasing infatuation with Molly and desire to escape her violent father. She is caught between childhood and adulthood and between classes (the students discuss their CVs and 'I … felt a thrill of fear, the backwash of my desperation to have such a thing, to leave childhood and dependence behind me, to enter the world') (29). She is also trapped by her abusive father: like other violent men, her father does not want his daughter to escape the home (not even to go for a Saturday job). Her teenaged desire for Molly grows throughout the novel. Inspired (and aroused) by Molly sea bathing, Silvie bathes in a stream and is seen by her father, who beats her with his belt: 'I'll not have my daughter a little whore' (62). Yet she defends her father when Molly expresses concern: 'Haven't you been listening, people don't bother to hurt what they don't love. To sacrifice it' (126).

The second story is her father's increasing radicalization during the 'experiment'. He is a violent, lonely, resentful and angry man (he does not 'like it when people laughed' (15)), racist, anti-Irish and anti-Catholic ('Foreigners coming over here, telling us what to think' (45)). He is obsessed with belonging to the chthonic roots of Englishness in the Iron Age, he 'wanted his own ancestry, wanted a linage, a claim on something … some tribe sprung from English soil' (45) ('like mushroom in the night' (45); Silvie adds that mushrooms grow on shit, of course). His interest in peat bodies has the same source: 'That's where you come from, those folk, that's how it used to be' (39). Even the Romans are the enemy and Hadrian's Wall is 'a physical manifestation of Ancient British resistance' (26). Significantly, for him, the remains of Ancient Britons are the same as those from the industrial age. Stopping off at Newcastle, he takes Silvie not to the Roman museum but to the docks:

> Cranes reared above is like the ceremonial pillars of lost civilisations, intricate with rust and disintegration ... Look at this, he said ... Used to send ships all over the world from here. Look at it now. (25)

This kind of scene – an older person mourning abandoned industrial site – is a cliché of what Kristian Shaw (2021) calls 'BrexLit' now: it occurs in a scene from Coe's *Middle England* (2018) in which the protagonist takes his father to where the Longbridge plant used to be (259); it suffuses Anthony Cartwright's *The Cut* (2017) in which 'everything above ground has gone, even the concrete floor of what had once been a factory building has disintegrated' (34), leaving the protagonist the job of digging up the pipes for salvage. In *Ghost Wall*, this loss leads to anger, resentment and violence. As the experiment goes on, the father becomes more extreme. At first cooking only a kind of gruel, he then hunts, skins and makes the group eat rabbits; he beats his wife and daughter more: 'it went on longer than usual, as if the open air invigorated him' (62). Finally, the men come to build the 'ghost wall' of the title. The archaeologist explains how as 'last-ditch defence against the Romans' (108) one of the tribes used magic and 'made a palisade and bought out their ancestral skulls and arrayed them along the top, dead faces gazing down' (108). Using animal skulls, the men build such a wall: 'the Rabbit Palisade', thinks Silvie dismissively, and Molly says that 'it kind of reminds me of Swallows and Amazons but they're grown men' (114). The men go on to have a ceremony, the Professor 'drumming with his head thrown back to the moon', Dad 'sitting straight as if in church and joining a wordless chant' (120).

Eventually – the foreshadowed sacrifice – the father and the men decide to 'sacrifice' Silvie: they 'wanted to kill me at sunset' (136), she says, re-enacting, or inventing, the ritual that created the bog bodies. Whether they actually plan to kill Silvie or not is moot (the novel is suitably ambiguous). But, as Molly says, 'they've completely lost the plot' (139). They tie Silvie and take her to the bog, beating the drums; they cut her with a knife ('there was pain' (144)), and she zones out just as she had when her father had beaten her earlier in the novel. But Molly has called the police and a local midwife they had met, Trudie. Silvie is rescued and spends the night at Trudie's, sleeping (not euphemistically) with Molly.

In contrast to her father's more racist chthonic mythic history, Silvie comes to her own ideas about the past. She does 'indulge' herself 'with the idea that ancient knowledge somehow runs in our blood' (107), but her realizations are more complex. She imagines the Roman army (correctly) as multicultural. She recalls Doggerland, the sunk land bridge to Europe, which meant, in contrast to John of Gaunt's endlessly reused 'Sceptre'd isle' speech, that the channel did not serve the office of a wall or moat but that anyone could walk from 'the marshy lowlands of Denmark to the Northumbrian Forest' (54). Silvie imagines the life of the bog girl, 'a young teenager, Dad had said, about your age … she had had a life before me, that bog girl' (69–70) and the life, too, of the Victorian girl whose shoe they recover from a peat bog. This allows her the crucial insight into the past, and into her father, that the 'bog people Dad loved who could exist as victims, as the objects of violence' (69). For her father they are both a sign of past grandeur and the focus of a resentment; they exist as destroyed, unheard and disempowered. He celebrates them as dead. By contrast, Silvie realizes the past is somehow in the present: the 'whole point' of the experiment is that 'we ourselves became the ghosts, learning to walk the land as they walked it two thousand years ago', and 'to do it properly, I thought, we would almost have to absent ourselves from ourselves' (34). Molly, too, realizes this: rather than celebrating the absence of the past, she says, 'I'd like to make things be alive again' (40). This awareness of the present-ness of the past allows Silvie to point out that, for example, the American military uses magic too (they paint slogans on their bombs, play heavy metal at their enemies). The professor agrees: 'one of the things you learn in my line of work is that there's no steady increase in rationalism over the centuries' (44).

In addition to this opposition over understanding the past, the novel draws out the polarizations I have discussed earlier, specifically over class. The professor and students are middle class, the family working class. The students take international holidays; Silvie says, 'we didn't have passports' (17). The students have not even heard of Burnley or Rochdale, where Silvie's family come from, and while Molly has a posh southern accent, Silvie's father is dismissive of the south as 'just traffic and throngs of people' (95). The father lacks status, and Silvie is aware he resents 'those other men who were paid to walk the places Dad loved and write the ideas he could have had' (93). His wife excuses his violence: 'He can't help it … he gets het up behind a wheel all day, a man like that, wanting to be outdoors, he weren't meant for it' (93–4). Even Silvie's name is cause of conflict. Silvie is short for 'Sulevia' as her father named her after 'an Ancient British goddess … he wanted me to have a proper British native name' (19). The students are critical of his idea that 'there's some original Britishness somewhere' and 'that if he goes back far enough he'll find someone who wasn't a foreigner' (20). They tell Silvia it is a Latinate name: she knows it is a 'Roman corruption of a lost British word. There are actually people who know Latin where I come from, we do have books' (20). However, as the chthonic past becomes more powerful over the course of the novel, that father takes the initiative from the middle-class professor. Activating the mythic past changes the social order in the present.

While many books, from canonical classics to cult hits, are adapted into comics/graphic novels, Barney Farmer's *Drunken Baker* (2018) is a rare example of a comic turned into a novel. The 'Drunken Bakers' are a strip from the popular monthly comic *Viz*. *Drunken Baker* is an utterly unpretentious late modernist stream-of-consciousness novel covering something like twelve hours in the life of a drunken baker, told by that baker in short, broken paragraphs, from his waking (with a tot of rum) to his work all day with another, also drunken, baker to leaving work that evening.

The story is a profoundly sad one. The bakery had been a success for three generations, customers 'a line along the pavement, along the street, past the bookies, down to the hairdressers' (Farmer 2018: 18) and the factory workers too, at lunchtime and in the evening: 'half the blokes in that factory would be up here for our pies' (43). But now it is more than precarious: it is failing but still just about open. The baker's memory is dominated by his surrogate father, the Gaffer, who owned the bakery and trained him, and the Gaffer's wife, Alice. The Gaffer taught him 'all the tricks and craft his dad and granddad passed to him, he passed that to us' (23), a chain of skill passing down through the generations. The town and the bakery are woven together: 'Bread of that family fed this town for 70 years' (20). Alice, too, tied the bakery into the whole community: she knew all the 'mums and wives and birds' (44). But now the factories are closed, the town is dying and the 'little pieces, the little links are broke, for good an' all' (21). The book, through the consciousness of this one baker, shows us the interlinked communal, professional and personal damage of this breakage: the baker's angry, self-destructive drunkenness is both a response to and a metaphor for this destruction.

The whole community has collapsed, although both the Gaffer and Alice 'went before the factory went' (44). The pubs have gone: 'They might have a fire lit in the Old England', says the other baker, but the protagonist replies, 'Old England's gone, every stone of it' (148). There is a vicious circle. The bakers and others buy black-market drink (and 'I hope that don't dry up now they've' fucked off out of

Europe. That'd be a ball ache' (109)) because the pubs are too expensive, which in turn leads to the pubs' closing, which in turn leads to more black-market drink which, in an epitome of loneliness, is consumed alone and not convivially.

The pubs and the bakery are 'little links', broken for good. Their bakery, and so the baker's professional craft and self-regard, has been destroyed by neoliberal capitalism: 'We can't compete with them shitty chains ... Two steak slices for a quid? A fucking quid? That's us fucked here. And Steak? Get to fuck is steak ... It's bleeding shit, bought by the tonne, blasted off fucking skeletons with a jetwash' (11). The bread sold by these chains is inhuman: 'frozen dough off an industrial estate two hundred mile away, done by the bloody tonne, all machines, no hands have been in it' (46). And while the Gaffer 'taught us never to cut a corner, not one, because you never know why people come back' (51), now, they have to 'cut a few corners ... to keep going' (21). 'We can only do what sells. What we can leave out longest, what we can afford to waste' (68). One of the many strengths of the novel is the detail of these cut corners: the Gaffer's recipe for Dundee cake calls for whiskey but instead they use some of the cheap black-market brandy which they drink all day.

This destruction is clear at the personal level too. The bakery itself is a dysfunctional community: the two bakers hate each other. We never learn his or his colleague's names; he is only called 'the cunt' (17 ff). While the other baker is a 'pissed-up cunt ain't made a cake you'd want to touch with your foot in 10 years' (21), the protagonist is also malicious and unpleasant. They steal from each other (94) and trick each other. They maintain long-standing grievances: the protagonist, for example, resents the way the other baker paid for his half of the business, borrowing from the Gaffer. Finally, in a dream sequence, it is revealed that the protagonist hit his ex-wife ('I never done that. I never done nothing like that' (87)) and that the other baker knows this. We hear his personal decline from a professional young man, meeting his wife-to-be for the first time, to a lonely, desperate, hate-filled alcoholic: 'we all have to go [urinate] in a cup sometimes, I know I do, then you forget and have a swig' (51).

When he was 'shitfaced' (121) the baker used to see a ghostly soldier covered in mud at the end of his bed. The ghost – as if from the Battle of the Somme – is a symbol of working-class pride and solidarity and at the same time an image of the betrayal of that solidarity by the officer class. This is the ghost that haunts the novel, the utter abandonment of this northern town, its businesses and people to the 'totalitarianism of the market'. The anger and resentment is turned inwards to the baker himself, to his colleague the other baker. He is existentially lonely; he has become uprooted and is losing his place it the world. As an illustration of the quantitative discussion of loneliness earlier, the strain of neoliberal capitalism is making him, and his bakery, superfluous, no longer part of the world at all. No wonder he 'gets out of it' on any drink he can lay his hands on. 'Out of it' is where he is.

The third novel I want to look at is Bernard Cornwell's *Warlord* (2020), the final instalment in a bestselling historical adventure series, which (in the words of the website) 'tells the tale of Alfred the Great and his descendants through the eyes of Uhtred, an English boy born into the aristocracy of ninth-century Northumbria, captured by the Danes and taught the Viking ways' (Cornwell n.d.). These are narratively compelling and well-crafted, if a little formulaic, books. Just as George Macdonald Fraser's Flashman appears heroic but is a cowardly poltroon, so also Uhtred is known by the sobriquet 'the Wicked' but is, in fact, quite good: loyal, oath-keeping and a good and thoughtful master. Cornwell's Napoleonic war hero Sharpe became an officer, and his working-class upbringing put him at odds with the military establishment; similarly, Uhtred is a pagan but serves and despite himself admires Christian rulers.

*Warlord* concerns the Battle of Brunanburh in 937 CE, which, Cornwell suggests, is the founding battle for England: 'before the battle there was no England … As dusk fell on that bloody field there was' (330) because Æthelstan, Alfred's grandson, had united the warring kingdoms within England as one by his victory. Like many bestselling writers, Cornwell keeps his personal politics close to his chest. For example, asked his opinion of Brexit on his website, he hedges, 'I suspect it's probably an error, or else it's the first lifeboat off the Titanic. One or the other' (Cornwell n.d.). But the politics of the books are clear: they are an epic of national creation. In the novel's metatext, Cornwell writes that 'the story of England's making is not well known, which strikes me as strange' (2020: 332) and these novels realize that story. In a neat summation of Lukács, Cornwell says in an interview that 'I had to write a book about the creation of England. Most historical novels have a big story and a little story, and the big story is the true story' (Flood 2020: n.p.). But, for Cornwell, these links to the past are powerful. After meeting his father for the first time as an adult, he learned that he 'was descended from this man who was the Lord of Bebbanburg' and this 'little story' gave way to the 'big story' (n.p.). Another material link is made in the afterword of the novel. In the main part of novel, the fictional Uhtred loses a small dining knife at Brunanburh: in the afterword, Cornwell thanks an archaeologist from Bristol University for giving him a small dining knife found, around twelve hundred years later, at the battlefield. One the one hand, this is a sweet and thoughtful gift from an archaeologist to a novelist who has both drawn on that archaeologist's work and amplified it through a bestseller. On the other hand, through its fictionalization (Uhtred to Cornwall), it has made it an uncanny and chthonic link to the fabricated past.

However, this series of books, cumulating in *Warlord*, is an ethnocentric nationalist epic and displays may of the qualities analysed by Ford and Sobolewska. Issues of race are dealt with in an interesting way. Uhtred's entourage is 'multiracial', comprising English, Irish and Viking warriors: he may seem wicked, but he is not racist. Moreover, he is notably 'progressive' in that, while disapproving of Christianity, he does not really mind people's religion: a proleptic protestant, English before the English, he refuses to open windows into men's souls, as Elizabeth I is reputed to have said. On the other hand, he and the novel are both profoundly ethnocentric: they are about belonging, allegiance and the conflict between different ethnic groups. Uhtred and others are firmly bound in place by oaths and ties of belonging. Moreover, their identities are bound to place: 'I am a Northumbrian and my life had been dedicated to regaining Bebbanburg' (103). This novel, and the series, glamorizes and celebrates such belonging in a clear masculine-gendered framework. (This is not, for example, a retelling of Alfred's story from a female perspective, although Alfred's daughter Æthelfaled had a major role in earlier novels.)

This is a chthonic nationalist history, of the sort that Silvie's father would approve, complete with its undertow of male violence. The epilogue begins:

> I am Uhtred, son of Uhtred, who was the son of Uhtred, and his father was also called Uhtred, and they were all lord of Bebbanburg. I am that too, though these days folk call me the Lord of the North … though I am old, my task is to stop the Scots coming south in to the land we have learned to call *Englaland*. (323)

Here, the chains of patrimony, the 'ancestry … linage' is foregrounded, the 'little links' have not fallen apart but appear in a kind of consoling historical myth. By myth I do not mean that these novels are not highly informed and draw on the historical record; rather, I mean that they offer a consoling, masculine, ethnocentric English nationalist story, matching Jones and Henderson's research on the rise of Englishness. No one here is lonely but lives in a fantasy of a strong community: the recurring trope of the novel series is the 'shield wall', both terrifying and held as the model of courage, in which warriors stand and fight their enemies shoulder to shoulder.

## Conclusion

What threads link these novels and the current state of the UK's community?

First, none of these novels offer to 'speak' for the whole community: they are not 'state-of-the-nation' novels. Indeed, such is the level of polarization revealed in the statistics that perhaps no state-of-the-nation novel is possible at the moment: there is nowhere outside the conflict from which to speak. Coe's *Middle England* has the generic markers of a 'state-of-the-nation' novel (many characters drawn from across the polity, fictionalized political reportage, real events recounted and so on), but in the end it wears its 'remain' heart on its sleeve and is part of the polarization. The three novels I have discussed are a literary fiction, literary fiction emerging from a subculture (if such a term is still relevant) and a bestseller. As such they stem from and perhaps reflect very different audiences. The two that are more literary are clearly more interested in the 'remain' politics, characterized by the so-called liberal elite: by contrast, Cornwell's bestseller displays a complex ambivalence. That said, each shows a community at war with itself: polarized by class and prosperity, region and ethnicity and (barring a bloody battle) with little sign of resolution. Oddly, it is the quantitative studies which suggest ways to solve our current situation: populist opposition in *Brexitland*; more local democracy in *Englishness*; rebuilding the fibres of community in Hertz and Pullman. None of the novels suggest anything like this, but they do explore a nostalgia for a lost past of communal connection. Two remain bleak: Silvie escapes her father and the police arrest him, but this is not a resolution but a respite; there is no way out for the drunken baker. *Warlord*, for all its craft, is a consoling historical fantasy.

Second, each is about a concern for the past and manifests a profound and painful nostalgia. Silvie's lonely and violent father's is the most extreme, a desire to root himself in the past and an awareness of loss in which the whole past is run together, 'Cranes' like 'ceremonial pillars of lost civilisations' (Moss 2018: 25). The baker's memory of the thriving town community and the chain of the generations, the bread which 'fed this town for 70 years' (20), is also painful. Both of these are the *-algia*, the illness of nostalgia. *Warlord* is both alive with these memories and a response to them, offering a nationalist epic consolation. Silvie, too, feels this, half playfully imagining 'ancient knowledge' in her 'blood' (107), although she does not feel the need to belong so strongly. This is how ethnocentrism inhabits a past.

This leads to a third point, one which the surveys fail, for the most part, to draw out: the gendered, masculine nature of this painful nostalgia. The male establishment elite are filled, writes Anne Applebaum in her savage *Twilight of Democracy*, with a conservative nostalgia and a belief in the 'restoration of English greatness' (2020: 89): these novels show the painful non-elite version of this nostalgia, which lacks any sense of 'restoration' and, instead, is filled with self-hate, despair, victimization and destruction. There is a search for a male patrimony: the Gaffer, the Ancient Britons, the fantasy consolation of the fortress owned by Uhtred's father and grandfather. This is so powerful in *Ghost Wall* that it 'wins over' the archaeologist and at least one of his male students, a gendered desire more powerful than class. It is tied as well to male violence against women.

Arendt wrote of how the 'visible and invisible threads' of society were severed, and Farmer's baker says that the 'little pieces, the little links are broke, for good an' all' (2018: 21). This past society was not, perhaps, as golden as the nostalgia paints it. But in its place, what is left appears to be a community totally ruptured and divided into profoundly opposed groups; individuals lost to loneliness and despair, turning to destruction and violence; false hope and hollow 'belonging' offered by dangerous people. The fiction I have looked at – and indeed a significant amount of British fiction of the past three or four years – is in the same vein. Some are escapist nostalgia, which may console, but the images of the past it offers may suggest something worse. Some are filled with warnings; some with nothing but despair.

## References

Applebaum, Anne (2020), *Twilight of Democracy*, New York: Doubleday.
Arendt, Hannah (1958), *The Origins of Totalitarianism*, London: Harvest.
BBC News (2018), 'Boris Johnson Challenged over Brexit Business "Expletive"', 26 June, https://www.bbc.co.uk/news/uk-politics-44618154.
Cartwright, Anthony (2017), *The Cut*, London: Peirine.
Clarke, Harold, Matthew Goodwin and Paul Whiteley (2017), *Brexit: Why Britain Voted to Leave the European Union*, Cambridge: Cambridge University Press.
Coe, Jonathan (2018), *Middle England*, London: Penguin.
Cornwell, Bernard (2020), *Warlord*, London: HarperCollins.
Cornwell, Bernard (n.d.), http://www.bernardcornwell.net/series/the-last-kingdom-series/.
Eaglestone, Robert (2018), 'Cruel Nostalgia and the Memory of the Second World War', in Robert Eaglestone (ed.), *Brexit and Literature: Critical and Cultural Responses*, 92–104, London: Routledge.

Farmer, Barney (2018), *Drunken Baker*, Hull: Wrecking Ball.

Flood, Alison (2020), 'I Play Merry Hell with History, I Admit It', *Guardian*, 15 October, https://www.theguardian.com/books/2020/oct/15/bernard-cornwell-history-uhtred-sharpe-war-lord.

Henderson, Alisa, and Richard Wyn Jones (2021), *Englishness: The Political Force Transforming Britain*, Oxford: Oxford University Press.

Hertz, Noreena (2020), *The Lonely Century*, London: Sceptre.

Mitchell, Peter (2021), *Imperial Nostalgia*, Manchester: Manchester University Press.

Moss, Sarah (2018), *Ghost Wall*, London: Granta.

Putnam, Robert (2000), *Bowling Alone: The Collapse and Revival of American Community*, New York: Simon and Schuster.

Shaw, Kristian (2021), *Brexlit: British Literature and the European Project*, London: Bloomsbury.

Sobolewska, Maria, and Robert Ford (2020), *Brexitland: Identity, Diversity and the Reshaping of British Politics*, Cambridge: Cambridge University Press.

Wellings, Ben (2017), *English Nationalism, Brexit and the Anglosphere*, Manchester: Manchester University Press.

Williams, Raymond (1954), 'Film and Dramatic Tradition', in R. Williams and M. Orrom, *Preface to Film*, London: Film Drama.

2

# 'Our uneasy mixed community': Cross-community romance, magic realism and Northern Ireland

Alison Garden

*They held their silence reverently and wondered if they loved the island enough to be neither north nor south, foreigner or familiar, but rather a brave new direction, balanced like a hairline fracture in the centre of everything.*

– Carson (2016: 190)

This is how Jan Carson concludes 'Children's Children', the final story from her eponymous collection *Children's Children* (2016). 'Children's Children' explores a brief interlude in the lives of two 'leftover children', on an unnamed but partitioned island, due to 'be married for the good of the island, both northern and southern sides' (184). The protagonists are the 'last' two young people on their respective sides of the border, '[a]ll the other young ones had left for the mainland with the notion of becoming beauty therapists or PhD students' (184). All is not quite as it seems in Carson's partitioned island, and this loss of people leads to a curious loss of landmass. In an earlier incident, 'in the 1970s, a half mile of the east coast had unhooked itself and floated off' as every year the island 'lost ten to twenty stones of weight' (186, 185). Carson's magic realist fable ends on a tentative moment of hope for this troubled island with her couple poised on the brink of a reconciliatory union. Her eponymous story is notably future oriented, 'Children's Children' gesturing towards the next generation and the hope that the young couple at the centre of Carson's story embody, 'balanced like a hairline fracture at the centre of everything' (190). This simile is ambivalent, a precarious stability that could crack open at the slightest disquiet. But it is the couple themselves, and their burgeoning union, who are the 'hairline fracture', and this gives them agency.

The word 'Ireland' is never used by Carson, but her story's imaginative geography of the 'northern and southern sides' maps neatly onto the latitudinally partitioned island that we know today as the Republic of Ireland and Northern Ireland. This narrative of a heterosexual couple 'married for the good of the island' is resonant, too, within Irish literary history. Carson's short story, Stefanie Lehner argues, 'imitates and parodies the fictional form that has become most notably associated with attempts to reconcile the ethnonational divide that has marked Ireland historically: the national tale' (2020a: 47). Much debated in recent scholarship, the hybrid genre of the national tale arose out of the unrest caused by the 1800 Act of Union, which took effect in 1801, resulting in the United Kingdom of Great Britain and Ireland. The national tale attempted to make this union palatable through a 'reliance on reconciliatory marriages' that took place, almost exclusively, between an Irish woman and a British, or Anglo-Irish, man (Connolly 2012: 94). 'Children's Children' is a contemporary take on a cultural form with a lengthy and complex history but particularly associated, in the latter end of the twentieth century, with the Northern conflict euphemistically referred to as 'the Troubles'. During the conflict, the reconciliatory 'love across the divide' narrative of a cross-community relationship became a staple motif utilized by writers of prose, poetry, film and theatre. Hugely popular with writers and readers, the motif has received scant critical engagement bar the exception of Joe Cleary who insists that the Northern Irish 'romance-across-the-divide is an anxious and contradictory literary mode' (2002: 112).

The romance narrative is not the only 'anxious and contradictory' element of Carson's story: her choice of genre, magic realism, embodies contradiction. Combining, as its name suggests, elements of both the real and magical, Stephen Slemon argues that magic realist texts enact a 'battle between two oppositional systems' or two 'different kind[s] of fictional world[s]' (1995: 409). The key effect of magic realist literature, Slemon insists, is the creation of 'two separate narrative modes [that] never manage to arrange themselves into any kind of hierarchy' (410). While this 'battle between two oppositional systems' mirrors the meeting of Carson's lovers from antagonistic communities, the literary history of the magic realist register adds another layer of complexity to Carson's use of the genre in a Northern Irish context. Magic realism, a term coined by art historian Franz Roh in 1925, has been associated most strongly with Caribbean and Latin American literature, especially that from the 1940s and 1950s. It is, then, a literary genre with a critical history that is firmly associated with the 'postcolonial'. The oppositional registers inherent in the hybrid genre are, Ben Holgate elucidates, indicative of 'the clash between the colonial culture and that of the indigenous population' (2015: 642). The use of the genre, Slemon proposes, is often read as political and notes the 'structure of perception ... in literary critical registers ... that magic realism, as a socially symbolic contract, carries a residuum of resistance toward the imperial system and to its totalizing systems of generic classification' (1995: 408). But what does this mean in an Irish or Northern Irish context, where there is no consensus as to whether Ireland ever was, used to be or, indeed, whether the North continues to be a colonial space?

The relationship of Ireland to its eastern neighbour has historically been, and continues to be, fraught. Historians and critics remain in dispute as to whether (Northern) Ireland has ever constituted a colony and as to the validity of postcolonial methods, theory and analysis to the study of Ireland.[1] In his contribution to *The Cambridge History of Postcolonial Literature*, Mario Siskind argues the genre of magic realism 'belongs organically to non-Western, or rather marginal, cultures' (2011: 835); Siskind's suggestion that non-Western and 'postcolonial' might be contiguous highlights some of the tensions inherent to the argument about the relevance of postcolonial theory to Ireland.[2] Carson is not the only contemporary author to turn to magic realism to tease out the complexities of romance between individuals from the North's ostensible 'two communities', and this chapter will discuss short stories by Bernie McGill and Róisín O'Donnell as well. Parsing these stories through the kinds of close reading so often denied to narratives of cross-community romance, this essay explores why these writers might have elected to use the magic realist genre to tell these particular romance stories. On the one hand, the generic choice is entirely unremarkable for Carson, whose fiction celebrates 'the domestic and the fantastic as everyday bedfellows' (Magennis 2021a: 35); likewise, O'Donnell uses the register frequently in her collection of short stories, *Wild Quiet* (2016). For Bernie McGill, however, the choice is more conspicuous, leading, perhaps, to the suggestion that ghosts, monsters and mock-heroic mating are more feasible than a happy union between lovers from the North's two communities. But, as this chapter will explore, narratives of cross-community romance, and their subversive potential, acutely embody the unsettling power of so-called domestic desires within a more transgressive political framework than they are often given credit for.

'Community' is a word that works hard in Northern Ireland. Used as a shorthand – perhaps euphemistically – for ethnopolitical identities, 'community' is heavy with the weight of history, politics and contested national allegiances. Across the island of Ireland, Brian Cliff agues, ideas 'of community have been answered for ... in terms of the nation' (2006: 116). As disputes continue about whether the contentious Northern statelet should be 'British', as part of the United Kingdom, or Irish, as part of a united Republic, there is no consensus about the national community of the six counties. In her powerful essay on Anna Burns's *Milkman* (2018), Patricia Malone opens by noting the enormous difficulties surrounding even the name of this north-eastern pocket of the island, claiming, 'Northern Ireland is an unspeakable state' and questioning whether she should use 'Northern Ireland' and 'in so doing tacitly endorse the existence of an unjustly gerrymandered territory'. Or should she instead go with 'the north' and overlook Donegal?' (Malone 2021: 1–2). Stephen O'Neill argues, 'as these terms suggest, this [is] more than just wordplay', with '[e]ach impl[ying] a particular political standpoint and reveal[ing] much about the user's attitudes towards the state' (2020: n.p.). As Malone summarizes, '[l]anguage is quite clearly a problem' in the North; shifting, slippery and 'innate[ly] politic[al]' (2021: 1, 9).

In Northern Ireland, the word 'community' has 'been hijacked as a synonym' for two dominant ethnopolitical identities that are strongly, although not exclusively, aligned to religious identities (Cliff 2006: 119). The North's 'two communities' are the largely Catholic Nationalist Republican (CNR) community, who identify as Irish, and the largely Protestant Unionist Loyalist (PUL) community, who identify as British (although, of course, Northern Ireland is not a part of the geographical landmass of Britain). The precarious peace engendered by the Belfast, or Good Friday, Agreement (GFA) enshrined these two communities in legislative terms and, as Lehner articulates, 'the consociational model that underpins the new devolved [Northern Ireland Assembly] naturalises rather than transcends the divisions of the two dominant ideological blocs' (2020b: 136). Due to the particulars of the GFA, 'members of the Northern Ireland Assembly must designate themselves as nationalist, unionist or other and that all decisions taken must have majority support from both the nationalist and unionist blocs' (Shirlow 2004: 196). Despite the enormous intersectional pressures that are brought to bear on these identities within these 'two communities', such as the vast inequities experienced due to class, gender and sexuality, 'there is no place within the new administrative order within which an accommodationist middle ground can develop' (196). This 'new administrative order' elides the North's other internal communities and fails to recognize that the statelet has always been shaped by other internal and external communities. Northern Ireland exists within a 'political system which undermines the power of appeals to cross-community sentiment' (196). Writing about love or desire that transcends this antagonistic bloc between communities is still subversive even if it is insistently fashioned as a phenomenon of the 'not yet', in a future time just beyond our reach.

## Jan Carson's 'Children's children': Desire and the magic of the 'not yet'

Jan Carson's turn to a symbolic and partitioned island, where 'you were north or south, or you left', satirizes the idea that the island's two communities are irreconcilably different (Carson 2016: 186). 'All the island's children had been formed from the same sandy soil', Carson declares, 'sprouting annually, in metric units, towards same sap-grey sky' (186). 'They spoke the same words ... and drunk from the same slow river', subject to the same weather '[w]hen it rained, as every day it did' from the 'same cloud sulk which settled on all their pitched roofs' (186). Countering their own insistence on their difference from one another, Carson writes that the 'people were as consistent as common spades, on either side of the border' (186). The islanders, north and south, become 'purple with indignation' at the suggestion that they might be similar: '[n]o true southerner wishes to be mistaken for an eejit from the north' (187). This 'indignation' can turn violent, too. 'In 1973, a young fella who'd come to make a documentary' found himself 'drowned ... and posted home in envelopes' for suggesting that the partition of the island 'was sheer stupidity' (186). Carson mixes her magic realist details here with a prescient note of grim reality; 1973 was one of the darkest years of the Troubles.

This moment is anomalous in Carson's story: an incident of extratextual violence rendered strange because of its incongruity within the magical world Carson has established. It is a clear nod to recent Northern Irish history and an intrusion of reality into Carson's fable-like world. But this acute tension between reality and its antithesis is 'the core paradox of magical realism' (Arva 2008: 68). Some authors and critics claim magic realism is a more effective way of representing, recreating or evoking 'the real' than realism. The Colombian author Gabriel García Márquez insisted in 1973 that the genre 'comes from the reality of Latin America' (Kennedy 1973: n.p.). For Márquez, 'Our reality is in itself out of all proportion' and so, for him, magic realism is more a veracious literary mode than traditional realism (Mendoza and Márquez 1983: 60). Elucidated above, magic realism is a genre that developed out of the oppositional encounter between colonial cultures and indigenous ones but it also enabled, Maria Takolander declares, writers to 'radically challenge colonialist constructions of the real' (2010: 169). The strangeness of the colonial experience, Márquez seems to suggest, is best depicted through a turn to magic realism.

However, Northern Ireland's ambivalent relationship to colonialism, as a statelet populated by communities with competing ideas about their own colonial status, elides any easy argument about Northern magic realism as a 'postcolonial' strategy. That said, all three of the stories discussed here deal with the violence of the Troubles, either explicitly or indirectly; this violence was a direct by-product of colonialism. What is more, the distinct nature of the Northern conflict distorted the putative ordinariness of everyday life beyond recognition, mutating reality into something nightmarish, where political violence and domestic life coalesced. If we tend to associate the ordinary or the everyday with the domestic, critics have made clear that there is nothing ordinary about the everyday domestic in the North. The Northern conflict ensured that the 'discrete categorizing of space into public and private, and the assumed privacy of the house are untenable' (Reid 2007: 935). Patricia Malone cautions against 'recuperative narratives that seek to stress the ongoing nature of "everyday life"', as if the Troubles were 'simply some sorts of backdrop against which life struggled to continue, instead of being an expression of longstanding and omnipresent hatreds that coloured the very texture of life itself' (2021: 3). This goes some way to account for the use of magic realism in the North, a genre where ordinary and extraordinary exist cheek by jowl, where 'uncanniness erupt[s] from a fissure in the ordinary' (Armitt 2012: 512). In all of the stories explored here, this tension between the ordinary and extraordinary is instructive to the ways in which normal life was malformed by the violence of the conflict. This use of the contradictory genre of magic realism is indicative of the anxiety and ambivalence that characterizes the relationships between Ireland, Britain and Northern Ireland. Carson's use of this intensifies the already 'anxious and contradictory mode' of the romance narrative which straddles the North's two antagonistic communities. After Carson's parabolic 'island had split in two', the two communities begin to circulate suspicious rumours about the other side with 'all sorts of stories' spreading 'backwards and forwards across the border' (2016: 187). Some are benign – northerners 'putting red sauce in [their] tea' – but others more pernicious, speaking to a fundamentally discordant difference in ways of living: 'the northerners kept their old ones in with the chickens; the folks of the south did not believe in dentists or even toothbrushes' (188). Underwriting this 'rumouring' is, of course, the rhetoric of suspicion of an alien other (187). These attitudes can be found within Northern Ireland itself where a 'devotion to community underpins the casting of the "other" community as treacherous, dangerous and untrustworthy'. Contrasted against this, '"the communal self" [is] trusted, safe, culturally homogeneous and morally superior' (Shirlow 2004: 201). Carson's fashioning of the two sides of the island reflects this distrust of one community for the other within Northern Ireland's borders. But once Carson's 'leftover children' actually meet one another, and confront these stereotypes, they warm to each other. She thinks the 'sound of him was a Continental holiday' and, in the kind of affective, embodied response Caroline Magennis writes so well about in *Northern Irish Writing after the Troubles*, she 'found herself goosebumpling up and down … much afraid and also excited' (Carson 2016: 189). However, the intrinsically political matter of the domestic undoes the partnership before it has begun: the two 'could not settle upon a side' of the border to live because of their worries about 'upset[ting] the balance and tip[p]ing' the island into the sea' (190). Despairing, the unnamed northern man declares, '[t]he weight of us combined could ruin everything'. The story, and collection, ends with the pair considering whether they are the start of a 'brave new direction, balanced', in an ambiguous simile that might talk back to Yeats's 'Second Coming' (1919), 'like a hairline fracture in the centre of everything' (Carson 2016: 190; Yeats 2000: 158). The third line of this Yeats poem – 'Things fall apart; the centre cannot hold' – has been much parodied and quoted (Yeats 2000: 158). Yet Carson's coupling is an active coming together that subverts Yeats's falling apart, the tautological 'centre of everything' emphasizing how cohesive the 'brave new direction' of the union could be for everyone (Carson 2016: 190).

As with its literary precursor, the nineteenth-century national tale, Carson's story transmutes the anxieties surrounding the political relationship between Ireland and its eastern neighbour, so potently compressed into the disputed six counties, into an intimate relationship between two individuals. The national tales were 'novels that absorb[ed] the anxieties generated by the passing of the controversial Act [of Union] in the Irish parliament into the sphere of fiction' (Connolly 2012: 106). Beneath Carson's parody of the national tale's symbolism, and her fantastical vision of 'leftover children', there are genuine concerns about migration, a diminishing population and what a united island might mean. Carson's divided island may lose landmass – 'in the 1970s, a half mile of the east coast had unhooked itself and floated off' – but it is the loss of people that is the cause of the most concern (2016: 186). The protagonists are the 'last' two young people on their respective sides of the border, '[a]ll the other young ones had left for the mainland' (184). 'Each year [the island] lost ten to twenty stones of weight as … the young ones' migrated (185).

Emigration has been a defining feature of Irish life for centuries; people from both the north and south, Catholics and Protestants, have emigrated to Britain, the United States and elsewhere. An overly deterministic interpretation of this story might read Carson's use of 'mainland' here as indicative of a particular sense of allegiance. The 'innate politicisation of language in the North' means that we could map this to the British mainland (Malone 2021: 9); the CNR community would likely say 'across the water', or similar, for Britain is not their 'mainland'. In this way, Carson's story could be seen as articulating intensifying PUL concerns about their diminishing majority and the increasing likelihood of a 'Border Poll' and, with it, the very tangible chance of a united Ireland. *Children's Children* was published in 2016: the year of the Brexit referendum. The results of this are still playing out, but it will undoubtedly radically resettle the political and emotional landscapes of Britain, Ireland and the United Kingdom.

The story speaks to broader anxieties that we may read from this slippage of language. As the only remaining young people, the unnamed protagonists are tasked with marrying and breeding: 'if more people were not soonly made, there would be no one left to keep the island afloat' (Carson 2016: 185). These biopolitical concerns are couched in a tone that seems both mythic and sardonic: these 'leftover children, too fat and faithful to consider leaving' are now compelled to reproduce and counter the receding of the 'island's tideline' due to its diminishing population and 'newfound lightness' (184, 185). But these biopolitical anxieties are acute in Northern Ireland, where there is a distinct nervousness about whether or not the population will reproduce appropriately and add to the 'right side' of the national family. The politician and activist Bernadette Devlin McAliskey encapsulated this with irreverence when she declared, '[u]nionists must ensure that nationalists don't outnumber them. On the other side what are we confined to – outbreeding them? Either we shoot them or we outbreed them' (Cahill 1995: 57). While these concerns were arguably more acute during the Troubles, there is a palpable anxiety in the North's PUL community about their current status within the United Kingdom. The past several census reports strongly suggest 'the trend away from a Protestant majority is likely to continue' (Morrow 2019: 11). When this chapter was written in spring 2021 (John Brannigan wryly observes, 'it is a necessary convention of every critical commentary on Northern Irish culture to include some such phrase indicating the provisional nature of what is to follow'), serious unrest has been fermenting in loyalist communities across the North, with violence directed towards Police Service Northern Ireland (PSNI) and interface areas between the two communities in Belfast (Brannigan 2006: 141). The factors leading to this are various and debated, but an important reason proffered is loyalist dissatisfaction with the 'Northern Ireland Protocol', legislation generated by Brexit that loyalists see as creating an economic block between Northern Ireland and Britain. This dissatisfaction is so severe that the Loyalist Communities Council (LCC) have temporarily withdrawn their support from the GFA.

What is fascinating about Carson's story is how it is the supposedly predictable, ordinary world of the domestic that unhinges the narrative of their symbolic union: everyday life in a cross-community setting seems impossible to sustain. Despite each being beguiled by the other, 'when they tried to imagine [life after their wedding], drinking tea and making up a stranger's bed, they could not' (Carson 2016: 185). The vital practicalities of their union, '[q]uestions such as which side of the island they might settle on, or who their children would marry, or where they would eat their Christmas dinner when Christmas made its annual appearance, had not been considered' (185). Numerous scholars have highlighted that the ostensibly private world of the domestic is never impermeable from external politics, but this is especially true of the North, Bryonie Reid argues, where 'private family homes in Northern Ireland have been made full participants in the public world in ways specific to the province's history and politics' (Reid 2007: 943). This is made visually apparent, Adam Hanna reminds us, as 'the working-class areas of Belfast and other urban areas that are divided into religiously homogenous zones, and whose domestic gable-end murals often declare the political and national allegiances of their inhabitants' (2015: 5). But there is an affective politics at play, too, in houses, and the domestic is a 'crucial political space', Eli Davies insists, even if the 'complicated reality of everyday domestic life is obscured' by dominant, recycled 'canonical political and cultural narratives' which foreground '(male) political violence' (2021: 71, 74). Highlighting the politicized nature of life in (post)colonial domestic spaces has also been a key feature of much magic realist fiction.[3] In her work on Salman Rushdie's novel *Midnight's Children*, Sara Upstone traces how, in the imperial project of British colonialism, 'home becomes a microcosm of the colony' (2007: 261). Magic realism, she argues, offers (post)colonial writers an imaginative space to deflect, resist and subvert the colonial politics of the home.

Carson's magic realism may be used to probe some substantial political concerns, but it is also cautiously optimistic in its vision for the future. The eponymous story is notably future oriented, 'Children's Children' gesturing towards the next generation and the hope that the young couple at the centre of Carson's story embody, 'balanced like a hairline fracture at the centre of everything' (2016: 190). As explored previously, this simile is ambivalent. Carson's coupling is an active coming together that subverts Yeats's falling apart, the tautological 'centre of everything' emphasizing how cohesive the 'brave new direction' of the union could be for everyone (2016: 190). Lehner sees Carson's story as 'anticipat[ing] an affiliative politics in its ending, which posits the seemingly impossible coming together of the two sides as a "brave new direction"', which she reads in light of Andrew Schaap's work in *Political Reconciliation* (Lehner 2020a: 50). 'Political reconciliation', Schaap argues, 'begins with the invocation of a "we" that is not yet and proceeds from the faith in its possibility towards a shared understanding of what went before' (2005: 77, also quoted in Lehner 2020a: 50). From this, Lehner grasps at the notion of a 'community that is "not yet"' to describe the imaginative project at the heart of 'Children's Children' (2020a: 50). Carson's story hints at a convivial, cosmopolitan future where neither is 'foreigner or familiar' but perfectly 'balanced' (2016: 190). Arguably, this idea of a future community is similar to the one envisaged in Paul Gilroy's *After Empire: Melancholia or Convivial Culture?* (2004). Here, Gilroy outlines a 'convivial' way of living in our contemporary (post)colonial moment. He describes it as a 'multicultural *future* prefigured everywhere in the ordinary experiences of contact, cooperation and conflict across the supposedly impermeable boundaries of race, culture, identity and ethnicity' (viii, italics mine). Carson's displacement of convivial community on to 'children's children' makes this a determinedly future focused aim.

There is a powerful futurity about desire. In her compelling criticism on contemporary Northern fiction, Caroline Magennis, drawing on the work of Lauren Berlant, Sara Ahmed and Audre Lorde, highlights the radical possibilities of the 'erotic as a political force' in the North (2021a: 5–6). Lauren Berlant elucidates this in *Desire/Love*, writing, 'desire describes a state of attachment to something or someone, and the cloud of possibility that is generated by the gap between an object's specificity and the needs and promises projected onto it' (2012: 6). This 'cloud of possibility', Magennis prompts, is the 'undefined future orientation of the love affair' (2021a: 46). Carson's reader is left to conclude that the fantastical and fable-like elements of 'Children's Children' are less unbelievable than a couple coming together from different communities. The magical 'not yet' of Carson's magic realism is the creation of a harmonious, everyday domesticity; a convivial future, imagined through desire, just out of reach. The magic realism of the stories engaged in this chapter works in multiple ways: creating hauntings, monsters and forced marriages that adduce the fundamental strangeness and horror of the reality of the Northern conflict. But Carson's ending introduces a different function of the magic realist elements of both this story and 'Children's Children' as a collection. In her final image of a magical cross-community coming together in the 'centre of everything', Carson's story articulates a burgeoning sense of a need to envision a new imaginative order for (Northern) Ireland (2016: 190).

## Bernie McGill's 'No angel': Care, forgiveness and cross-community compassion

Whereas Jan Carson's use of magic realism is distinctive and Róisín O'Donnell writes in a variety of genres, Bernie McGill's use of magic realism in her short story 'No Angel' is unusual (Magennis 2021a: 15). Noting the use of the genre in recent fiction, Dawn Miranda Sherratt-Bado argues the 'generic slipperiness of magical realism makes this an appropriate narrative mode for writing about Northern Ireland, a polity whose status is also problematic to define' (2018: 7). Testament to this 'generic slipperiness', Bernie McGill's 'No Angel' could be read as a ghost story, rather than as an example of magic realism, but there is none of the dread or horror that we might associate with a ghost story. Instead, the ghost is presented to us in entirely sober terms: '[t]he first time I saw my father after he died I was in the shower, hair plastered with conditioner' (McGill 2013: 39). Writing about the overlap between magic realism and the ghost story, Lucie Armitt notes their different treatment of ghosts. She suggests, in 'magic realism, ghosts are simply "there," usually giving testimony to the voices of those whom society has silenced or rendered "disappeared," but rarely the primary focus of the mystery of a text' (Armitt 2012: 519). In McGill's story, the extraordinary presence of the spectre is offset by the most quotidian details of everyday life; the first thing that the ghost of Annie's father says to her is that her tiles 'need re-grouting', complaining about the 'the salmon pink mould' (2013: 39). The mundane nature of this ghost's opening intervention – to comment on something as nondescript as bathroom mould – punctures any sense that this is an ominous haunting. And, yet, this presence appears to Annie in one of the most private places imaginable, the bathroom: it seems even in the most intimate spaces that Annie cannot be free of her father's hold.

As the story unfolds, we learn that Annie had lived with her father in their shared house after a fatal sectarian attack on her brother, Jamesie, caused her mother to die of heartbreak and grief. The horrifically violent murder of Jamesie happens simply because Annie's family are 'the wrong sort ... in the wrong place' in their 'uneasy mixed community' (McGill 2013: 42, 45). The resulting grief kills Annie's mother and makes her father 'bitter' against the other community: 'they're all the same', he declares, 'hungry land grabbers every last one of them' (42). This tension becomes especially pronounced when Annie's relationship with her boyfriend Thomas becomes serious and she meets his parents as a 'prospective daughter-in-law' (41). It is clear that the two come from different backgrounds when Annie remarks that his parents 'were far too middle-class for religion to be an issue' (41). Thomas's parents might not mind the cross-community dimension to their romance, but the ghost of Annie's father is incandescent with rage. In another visit, he demands to know if Annie is 'going to marry thawn boy' (41). In a curt exchange, Annie retorts, 'You know his name, Daddy', but the ghost of her father refuses to name him because his fear and distrust of 'the other' has led him to believe 'they're all the same' (41, 42). Her father's belief is briefly put under pressure when Annie ironically confesses that her initial attraction to Thomas stemmed from the ways in which he 'reminded [her] of Jamesie' (47). Despite this, the couple later break up, and Annie reveals that the relationship between the two 'was never going to work' (47). The exact reasons for the fatalism are only hinted at but we can presume that differences of both class and religion play at significant role in the failure of the relationship. Annie wryly observes that she 'couldn't have kept up the suitable-daughter-in-law show for a whole lifetime' (47). This idea of suitability clearly suggests that communal loyalties are still keenly observed, despite the polite veneer of 'middle-class' liberalism.

Even though the relationship between Annie and Thomas does not last, it is this, and her father's anxieties about it, which acts as a catalyst for, in that most poignant of phrases, 'dealing with the past'. At the story's close, we see Annie in Belfast's Opera House, attending a production of *The Bartered Bride*. Here, she has a final encounter with the ghost of her father, as well as a first and last encounter with the ghosts of her brother and mother. This choice of opera is pertinent: Bedřich Smetana and Karel Sabina's *The Bartered Bride* (1866) celebrates the romance between Mařenka and Jeník but only after many obstacles are overcome, including an attempt to convince Mařenka's overbearing parents that she should be allowed to choose her own lover. This is echoed in Annie's penultimate sentence to her father when she forcefully declares, 'I won't be told who to love by you', and her father's ghost responds with, 'I know' (McGill 2013: 48). McGill's story concludes with a 'kind of recovery', Caroline Magennis suggests, in that Annie's three family members are reunited and we, as readers, can assume that these spectres are finally at rest (Magennis 2021a: 124). It is telling that the story concludes here. Regardless of Annie's insistence that she can pursue romance with whoever she wants, whatever their ethnopolitical identity, the nuclear family remain siloed together – even in death.

However, if we think through the generic conventions associated with ghosts and haunting, McGill's subversion of them embeds an act of restitution that gestures towards the kind of hopeful futurity in Carson's story. While McGill's story is more accurately described as an example of magic realism rather than a Gothic ghost story, where 'ghosts are simply "there", … but rarely the primary focus of the mystery of a text', the ghost is still a literary device that we associate with generic conventions (Armitt 2012: 519). Traditionally, Julia Briggs articulates, the ghost 'represent[s] the return of the repressed in its most literal and paradigmatic form' and that generic traditions often invoke the ghost to 'deal with the most primitive, punitive, and sadistic of impulses, revenge being one of the commonest motifs' (2012: 178, 182). When McGill raises the story of Jamesie's murder, rendered in all its gruesome, heart-breaking detail, 'eyebrow like a burst plum, his buckled nose, the rainbow of bruises that spanned his face', readers may well expect that Annie's father has returned for revenge (2013: 43). After all, Avery F. Gordon insists, haunting is 'an animated state in which a repressed or unresolved social violence is making itself known' (2011: xvi). But, as the conclusion of McGill's story makes clear, the 'unresolved social violence' here is not Jamesie's murder but the desperate need of Annie's father to forgive those who killed him (Gordon 2011: xvi). The ghost, Gordon maintains, 'produc[es] a something-to-be-done' (xvi). For Annie's father, this means to find a way to be at peace and forgive Thomas, his community and 'his kind' (McGill 2013: 42). This is evident in the reveal of the story's final moments that, despite the ghosts of both her brother and mother being present in Annie's world, neither have ever visited her; when she encounters them in the Opera House, they do not even look at her. They have no cause to haunt the living because they have reconciled themselves to the past. Annie's father can only locate these ghosts, and find peace, after he has realized that Annie is free to love whom she wishes; forgiveness for Thomas and what he represents is an act of redemption. 'No Angel' foregrounds emotional recoupment and connection, where future reconciliation and peace can only be built through tentative, tender forgiveness of the past and engagement with communities beyond one's own.

## Róisín O'Donnell's 'Ebenezer's memories': Memory, family and communal identity

If we are to follow Jacques Derrida's (1994) intervention, the ghost is much more than an embodiment of past trauma: it is both *revenant* and *arrivant*, marker of an irrepressible history and speculative future. Like Carson, McGill's story is as acutely concerned with the future as with the past. This is also apparent in Róisín O'Donnell's short story, 'Ebenezer's Memories', from *Wild Quiet* (2016), which is relayed to readers through temporal play that ricochets back and forth like snatches of memory. 'Ebenezer's Memories' is the story of two English children of Irish parents, siblings Catherine and Jack, who spend their school holidays at their grandfather's house in Derry only to discover 'there's a monster living in [the] cupboard' under the stairs 'and his name is Ebenezer' (O'Donnell 2016a: 2). This monster, we learn, is 'hungry' and needs to be fed 'newspapers every day, and other … scary things … Things we'd rather forget' (3). It is later revealed that the monster, in addition to 'being a great devourer of newspapers … was a fairly ferocious consumer of unwanted memories too' (8). Sherratt-Bado (2018) reads this story in light of the trauma and the politics of Northern Ireland, as a statelet ghosted by the irrepressible nightmares of the Troubles. While O'Donnell's story is clearly haunted by the past, what interests me is how Catherine's status as the 'poor wain from the *Mixed Marriage*' is as unsettling as the magic realist genre the story is written in (O'Donnell 2016a: 3, italics original). As the daughter of a cross-community romance, we might read Catherine as an embodiment of the kinds of convivial futurity that Carson's story gestured towards.

Early into the story, the older narrator, Catherine, looks back to a moment from her childhood when she was very young, 'six or seven', and overhears some neighbours gossiping about her as she plays on the street outside her grandfather's house; the two women remark, '[t]here's that poor wain from the *Mixed Marriage*' (O'Donnell 2016a: 3). O'Donnell's use of italics mimics Catherine's intense awareness that this is something about her that is noteworthy. This realization leaves Catherine with a 'feeling like fear [which] made [her] pulse quicken' and 'the moment was stored in [her] memory as a hurt foretold' (3). Although she is too young to really comprehend the situation, she feels it as 'something that upset [her then] and would anger [her] later, in a way [she] didn't yet understand' (3). Catherine's mixedness marks her out amongst the residential streets of Derry where each community is strictly separated from the other. In the Waterside, where her mother's family are from, '[b]ands of red-white-and-blue paint wrapped the kerbs'; in Rosemount, where her father's family are from, 'green-white-and-orange lined the pavements' (10). It is only towards the end of the story that Catherine begins to understand what mixed marriage means and the enormous cost that her parents' marriage had for her mother and father: 'both families refused to speak to them', all 'locked in a stand-off that lasted nearly a decade' and, in her parents having to leave Derry to elope, 'something undefinable had been lost' (20).

This intergenerational narrative of trauma and loss is passed on to Catherine through her encounters with Ebenezer, the monster who lives under the stairs of her Grandad's house, eating memories and newspapers. After summoning the courage to engage with the monster, Catherine is subject to a montage of 'half-remembered faces, and others I had only seen in photographs' (O'Donnell 2016a: 7). 'Each time I slipped my fingers under the door', Catherine tells us, 'I'd witness episodes of family history, like snatches of a stolen documentary' (8). None of these memories are hers but those of her other family members; most frequently, they are the memories of her mother and Grandad.

Indeed, the role of memory in 'Ebenezer's Memories' is intricate and complex: it is a story of family memory narrated through the memory of an individual, Cathy. But, also, in telling a family story, O'Donnell evokes the collective identities sustained through the memory cultures of the North's two dominant communities. The vital role that memory plays in creating and sustaining collective identity has been well established by critics such as Benedict Anderson and Maurice Halbwachs; more recently, the complex interaction between collective identity and cultural memory has been thoughtfully mapped by individuals such as Astrid Erll and Ann Rigney.[4] Guy Beiner and Graham Dawson have been key figures in thinking about the role of memory in Irish history and culture. Dawson has powerfully demonstrated that the 'different and mutually antagonistic ways of telling the story of Ireland' has resulted in two distinct memory cultures (2007: 33). The role of family, Erll delineates, is 'an important link between the individual memory and larger formation of collective memory' within communities (2011: 308). The mixed marriage of Cathy's parents, and her father's death, means that she has been cut adrift from the communal memories, and identities, of both sides of her family.

In her imaginative engagement with family memories from the North's two dominant communities, O'Donnell's offers us a novel way of revealing how painful the past is for both. During one of the most distressing encounters with Ebenezer, Catherine learns that her father's death was 'not in a crisp-sheeted hospital bed as [her] Mammy had described it' but that he was murdered 'in a docklands alley' on his first trip back to Derry after leaving for England (O'Donnell 2016a: 12). At this point in the story, we might assume, given our knowledge of the upset that the mixed marriage caused and how viscerally others have reacted, that this murder was related to his romantic choice. Readers familiar with literature about the North – or perhaps even those primed by BBC police dramas – expect politically motivated murders and violent sectarian crimes in cultural texts about Northern Ireland.[5] As McGill achieved with her story 'No Angel', O'Donnell undercuts her reader's expectations of the genre towards the end of the story when Catherine discovers the murder of her father 'wasn't a political killing as such; more a chance; a misfortune' after he stumbled upon '"someone up to something" in the docklands' (O'Donnell 2016a: 20). The tragic mundanity of this is juxtaposed against the paranormal monster who magically feeds these memories back to Catherine like 'moving pictures were being projected inside [her] eyelids from an invisible cinema reel' (7). The past is revealed to be so unpleasant that there must be 'supernatural presence' at work; it is hard to 'believ[e] that the human mind could, by itself, conjure such nightmares' (17). This play on the unreality of reality fits with the generic conventions of magic realism and reiterates the true horror that people lived through.

It is significant, too, that these intergenerational family memories and this knowledge is shared in the domestic space of her family home, through the monster that lives under her Grandad's stairs. Earlier in this essay we noted the intensely political importance of the domestic in Northern Ireland, and all three stories discussed here foreground the centrality of the putatively ordinary domestic setting as a locus for extraordinary encounters. Bryonie Reid insists the 'discrete categorizing of space into public and private, and the assumed privacy of the house are untenable' in the North, where 'the assumed privacy' of domestic life and the home are co-opted into the public world of politics because of the specific nature of the conflict (2007: 935). Even houses themselves, Eli Davies maintains, 'become commemorative objects' and 'murals are painted on the gable ends of houses and blocks of flats' (2018: 11). We see this in O'Donnell's Derry, where 'the skull of a paramilitary was painted on a gable-end near Grandad's house with the words *No surrender* written on a scroll above it'; 'a gable-end at Rosemount' is adorned with a mural of a 'tricolour tied to a machine gun' (O'Donnell 2016a: 10). But this public commemoration, 'the bigger stories of collective suffering and struggle told on the outside' houses, Davies warns, obscures the 'domestic, emotional and physical labour that takes place *inside*' these houses (Davies 2018: 11, italics mine). The monster in 'Ebenezer's Memories' stalks the entire city, O'Donnell makes clear, with multiple private houses ghosted by the horrors of the North's public political conflict: 'Ebenezer had hidden in every house in this city at one time or another' (O'Donnell 2016a: 15). The whole city – and the various communities contained within – is at the mercy of a fantastical beast that terrorizes domestic spaces and feasts on memories.

O'Donnell's story also emphasizes the enormous amount of emotional labour and care that takes place within these domestic settings. Catherine's Grandad is especially important in this regard, introducing Catherine to the Ebenezer and so, by extension, the family memories that Ebenezer has access to. He is also responsible for soothing Catherine after she mistakenly assumes that she has let Ebenezer escape and that Ebenezer was subsequently responsible for the Omagh bombing of 15 August 1998, where twenty-nine people were killed by the Real Irish Republican Army. In the midst of what readers know to have been an atrocity, the kindness of Catherine's Grandad sings out as he puts her on his knee in 'the good room, which we were only allowed to use if it was Christmas' and reassures her, 'It wasn't you caused anything, darlin'' (O'Donnell 2016a: 19). With her 'head on Grandad's shoulder', Catherine is consoled by this act of care in a room where a 'gilt-framed photo of Granny Nora was propped proudly on the mantelpiece, its glass dustless' (19). As further proof of the reparative potential of domestic spaces and the great love, and memory work, that houses can sustain, Catherine reflects 'Grandad must have cleaned this room every day' (19). Rather than read this story as purely marked by trauma, as some might advocate, it seems more productive to follow Magennis in acknowledging that 'loss, recovery and memory are multifaceted processes' that encompass many emotional states (2016: 48). As Davies's work makes clear, the domestic in the North can be sites of extreme pain and powerfully restorative sites of care and emotional labour. The story concludes with an adult Catherine '[w]alking down a Dublin street' when she is 'suddenly arrested by the scent of a real coal fire' and a memory of her Grandad in his house, the thought of which, she says brings her 'some comfort' (O'Donnell 2016a: 21). The future ends with a happy memory of the past, revealing how pivotal individual memories can be in adding texture and nuance to the sometimes monolithic nature of community memory.

## Conclusion

The 'anxious and contradictory' genre of magic realism combines binary opposites in what Young and Hollaman term a 'hybrid' mode of writing (1984: 2). The 'anxious and contradictory' romance narratives engaged here highlight the potentially radical possibilities engendered by desiring outside one's own community in an active thematization of the 'impossible binary' that structures much of life in the North (Garnett 2021: 91). Recent scholarship has sought to interrogate other supposed binaries in the North, and the work of Davies and Reid illustrates strikingly how the private domestic and public political are irrevocably permeable in the North. The political, transgressive power of desire within the North is acute as a force that 'both constructs and collapses distinctions between public and private: it reorganizes worlds' (Berlant 2012: 14). The stories discussed here all engage the cross-community love story; romantic union and happiness may escape its lovers but the power of desire, Berlant reminds us, 'is a source of creativity that produces new optimism, new narratives of possibility"' (43). The 'community that is "not yet"', a convivial futurity that Lehner, Gilroy and Schaap all circle around, is central to Bernie McGill's 'No Angel', Róisín O'Donnell's 'Ebenezer's Memories' and Jan Carson's 'Children's Children' (Lehner 2020a: 50). All of these stories play with the uniquely enabling 'disruptive narrative mode' of magic realism to explore this 'community that is "not yet"' (Bowers 2010: 4). In this way, these stories reach towards a future for the North where 'community is less a fixed thing than a fluid process, one that, like desire itself, is manifested through multiple, overlapping relationships' (Cliff 2006: 118). The unruly, chaotic power of desire is well suited to the unsettling, disruptive genre of magic realism, and these stories seek to imagine a future where such happy cross-community romance is less the terrain of magic and more the realm of the real.

## Notes

1 This critical conversation is beyond the scope of this chapter but a comprehensive overview can be found in Hooper (2002) and González-Arias (2007). The debate was recently revived by Hassett, Omar and McAtackney (2021).
2 Hooper articulates this line of argument when he notes many doubt that Ireland, as a 'white, literate and Christian society on the edge of Europe[, has] anything like the

necessary credentials to discuss the realities, never mind the oppressions, of colonial endeavour' (2002: 12).

3 I use the (post)colonial when writing about Ireland, north and south, in recognition of the partitioned nature of the island and disputed status of Northern Ireland; for some, the Northern statelet is still a British colony. I use 'postcolonial' when referring to the body of academic work concerned with the processes, and afterlives, of colonialism and imperialism.

4 See Anderson (1991); Halbwachs (1997); Erll and Rigney (2009) and Erll (2009).

5 For more on the phenomenon of Northern Ireland and Northern Irish characters in BBC dramas, see Magennis (2021b). For more on violence and Northern Irish literature, see Hughes (2001) and Pelaschiar (2009).

# References

Anderson, Benedict (1991), *Imagined Communities: Reflections on the Origins and Spread of Nationalism*, London: Verso.

Armitt, Lucy (2012), 'The Magical Realism of the Contemporary Gothic', in David Punter (ed.), *A New Companion to the Gothic*, 510–22, Oxford: Wiley-Blackwell.

Arva, Eugene (2008), 'Writing the Vanishing Real: Hyperreality and Magical Realism', *Journal of Narrative Theory*, 38 (1): 60–85.

Berlant, Lauren (2012), *Desire/Love*, New York: Punctum.

Bowers, Maggie (2010), *Magic(al) Realism*, London: Routledge.

Brannigan, John (2006), 'Northern Irish Fiction: Provisionals and Pataphysicians', in James F. English (ed.), *A Concise Companion to Contemporary British Fiction*, 141–66, Oxford: Blackwell.

Briggs, Julia (2012), 'The Ghost Story', in David Punter (ed.), *A New Companion to the Gothic*, 176–85, Oxford: Wiley-Blackwell.

Cahill, Sean (1995), 'Occupied Ireland: Amid Hope of Peace Repression Continues', *Radical America*, 25: 51–6.

Carson, Jan (2016), *Children's Children*, Dublin: Liberties.

Cleary, Joe (2002), *Literature, Partition and the Nation State: Culture and Conflict*, Cambridge: Cambridge University Press.

Cliff, Brian (2006), 'Community and Contemporary Irish Literature', *Irish Review*, 34: 114–29.

Connolly, Claire (2012), *A Cultural History of the Irish Novel*, Cambridge: Cambridge University Press.

Davies, Eli (2018), 'Domestic Space and Memory: Remembering Deirdre Madden's *One by One in the Darkness* and the Belfast Agreement', *Open Library of Humanities*, 4 (2): 34, 1–27, https://doi.org/10.16995/olh.359 (accessed 13 November 2019).

Davies, Eli (2021), '"At Least We Can Lock the Door": Radical Domesticity in the Writing of Bernadette Devlin and Nell McCafferty', *Journal of War & Culture Studies*, 14 (1): 70–88.

Dawson, Graham (2007), *Making Peace with the Past? Memory, Trauma and the Irish Troubles*, Manchester: Manchester University Press.

Derrida, Jacques (1994), *Specters of Marx: The State of the Debt, the Work of Mourning, and the New International*, London: Routledge.

Erll, Astrid (2009), *Memory in Culture*, Basingstoke: Palgrave.

Erll, Astrid (2011), 'Locating Family in Cultural Memory Studies', *Journal of Comparative Family Studies*, 42 (3): 303–18.

Erll, Astrid, and Ann Rigney (eds) (2009), *Mediation, Remediation, and the Dynamics of Cultural Memory*, Berlin: Walter de Gruyter.

Garnett, Mariah (2021), 'An Interview with Mariah Garnett by Alison Garden', *Tangerine*, 10: 89–94.

Gilroy, Paul (2004), *After Empire: Melancholia or Convivial Culture?*, London: Routledge.

González-Arias, Luz Mar (2007), 'Postcolonial Locations: Ireland', in John McLeod (ed.), *The Routledge Companion to Postcolonial Studies*, 108–19, Oxon: Routledge.

Gordon, Avery (2011), *Ghostly Matters: Haunting and the Sociological Imagination*, London: University of Minnesota Press.

Halbwachs, Maurice ([1950] 1997), *La Meìmoire Collective*, ed. Geìrard Namer, Paris: Albin Michel.

Hanna, Adam (2015), *Northern Irish Poetry and Domestic Space*, Basingstoke: Palgrave Macmillan.

Hassett, Dónal, Hussein Omar and Laura McAtackney (2021), 'The Case for Rethinking Ireland and Empire', *RTÉ Brainstorm*, 19 April, https://www.rte.ie/brainstorm/2021/0419/1210712-case-rethinking-ireland-empire/.

Holgate, Ben (2015), 'Unsettling Narratives: Re-evaluating Magical Realism as Postcolonial Discourse through Alexis Wright's *Carpentaria* and *The Swan Book*', *Journal of Postcolonial Writing*, 51 (6): 634–47.

Hooper, Glen (2002), 'Introduction', in Glen Hooper and Colin Graham (eds), *Irish and Postcolonial Writing: History, Theory, Practice*, 3–18, Basingstoke: Palgrave Macmillan.

Hughes, Eamonn (2001), 'Fiction', in Mark Carruthers and Stephen Douds (eds), *Stepping Stones: The Arts in Ulster 1971–2001*, 79–102, Belfast: Blackstaff.

Kennedy, William (1973), 'The Yellow Trolley Car in Barcelona, and Other Visions', *Atlantic*, January, https://www.theatlantic.com/magazine/archive/1973/01/the-yellow-trolley-car-in-barcelona-and-other-visions/360848/.

Lehner, Stefanie (2020a), 'Nation: Reconciliation and the Politics of Friendship in Post-Troubles Literature', in P. Reynolds (ed.), *The New Irish Studies*, 47–62, Cambridge: Cambridge University Press.

Lehner, Stefanie (2020b), 'Crossings: Northern Irish Literature from Good Friday to Brexit', in E. Falci and P. Reynolds (eds), *Irish Literature in Transition: 1980–2020*, 136–51, Cambridge: Cambridge University Press.
Magennis, Caroline (2016), '"My Narrative Falters, as It Must": Rethinking Memory in Recent Northern Irish Fiction', in Chris Andrews and Matt McGuire (eds), *Post-Conflict Literature*, 44–53, London: Routledge.
Magennis, Caroline (2021a), *Northern Irish Writing after the Troubles: Bodies, Intimacies, Pleasures*, London: Bloomsbury.
Magennis, Caroline (2021b), 'Line of Duty: Why There Are So Many Northern Irish Coppers in British Crime Dramas', *Conversation*, 16 April, https://theconversation.com/line-of-duty-why-there-are-so-many-northern-irish-coppers-in-british-crime-dramas-158919.
Malone, Patricia (2021), 'Measures of Obliviousness and Disarming Obliqueness in Anna Burns' *Milkman*', *Textual Practice*, https://www.tandfonline.com/doi/abs/10.1080/0950236X.2021.1900357.
McGill, Bernie (2013), *Sleepwalkers*, Belfast: Whittrick.
Mendoza, Plinio Apuleyo, and Gabriel García Márquez (1983), *The Fragrance of Guava*, trans. Ann Wright, London: Verso.
Morrow, Duncan (2019), 'Sectarianism in Northern Ireland: A Review', University of Ulster, https://www.community-relations.org.uk/sites/crc/files/media-files/A-Review-Addressing-Sectarianism-in-Northern-Ireland_FINAL.pdf.
O'Donnell, Róisín (2016a), *Wild Quiet*, Dublin: New Island Books.
O'Neill, Stephen (2020), 'The Twists and Turns from the Irish Free State to Ireland', *RTÉ Brainstorm*, 12 March, https://www.rte.ie/brainstorm/2020/0310/1121406-irish-free-state-ireland/.
Pelaschiar, Laura (2009), 'Terrorists and Freedom Fighters in Northern Irish Fiction', *Irish Review*, 40/41: 52–73.
Reid, Bryonie (2007), 'Creating Counterspaces: Identity and the Home in Ireland and Northern Ireland in Environment and Planning', *Society and Space*, 25: 933–50.
Schaap, Andrew (2005), *Political Reconciliation*, London: Routledge.
Sherratt-Bado, Dawn Miranda (2018), '"Things We'd Rather Forget": Trauma, the Troubles, and Magical Realism in Post-Agreement Northern Irish Women's Short Stories', *Open Library of Humanities*, 4 (2): 12, 1–30, https://doi.org/10.16995/olh.247.
Shirlow, Peter (2004), 'Northern Ireland: A Reminder from the Present', in C. Coulter and S. Coleman (eds), *The End of Irish History?*, 192–207, Manchester: Manchester University Press.
Siskind, Mariano (2011), 'Magical Realism', in Ato Quayson (ed.), *The Cambridge History of Postcolonial Literature*, 833–68, Cambridge: Cambridge University Press.
Slemon, Stephen (1995), 'Magic Realism as Postcolonial Discourse', in Lois Parkinson Zamora and Wendy Faris (eds), *Magical Realism: Theory, History, Community*, 407–26, Durham, NC: Duke University Press.

Takolander, Maria (2010), 'Magical Realism and Fakery: After Carpentier's "Marvelous Real" and Mudrooroo's "Maban Reality"', *Antipodes*, 24 (2): 165–71.

Upstone, Sara (2007), 'Domesticity in Magical-Realist Postcolonial Fiction Reversals of Representation in Salman Rushdie's *Midnight's Children*', *Frontiers: A Journal of Women Studies*, 28 (1/2): 260–84.

Yeats, W. B. (2000), *The Collected Poems of W.B. Yeats*, Ware: Wordsworth Editions.

Young, David, and Keith Hollaman (eds) (1984), *Magical Realist Fiction: An Anthology*, New York: Longman.

3

# Incomers and settlers: Nomadism and entanglement in contemporary Scottish fiction

Timothy C. Baker

## Settlers, colonists and new Scots: Changing Scottish communities

In the summer of 2020, Val McDermid and Jo Sharp published a collection of over one hundred short pieces by 'a cross-section of Scottish society', asking them to describe, in a few hundred words, 'a country where you'd feel truly at home' (2020: 1). The majority of contributors were writers, particularly novelists, although the volume includes a wide array of voices. Not surprisingly, many of the pieces emphasize ideas of community, defined most frequently in terms of shared responsibility and stewardship for the land, as well as a welcoming ethos. A. L. Kennedy envisions the country as a family that 'makes you a member as soon as you join it'; Alexander McCall Smith emphasizes '[t]he idea of community, of being / In it together'; the songwriter Ricky Ross yearns for communities where 'happiness and joy is not limited to the wealthy, and no one is excluded' (McDermid and Sharp 2020: 123, 145, 214). This desire for community is not intrinsically utopian; Malachy Tallack, whose work is discussed below, emphasizes the vulnerability of rural communities and the difficult relation between centre and periphery in any Scottish political imagining (McDermid and Sharp 2020: 243). The volume as a whole, however, repeatedly returns to the claim that a future Scotland is one based on the principles of community and care.

If questions of community are often particularly visible 'at times of profound social transformation or of great turmoil' (Nancy 2010: 147), and have consequently been central to discussions of the possibility of an independent

Scotland, they are just as much endemic to Scottish literature itself. The idea of community is not only a 'key thematic concern in Scottish literary representations', as Scott Lyall argues, but has 'also been a bulwark of the Scottish tradition, helping to form Scottish literature as a subject-area' (2016: ix). Community, treated positively or negatively, is seen both as a primary theme of Scottish fiction, in particular, and as a necessary approach to the study of that literature. For Kurt Wittig, in one of the most important early surveys of Scottish literature as a distinctive subject area, Scottish literature must be perceived as 'grow[ing] out of the life of the community' (1958: 3). Two decades later, Francis Russell Hart emphasizes the principle of nostalgia in literary representations of community: community is a central theme in Scottish fiction, he argues, because it creates a 'compensatory myth' where Scotland can be seen whole and complete, despite widespread emigration and precarity (1978: 205). If a national community is subject to fracture, a localized community, particularly the village or small town, might suffice to replace it in the imagination. A further two decades later, Cairns Craig suggests that these localized Scottish communities in fiction are themselves characterized not by unity but by a sense of fear that becomes 'the very essence of the whole pattern of [communal] life' (1999: 48). The harmonious local communities found in the kailyard novels of writers such as J. M. Barrie in the nineteenth century have been derided by writers and critics throughout the twentieth century, but community – whether seen in terms of geographic locality or the imagined community of the nation – has remained a dominant concept in both critical and creative writing in Scotland, perhaps more so than in other parts of the UK. While regional communities should not be taken as a metonym for a national community, the continued emphasis in Scottish fiction on small communities is often used to interrogate ideas of Scottishness and national belonging.

The twentieth-century critics discussed above write largely in relation to a Scotland defined by emigration. From the legacy of the Highland Clearances in the eighteenth and nineteenth centuries to the disproportionate involvement of Scots in colonial endeavours and the continued mass emigration that defined the twentieth century, the Scottish community in question has been seen as what is left behind. In the past twenty years, however, the demographics of Scotland have begun to shift dramatically: while in the second half of the twentieth century the Scottish population continued to decrease by almost 6 per cent per decade, a figure unmatched elsewhere in the UK, immigration by individuals born outside the UK increased from the late 1990s onwards, such that the foreign-born population almost doubled between 2001 and 2011 (Devine and McCarthy 2018: 5, 7). As the poet Bashabi Fraser argues, in particular relation to Scotland, diaspora is 'a reality that has shaped the socio-cultural fabric of nations' (Mallick 2018: 190). Fraser employs Steven Vertovec's 'triadic relationship' between self-identified ethnic groups, the states and contexts where those groups reside, and their states or contexts of familial or ancestral origin to study the work of Scottish South Asian poets, arguing that even as 'a new nation is embraced, the nation of origin is the invisible bond that knits diasporic communities together' (2016: 216–18). 'New Scots' write, as will be particularly explored below in relation to the work of Leila Aboulela, from and to both Scottish and international communities, as well as in relation to more localized communities. While Scotland is often positioned in the popular press as being more welcoming to immigrants than the rest of the UK, particularly in light of a majority vote of 62 per cent for Remain in the EU Referendum, recent studies show that anti-immigrant sentiment in Scotland is not particularly different from that in England and Wales (Sime 2020: 338). This shifting demographic has required new literary strategies and a reconsideration of both local and national communities.

The urgency of finding a new model to describe this population, including immigration from other parts of the UK, was most clearly illustrated by the furore over the publication of Alasdair Gray's brief essay 'Settlers and Colonists' in 2012. Writing in a collection of essays by Scottish writers on Scottish independence, Gray characterizes colonists and settlers as 'two sorts of invader'; he is keen to praise the contribution of English, Asian and Italian 'settlers', or immigrants who have made Scotland their home and contributed to the Scottish economy and culture, but reserves his ire for English 'colonists' who live and work briefly in Scotland before returning to England, particularly in relation to foreign-born arts administrators (100). That Scotland would invite external figures to oversee its arts sector speaks, Gray argues, not only to a tradition of English colonialism and paternalism but also to a lack of Scottish confidence. Gray's framing of English immigration to Scotland in terms of colonialism generated an unprecedented amount of media coverage, with 119 articles on Gray appearing in the UK press in December 2012, along with tens of thousands of tweets, blog comments and other social media engagements (Hames 2014: 75).

As Scott Hames notes, much of the criticism directed at Gray was not based in a close reading of the initial essay but in response to newspaper summaries of the work, which were frequently framed in terms of anti-English rhetoric. Yet the extent of the controversy reveals the extent to which discussions of Scottish identity, particularly in relation to literature, remain predicated on the idea of a knowable and often homogenous community that may no longer exist in a post-imperial Britain that Paul Gilroy characterizes in terms of 'loss and what might be called an identity-deficit' (2011: 190). Scotland's complicated role as both colonizer and colonized, coupled with the continual presence of discussions surrounding independence and devolution, make the nature of a national community an often-vexed question; likewise, the continued importance to Scottish cultural and political life of the Central Belt of Edinburgh and Glasgow, at the frequent expense of the rest of the country, invites further discussion of how local communities might relate to a national one. Scottish literature is only gradually responding to increased immigration both from England and further afield: fiction has increasingly begun to examine how 'incomers' might reshape a given community, and whether this might lead to the cosmopolitan, polyvocal, caring community envisioned by McDermid and Sharp's contributors or bring about the hostility towards outsiders that Gray's less generous critics found in his essay.

The four texts discussed in this chapter approach the question of community from a variety of angles. Malachy Tallack's *The Valley at the Centre of the World* (2018) and Linda Cracknell's *Call of the Undertow* (2013) both depict rural communities, in Shetland and Caithness, respectively, that are changed by the arrival of incomers. In both novels, the community is sometimes hostile to outsiders but also requires new perspectives in order to survive. If immigrants are treated with suspicion, they are also necessary to ensure the continuity of a particular community. Leila Aboulela's story collection *Elsewhere, Home* (2018) and Sarah Moss's *Summerwater* (2020) take more cosmopolitan approaches to examine the friction between different racial, ethnic and cultural identities, and to assess what possibility for community coherence remains. These four texts are notable both for their nuanced approach to representations of community and for their frequent emphasis on non-human, or more-than-human, agents: in Tallack's and Moss's novels, especially, the principle of community is extended beyond the human. None of these texts, notably, comments extensively on the idea of a national community or ideas of Scottish identity as such. Instead, each focuses on self-defined communities, whether in terms of geography or ethnicity, in order to depict the necessity and difficulty of communal living and the importance of individual, material encounters over preordained ideas of unity. In their representation of immigration, nomadism and settling, these texts highlight the importance of belonging and the simultaneous fragility and continued promise of community.

## Precarious communities

*The Valley at the Centre of the World* and *Call of the Undertow* are both set almost exclusively in the sort of small rural community that dominated much of twentieth-century Scottish fiction. Tallack's novel depicts a life of 'the valley', a small crofting community on the Shetland mainland, while Cracknell's novel is set in Dunnet, the northernmost point in mainland Scotland, just west of John O'Groats. Island, and implicitly coastal, settings have long been used in Scottish writing to emphasize the primacy of community. The writer Iain Crichton Smith, who spent his childhood in Lewis, claims that it is a 'sense of community' that differentiates island and city life, making exile from the community 'desolate and frightening': such communities provide a 'sense of warmth, settledness', even as they are often conservative (1986: 23–4). As the title of Smith's essay in *Towards the Human: Selected Essays*, 'Real People in a Real Place', suggests, this sense of community, however limited it might appear, must be taken seriously: 'This is a real society in a real world and it will therefore be characterised by the particular reality to which it belongs' (49). Focusing on small communities is not a fundamentally nostalgic act but recognizes a truth of social construction that is often overlooked. As Alice, one of the central characters in *Valley*, ponders: 'The thing about an island ... is that you feel you can know it. You feel your mind can encompass everything in it, everything there is to see and to learn and to comprehend. You feel you can contain it, the way it contains you' (Tallack 2018: 26). This focus on the local is not inherently romantic: Maggie Thame, the protagonist of Cracknell's novel, notes Dunnet's lack of employment and empty streets, reflecting that '[i]t was as if time had forgotten this place' (2013: 10). For both characters, however, part of the value of a remote community is that it can be known and understood, in its complexity, in a way that larger urban environments cannot.

While this view of community is common to Scottish fiction, Tallack's and Cracknell's novels are differentiated by using incomers as focalizers. Maggie, in *Call*, is a cartographer from Oxford who has moved, for a fixed stay of six months, to Dunnet in order to work on an atlas of West Africa; as much as she is interested in the local community, 'charting it with her feet in her usual way' (2013: 5), its primary value is that it allows her to imagine a different community, specifically Lagos. Although she notes that the community is not unfriendly, she largely, through the first half of the novel, keeps herself at a remove and is unable to decide if she is tourist or resident. Her work with local schoolchildren affords her some interaction with the villagers, but her own 'inquisitive' spirit is interpreted by the locals as '[i]ntrusive' (171). Her clearest moment of belonging comes when she is attacked on the beach by Arctic terns and is pleased 'that it was not the place attacking her, but its immigrants' (111). Belonging to the community is a matter of defining oneself against outsiders. Maggie's status as incomer gives her a privileged vantage point, where she is able to investigate the town's history, and the relations between its present inhabitants, from an academic perspective, even as she is sometimes treated with distrust. Alice, in *Valley*, is another English incomer: a crime writer from York, she moves to Shetland after her husband's death in order to write, and experience, 'something *real*' (Tallack 2018: 23). Both artists come to realize that detached observation is insufficient: instead, their work ultimately involves constructing a series of layers. As Alice reflects, '[t]he closer she looked, the more the valley would expand … The present day could not be understood – it couldn't even be seen properly – without understanding the layers upon which it rested' (62, 68). Likewise, when Maggie finally draws a map of Dunnet, she incorporates her own experiences, 'all the places she'd been to in the last days' and is 'surprised to see how densely marked she made her map of this "empty" place' (Cracknell 2013: 230). In both novels, understanding community is made possible only by active attention; Alice and Maggie's status as newcomers forces them to observe the life around them without preordained hierarchies or assumptions. In this sense, both novels highlight the possibility that an incomer, however accepted they may or may not be, can provide a new, more comprehensive, perspective on a community.

Maggie and Alice are not, however, the only incomers in the novels. Sandy, in Tallack's novel, is a young man who has recently become part of the crofting community; although his childhood was spent in Lerwick, he does not consider Shetland home: 'He'd never thought that much about it. The question just didn't seem important' (2018: 5). Sandy moves to the valley with his partner Emma, who comes from the valley and returns there to be close to her parents, David and Mary, explaining,

> We're tied to da islands by elastic … Du just has to decide how du lives wi it. Either du goes awa and stretches that elastic – gradually it'll slacken aff and du can breathe easier – or else du just gives in. Let it pull dee back. Let it carry dee home. (5)

Shortly before the novel's opening Emma leaves for Edinburgh, but Sandy remains, working alongside his father-in-law David. David sees his position as the oldest person left in the valley, and the only one to be born there, as 'a responsibility, a weight that couldn't be lifted': he lives in an 'eternal present' where his own survival becomes a metonym for the survival of the community (30, 117). The triadic relationship of David, Emma and Sandy exemplifies multiple ways of belonging to a community, and a place. For David, the small crofting community is the only reality he has known, while for the younger generation, living there and contributing to the community is a choice. Yet while Sandy is an outsider, his willed belonging is a form of integration. Emma, who never directly appears in the novel, may speak of the importance of her ties to home, but Sandy develops them through lived experience. Sandy explains his position to Ryan, a neighbour to whom David has sold a house, in the hopes that more young people will 'become part of the community' (106), but who simply intends to refurbish it and move on. Ryan laments that in the community 'it's lik du has to live by stricter rules to fit in. Lik du has to conform' (158). For Sandy, on the other hand, communal life is a path towards individual freedom: 'I couldna be *this* person then because I wasna *here*. And I prefer this person to that one' (158–9, original emphases). The choice to become part of a community is itself a path to acceptance: while despite the oddity of the arrangement David welcomes Sandy, he evicts Ryan from the community when he discovers he does not intend to stay.

The intentional nature of belonging is highlighted in Jacques Rancière's definition of 'community', which he defines not as 'a reunion of persons sharing a common identity' but as 'a certain fabric made of things that individuals can perceive as constituting their lived world': a community is formed through 'a broadly shared sense of what is given and what is happening' (2016: 93). Sandy's original move to Shetland is predicated on a longing for unity, where '[h]is wholeness was subsumed within a larger whole' (Tallack 2018: 101–2), but with the dissolution of his relationship he realizes that such wholeness may have always been a myth. Instead, in finding common purpose with David, through their collaborative working of the land and their desire to see the community survive, he arrives at a sense of community that is based not in a common identity but in shared experience. The community in *Valley* exemplifies what Roland Barthes, in a discussion of the monks of Mount Athos, terms idiorrhythmy, where 'each subject lives according to his own rhythm' (2013: 6). Collective life does not subsume or replace individual life but rather is comprised of individuals working both independently and together. David and Sandy arrive at their shared sense of the world through different avenues – as does Alice – and yet their community provides a framework for their individual and collective flourishing. For Sandy, belonging to the community is not a matter of conforming, or leaving the world behind, but of becoming the person he is happiest being.

The community in *The Valley at the Centre of the World* is undeniably precarious: it is only because certain individuals choose to inhabit it that it can survive. In *Call of the Undertow*, on the other hand, the precarity of the community is made visible by the appearance of another outsider. One of the central strands of the novel is Maggie's friendship with a local boy, Trothan, who may be a selkie. Trothan is initially presented as having an indeterminate gender, and compared to an 'imp' and a 'wild thing' (2013: 37–8); he is known simply as unlike other children. While Maggie can choose her level of involvement with the community, to an extent, Trothan is far more ostracized; the other children find his difference 'so fundamental that he didn't even cross their radar' (54). Trothan develops his interest in mapmaking through conversations with Maggie and charts the village in a unique way, developing techniques that Maggie herself will later adopt. In so doing, he exposes the village's secrets, from its legacy of slavery to present black-market fish sales. At the novel's end, he disappears, either returning to the seals from whom he has come or simply running away from a community that has never wholly welcomed him. Although Maggie eventually comes to believe that he is a selkie, her initial response to the idea is to see selkie stories as a metaphor for '[p]eople who feel pulled between two worlds, who're not sure they fit in' (81). Her attraction to the boy, which is viewed by the villagers as potentially harmful, instead stems from a connection between outsiders: Maggie and Trothan both try to understand a world that does not wholly include them. While the community in Tallack's novel is precarious itself, precarity in Cracknell's novel is experienced at the level of the individual. In Anna Lowenhaupt Tsing's words, precarity 'is the condition of being vulnerable to others. Unpredictable encounters transform us; we are not in control, even of ourselves. Unable to rely on a stable structure of community, we are thrown into shifting assemblages' (2015: 20). Maggie and Trothan are unable to form, or become part of, a community but are known in their transformative vulnerability. Rather than the community being formed through individual relations, it is a backdrop for those relations.

Cracknell's and Tallack's novels ultimately reveal opposed perspectives on rural communities. In *Call of the Undertow* community is stable, but external: a community exists in a given location, where the land and its people are known to each other. Whether or not such a community is hostile to outsiders, it can be known in itself. In *The Valley at the Centre of the World*, on the contrary, the act of knowing the land and its people is intentional and manifested at the level of the individual: community cannot pre-exist the people who constitute it. Both novels, however, argue that the presence of incomers is not inherently disruptive. For critics such as Roberto M. Dainotto, regional communities can be defined as 'what has never been debased by industry, capital, and, above all, immigration': regionalism is, most simply, 'the erasure of the other' (2000: 22–3, 72). These novels show, however, that communal life is not, and cannot be, homogenous in this sense: instead, community is formed in relation to incomers. Incomers are catalysts for change, but also for continuity: it is only as community is actively willed through the presence of individuals that it becomes sustainable.

## Integration and disaster

While Cracknell's and Tallack's novels depict communities centred on a particular location, Aboulela's and Moss's texts reveal, often more cynically, the way that immigrant populations often fail to be included in placed communities and are instead defined in relation to pre-existing identities. Both authors examine the nature of a globalized, cosmopolitan Scotland, echoing the tension between attachment and detachment described by Rebecca L. Walkowitz (2006: 9) or rupture and reassemblage noted by Berthold Schoene (2010: 21). These tensions often appear in discussion of Scottish multiculturalism; Maggie Scott, for instance, examines the use of Scots in contemporary texts in reference to Gilroy's concept of postcolonial melancholia, arguing that use of vernacular language 'demonstrat[es] the practical positivity of the creative imagination to address complex and contested ideas of cultural, national, and personal identity' (2017: 23). Suhayl Saadi's Glasgow-set, Scots-language *Psychoraag* (2004), for instance, has often been heralded as suggesting new possibilities for Scottish fiction in its blend of Scots, Panjabi and Urdu. Yet Saadi's foundational work has rarely been followed up: while the voices of New Scots are increasingly heard in poetry and drama, however, they remain sorely underrepresented in mainstream fiction.

Aboulela's work frequently addresses this absence, often examining the way reassemblage and integration are impossible. Her early story 'The Museum', for instance, depicts the arrival of a wealthy Sudanese student, Shadia, at the University of Aberdeen. She instantly finds herself part of a hybrid 'congregation from the Third World [who] whispered their anxieties in grim Scottish corridors', separating their fellow students into '[u]s and them' (Aboulela 2018: 158). The community of outsiders provides a form of safety, even as it is also externally imposed: not being Scottish becomes a form of identity that supercedes the students' own ethnic and cultural differences. Anti-immigrant racism is pervasive, although Shadia also mocks a local student's use of Scots, as well as his working-class background. When that student, Bryan, takes Shadia to a local museum to look at their collection of African artefacts, she finds that '[n]othing was of her, nothing belonged to her life at home, what she missed' (177). There is nothing for her in Scotland, she believes. Her life will always be understood in relation to a history of colonialism and objectification that does not reflect her life in Khartoum. Although Shadia has come to Aberdeen by choice, her experience echoes Edward Said's description of exile as 'nomadic, decentered, contrapuntal', where new experiences are always held against the memory of a previous environment (2000: 186). Shadia is dissatisfied by the constraints of the self-identified immigrant community but at the same time can only find in Aberdeen inadequate reminders of home. Home is, as the collection's title suggests, always elsewhere. In 'The Museum', this failure to be included is ultimately framed as an individual failing. The story concludes with Shadia's self-remonstration: 'If she was strong, she would have explained and not tired of explaining' (Aboulela 2018: 182). There is no hope for communal acceptance but only the will of the individual to explain themselves or not, always at a remove.

While many of the stories in the collection repeat this theme, the volume as a whole points towards a new form of reconciliation and community that might be more closely connected with Rosi Braidotti's account of nomadism than Said's. Braidotti defines 'nomadic subjectivity' as 'a creative alternative space of becoming that would fall not between the mobile/immobile, the resident/the foreigner distinction, but within all these categories' (2011: 7). This alternative space is provided not within the stories but between them. The various stories are set in Cairo, Khartoum, Aberdeen, Edinburgh and elsewhere; if many of the stories depict Africans who are unable to settle in Scotland, there are also stories that show Scots unable to settle in Africa, or Africans who find themselves adrift in Africa. In 'Summer Maze', for instance, Nadia, born to Egyptian parents in England, visits Cairo: 'In Cairo she was a stranger, but a stranger who went unnoticed, who was not tricked into paying extra for taxi rides and souvenirs. The effect was like a disguise' (Aboulela 2018: 3). If African characters find themselves 'alienated from this place where darkness descended unnaturally at 4pm' (148), there is also no return to an imagined home. The experience of having been an immigrant is a perpetual force of segregation. Instead, Aboulela's characters find community not in particular locations but in shared experience. As Lindsey Moore writes, Aboulela 'has described her work as "Muslim immigrant fiction" indicating that geographical specificity is less central to her vision than faith-based identification' (2012: 75). Community is not found in a particular place but in the links between places and in the connections made by people of shared faith, rather than shared ethnicity.

Many of Aboulela's Scottish stories, however, do depict placed community. Rather than focusing on the village or city, however, these communities are located in specific buildings, such as the Nile Café, a Sudanese restaurant in Edinburgh, or the University of Aberdeen Chaplaincy, that provide gathering spaces for the local Muslim population. It is central to Aboulela's work that these are real, rather than imagined, spaces, although they may not be familiar to many of her readers. Aboulela's work, in its construction of faith-based communities, is as dependent on physical geography as Cracknell's or Tallack's novels; it is still only within a particular space that community can be formed. These are not always necessarily homogenous or harmonious spaces. For example, in 'The Boy from the Kebab Shop' an Aberdeen student is shocked, visiting a new friend at the kebab shop where he works, to see him pray. Although she is descended 'from generations of Muslims, she had never seen anyone praying' (2018: 132). While she realizes that the experience is an invitation for her to explore her own faith, she turns away in surprise. Yet the story emphasizes the contingent nature of immigrant communities: even a kebab shop can be a place for community-building and transformative encounters. At the same time, however, the dialogue between the stories suggests the possibility of a fundamentally literary community in Rancière's definition, where a 'community of the atoms, the patterns that they draw under the name of individual feelings' replaces an idea of community as 'an organic body' (2016: 101). Each atomized individual in the collection can be seen in relation to the patterns they make in relation to each other individual, and so community is formed. It is precisely because community is not a given, knowable commodity that individuals, both within and between the stories, can be seen in relation.

The possibility that literature is a central grounding element of community is particularly prominent in the collection's final and most recent story, 'Pages of Fruit'. The story is written as a letter from a devout Muslim woman initially based in Aberdeen to a more prominent Arab novelist. The narrator describes how in reading these novels she felt an immediate kinship and sense of community with the famous author and believed her experiences were manifested on the page. Meeting the author, however, first in Charlotte Square at the Edinburgh International Book Festival and later in the Emirates Palace Hotel in Abu Dhabi, the narrator finds herself dismissed, both for her class and her religion. At the end of the story, the narrator, disappointed with her encounters, 'start[s] to read, again, my favourite novel' (2018: 214). The community and connection found in fiction is more valuable, in a sense truer, than that found in human encounter. While Alice, in *Valley*, finds that her writing cannot encompass the full nature of her community, the unnamed narrator of Aboulela's story finds that it is only in writing that community can be found. The imagined community is grounded in relation to real people in real places, but it is also, in this story, experienced in solitude.

The idea of a community that is not depicted within but between stories is echoed, to a different effect, in Moss's *Summerwater*. The novel is divided into twenty-four chapters, twelve short chapters that emphasize elements of the natural world and twelve longer chapters that are focalized through different residents of a Scottish chalet park, somewhere near Stirling, on a single rainy summer day. The twelve central characters encompass a range of ages and life experiences; some are English and some Scottish; few are happy to be stuck in a dilapidated chalet in the rain. While the twelve individuals often observe their neighbours and comment on their activities, there is very little interaction between the various households. Each focalizer sees themselves as distinct, and the reader alone is able to understand how these lives work in relation. In this fundamental emphasis on difference, Moss's novel can be understood in relation to Sarah Kofman's claim that

> only the foreignness of that which can never be held in common can found the community. An idyllic community which erases all trace of discord, of difference, of death, which pretends to rest on a perfect harmony, a fusion conferring immediate unity, can only be a fictional community, a beautiful (psychotic?) story. (1988: 30)

The discord that Kofman highlights is often presented not simply in terms of class and intergenerational conflict but also in terms of anti-immigrant sentiment. Justine, the novel's first focalizer, is from Manchester but congratulates herself on choosing this remote site, as opposed to 'every English family' that has ventured to the Highlands: here, she reflects, '[y]ou should get a different kind of person' (Moss 2020: 17). David, an older Scottish character, makes the same point, lamenting 'those English accents evolved to be audible from High Table' at the same time that he sees the loch where the chalet park is located as 'the best place of his life', where he can retreat for 'peace and quiet' (40). Claire, who is English but lives in Edinburgh, imagines her neighbours complaining about the way Scotland is 'full of the English these days, can't stand their own country any more' (116), while Becky, a Glaswegian teenager, imagines going to Claire's chalet and inviting her to '[f]uck off back to England, then, if you don't like it here' (147). The vast majority of characters position themselves as authorities on the location and the right people to be there, whereas others are dismissed as interlopers. Scotland is full of natural beauty, but the English, or the uneducated, or the poor, are not well-placed to appreciate it and are only tourists. Just as importantly, however, it is only the reader who can appreciate the patterns these individuals make. Claire and Becky imagine speaking to each other and are roughly accurate in their prediction of how the conversation would go, but they do not speak: instead, the reader can connect their conversation.

Although the novel is filled with atomized individuals, the desire for community remains a constant. Milly and Josh are a young couple contemplating moving to Barra, mostly at Josh's insistence. As Milly reflects:

> Good practice, then, anyway, this holiday, though on the island there'll be things to do, work, community events. Joining in, that's what they're after, a collective, a way of life that recognises people's dependence on each other and the land. She just hopes it turns out to be worth leaving all her friends. (2020: 62)

Community, as an organic whole, is positioned elsewhere, and as part of an imagined future. The fractured community within the novel, as well as its temporary and contingent status, reflects the challenges of any community. As Josh himself thinks, 'the closeness of the community is also the challenge of living there' (161). Just as much as in Tallack's novel, community is presented as an act of individual will; as much as in Aboulela's stories, community is often framed as a force of separation, rather than integration. This is nowhere more apparent than the way many of the focalizers are unwittingly united in their hatred of the one non-British family present at the park. The family is Ukranian, although various characters call them Romanian, Polish or Bulgarian; they are based in Glasgow, although perceived as outsiders. For the majority of the novel, characters treat the family with disdain and barely suppressed racism: they are perceived as being too loud, too given to inviting their friends over for parties and not fit residents. Lola, one of the teenage characters, is one of the few to speak to the Ukranians, but her conversation largely consists of mocking their names, turning Violetta Shevchenko into 'Shit-chenko', and asking, '[s]o where are you really from' (74–5). If the various focalizers largely concentrate on their differences, their point of common purpose is their hostility to non-British immigrants, a feature that is emphasized by the fact that no member of the family is given a chapter of their own.

The community of hostility is developed in two ways. Midway through the novel Mary, David's wife, remembers a host of quotations, from French grammar to Christmas carols. The chapter is immediately marked as significant because it is the first in the novel that returns to a household the reader has already encountered; while Mary's disability means that she is unable to venture far from her house, the reader discovers that she has been watching all of the other characters, seeing many of the same scenes as the reader. At the centre of her reminiscences is William Watson's ballad 'Semmerwater', which Mary keeps calling 'Summerwater'. The ballad, more properly spelled 'Semerwater', tells the legend of a prosperous Yorkshire city in which an outsider finds no welcome, except for a poor couple on the outskirts of the town; he curses the city with a great flood, creating a large lake. It is, thinks Mary, an 'odd choice, really, for a young child, though people worried less about that kind of thing in those days' (129). The poem is clearly an index to the novel, as it similarly concerns a community's hostility to outsiders and its resulting destruction. Yet the poem's appearance in the private reflections of one of the most isolated characters means that the poem is not necessarily explanatory but forms part of a recurring pattern. The bias and distrust manifested in the novel are not specific to twenty-first-century Scotland but occur in multiple times and places. This patterning is visible outside the novel as well: Jan Carson's collection *The Last Resort* (2021) presents a very similar set of stories, each with a different narrator, set in a decaying caravan park in Northern Ireland, with a similar focus on racism towards Eastern Europeans. While the hostility both between English and Scottish characters, and between British and Eastern European characters, can easily be read as an allegory for Brexit, the use of Watson's poem, which in its misremembered form grants the novel its title, indicates the extent to which this fracturing is perhaps endemic to all communities.

As much as *Summerwater* can be read allegorically, its shocking ending also indicates how these, too, are real people in a real place. As the Ukranians and their friends begin another party, men from the various houses go to investigate. Rather than fighting, however, the various British characters appear to be integrated, joining in the fun. The chapter is focalized through Jack, a small boy, who does not quite understand what is happening but dances alone in his room in emulation of what he imagines happening in the neighbouring chalet, and 'the dancing around the room, he'll think later, later and often, was why he didn't see the flames sooner' (Moss 2020: 196). The chalet burns down, and Jack and the reader are fairly certain that Violetta, and possibly others, have died inside, although this is not depicted. This sudden, apocalyptic ending echoes both the ambiguous death or disappearance of Trothan in *Call of the Undertow* and more specifically a giant fire at the end of *The Valley at the Centre of the*

*World*. In Tallack's novel the fire destroys not only a house but the possibility of communal memory. While Alice originally envisions ending her book about the community with the story of Maggie, the old woman whose house has burned, the fire 'changed everything. The box Sandy found in the loft had been the first thing to burn. The diary and photographs were destroyed' (2018: 321). The fires, even if accidental, illustrate the precarity of community, the way each of these communities was only moments away from destruction.

In each of the three novels the solution is, to an extent, the same as the one presented in Aboulela's 'Pages of Fruit'. Maggie, in Cracknell's novel, moves to a neighbouring community and begins a new mapping project, employing what she has learned. Alice, in Tallack's novel, learns that while no single life can illuminate a community, she must make her account more autobiographical. While Moss's novel is more abrupt in its ending, the suggestion, in the passage quoted above, that Jack will ponder and re-evaluate these events later in life carries a similar suggestion of individuation. In each of the four texts, then, the hope for an integrated community is replaced by a focus on the individual. This is not, especially in Tallack's novel, at the expense of the community. Rather, the authors insist that community cannot first be understood as an organic whole but must always be considered in relation to individual actions and desires. If, as Nancy has argued, community means 'that there is no singular being without another singular being' (1991: 28), these texts repeatedly emphasize the primacy of that singularity. Community cannot be naively approached as a pre-given thing, stable and secure, but is always precarious and contingent.

## Conclusion: Towards a more-than-human community

As Carole Jones notes in a study of queer communities in Scottish fiction, the 'notion of community in itself … has oppressive consequences, with rules of inclusion and policed boundaries of normativity' (2016: 184). This potential oppression is particularly highlighted in recent Scottish fiction that considers the place of incomers; as much as integration might be desirable, each of these texts shows the extent to which it often fails. As much as localized communities might require new inhabitants in order to survive, communities themselves, even when perceived as a pre-existing whole, often remain hostile and are revealed to be fundamentally unstable. Each text discussed in this chapter reveals a very real desire for community and strongly suggests the possibility of community in the present. Nonetheless they also acknowledge that the very idea of a homogenous, localized, harmonious community that has underpinned so much of Scottish fiction over the past two centuries was, perhaps, always a myth. Community, in these texts, is precarious, contingent and often momentary: it is constructed through acts of individual will and is a necessary fiction, both comforting and destructive.

Although these texts clearly reflect the state of Scotland in recent years, with a particular focus on demographic shifts, political ideologies and economic centralization, this scepticism towards community is familiar both in earlier Scottish fiction and in texts from other nations and cultures. The texts discussed above, however, are differentiated in two ways. Firstly, the focus on polyvocal perspectives in Aboulela's, Moss's, and Tallack's texts leads to a conception of community as an ideal that is manifested in fiction, or in text, even when it represents difficulty for the characters. The reader is the true denizen of community, given a privileged perspective on how the atomized individuals depicted in the pages form patterns and share a common purpose of which they themselves may be unaware. The text itself is a communal endeavour, an interaction between language and reader that creates its own sense of purpose. Just as importantly, these texts also gesture towards the importance of a more-than-human community. Trothan's, and eventually Maggie's, maps of the local area in *Call of the Undertow* incorporate the appearance and actions of birds and seals as much as humans. In *The Valley at the Centre of the World* not only does Alice seek to tell the story of the community through all of its inhabitants, human and non-human alike, but Sandy and David's work with their sheep is presented as being as vital a form of relation as the connections between human inhabitants. While the stories in *Elsewhere, Home* are exclusively focused on the human, Aboulela's more recent novel *Bird Summons* (2019) likewise incorporates both mythical and real birds in its stories of human encounters. In this way, these authors illustrate the material ecocritical emphasis on the way humans 'are entangled with [non-humans'] material agency' such that all material forms 'emerge *together* as storied beings' (Iovino and Oppermann 2014: 8, original emphasis). If community is a story we tell, then it is a story that can include not only human agents but multiple forms of life and relation.

This emphasis on more-than-human stories is most clearly presented in Moss's novel. The twelve chapters focusing on the natural world are often brief and fragmentary. At times they reflect the actions of the novel, as when a fox eats discarded food the reader has seen, in passing, in earlier chapters. At times they prefigure events. The first chapter describes the sound of the rain, which '[y]ou would notice soon enough, if it stopped' (Moss 2020: 1). The novel's final sentence describes the sound of a mother grieving for her child:

> And then the music did stop and then there came a human sound he never wants to hear again and will always be hearing, somewhere in his head, and he was right, Jack, you notice, when it stops. (200)

Rather than making a point as banal as the inevitability of both rain and grief, Moss's echoing line suggests that human concerns always exist within a material environment. In a chapter on geology she states: 'In the beginning was earth and fire. Was there here, then? Was Scotland?' (26). If place is central, it is also precarious; if community is a form of knowing, it is also liable to rupture.

Community is both a placed experience and an act of will; it is known through encounter and through fiction. Communities, in Scottish fiction, are often hostile to the presence of newcomers, and yet this presence not only demonstrates the centrality of community to Scottish life but also allows for new forms to emerge. None of these texts can state unequivocally that a welcoming community, based in the land but exceeding it, is the future, or present, of Scotland. Yet fiction remains a way of thinking through and with community and understanding both its continuity and its necessary change.

## References

Aboulela, Leila (2018), *Elsewhere, Home*, London: Telegraph.
Aboulela, Leila (2019), *Bird Summons*, London: Weidenfeld and Nicolson.
Barthes, Roland (2013), *How to Live Together: Novelistic Simulations of Some Everyday Spaces*, trans. Kate Briggs, New York: Columbia University Press.
Braidotti, Rosi (2011), *Nomadic Subjects: Embodiment and Sexual Difference in Contemporary Feminist Theory*, New York: Columbia University Press.
Carson, Jan (2021), *The Last Resort*, London: Penguin.
Cracknell, Linda (2013), *Call of the Undertow*, Glasgow: Freight.
Craig, Cairns (1999), *The Modern Scottish Novel: Narrative and the National Imagination*, Edinburgh: Edinburgh University Press.
Dainotto, Roberto M. (2000), *Place in Literature: Regions, Cultures, Communities*, Ithaca, NY: Cornell University Press.
Devine, Tom M., and Angela McCarthy (2018), 'Introduction: The Historical and Contemporary Context of Immigration to Scotland since 1945', in T. M. Devine and Angela McCarthy (eds), *New Scots: Scotland's Immigrant Communities since 1945*, 1–20, Edinburgh: Edinburgh University Press.

Fraser, Bashabi (2016), 'The New Scots: Migration and Diaspora in Scottish South Asian Poetry', in Scott Lyall (ed.), *Community in Modern Scottish Literature*, 214–34, Leiden: Brill Rodopi.

Gilroy, Paul (2011), 'The Closed Circle of Britain's Postcolonial Melancholia', in Martin Middeke and Christina Wald (eds), *The Literature of Melancholia: Early Modern to Postmodern*, 187–204, Basingstoke: Palgrave Macmillan.

Gray, Alasdair (2012), 'Settlers and Colonists', in Scott Hames (ed.), *Unstated: Writers on Scottish Independence*, 100–10, Edinburgh: Word Power Books.

Hames, Scott (2014), 'The "Settlers and Colonists" Affair', in Camille Manfredi (ed.), *Alasdair Gray: Ink for Worlds*, 73–104, Basingstoke: Palgrave Macmillan.

Hart, Francis Russell (1978), *The Scottish Novel: A Critical Survey*, London: John Murray.

Iovino, Serenella, and Serpil Oppermann (2014), 'Introduction: Stories Come to Matter', in Serenella Iovino and Serpil Oppermann (eds), *Material Ecocriticism*, 1–17, Bloomington: Indiana University Press.

Jones, Carole (2016), 'From Subtext to Gaytext? Scottish Fiction's Queer Communities', in Scott Lyall (ed.), *Community in Modern Scottish Literature*, 179–95, Leiden: Brill Rodopi.

Kofman, Sarah (1988), *Smothered Words*, trans. Madeline Dobie, Evanston, IL: Northwestern University Press.

Lyall, Scott (2016), 'Preface: In Search of Community', in Scott Lyall (ed.), *Community in Modern Scottish Literature*, vii–xiii, Leiden: Brill Rodopi.

Mallick, Saptarshi (2018), 'Professor Bashabi Fraser in Conversation', *Asiatic*, 12 (1): 180–95.

McDermid, Val, and Jo Sharp (eds) (2020), *Imagine a Country: Ideas for a Better Future*, Edinburgh: Canongate.

Moore, Lindsey (2012), 'Voyages Out and In: Two (British) Arab Muslim Women's Bildunsromane', in Rehana Ahmed, Peter Morey and Amina Yaqin (eds), *Culture, Diaspora, and Modernity in Muslim Writing*, 68–84, New York: Routledge.

Moss, Sarah (2020), *Summerwater*, London: Picador.

Nancy, Jean-Luc (1991), *The Inoperative Community*, ed. Peter Connor, trans. Peter Connor, Lisa Garbus, Michael Holland and Simona Sawhney, Minneapolis: University of Minnesota Press.

Nancy, Jean-Luc (2010), 'Communism, the Word', in Costas Douzinas and Slavoj Žižek (eds), *The Idea of Communism*, 145–53, London: Verso.

Rancière, Jacques (2016), 'Literary Communities', in T. Claviez (ed.), *The Common Growl: Toward a Poetics of Precarious Community*, 93–110, New York: Fordham University Press.

Saadi, Suhayl (2004), *Psychoraag*, Edinburgh: Black and White.

Said, Edward (2000), *Reflections on Exile and Other Essays*, Cambridge, MA: Harvard University Press.

Schoene, Berthold (2010), *The Cosmopolitan Novel*, Edinburgh: Edinburgh University Press.
Scott, Maggie (2017), 'Melancholia and Conviviality in Modern Literary Scots: Sanghas, Sengas and Shairs', *C21 Literature: Journal of 21st-Century Writings*, 5 (1): 1–29.
Sime, Daniela (2020), 'New Scots? Eastern European Young People's Feelings of Belonging and National Identity in Scotland Post-Brexit', *Scottish Affairs*, 29 (3): 336–53.
Smith, Iain Crichton (1986), *Towards the Human: Selected Essays*, Edinburgh: MacDonald.
Tallack, Malachy (2018), *The Valley at the Centre of the World*, Edinburgh: Canongate.
Tsing, Anna Lowenhaupt (2015), *The Mushroom at the End of the World: On the Possibility of Life in Capitalist Ruins*, Princeton, NJ: Princeton University Press.
Walkowitz, Rebecca L. (2006), *Cosmopolitan Style: Modernism beyond the Nation*, New York: Columbia University Press.
Wittig, Kurt (1958), *The Scottish Tradition in Literature*, Edinburgh: Oliver & Boyd.

# Part 2
# Speculative Community

4

# Beyond the multicultural: Queer community in Jackie Kay's *Trumpet*

Peter Ely

## Introduction

This chapter situates the work of Jackie Kay alongside the development of 'multicultural nationalism' in Britain during the 1990s under the Labour government led by Tony Blair. Drawing attention to the ways in which an optimistic, broadly Liberal consensus was built during the Blair years, where plurality, diversity and hybridity were proposed as progressive emblems of a new political future for Britain beyond the divisiveness of class politics and ethnonationalism, close attention to the rhetoric of New Labour reveals an enduring nationalist strand. Multiculturalism was aligned with figures of national unity, security and neoliberal economic policy in ways that had significant consequences for community, reimagining the bonds of social solidarity in 'cultural' terms that diminished their political potential (Bewes and Gilbert 2000: 7). If some commentators have argued British politics since 2016 has exhibited a 'nationalist turn', where more strident, overt and confident forms of nationalist rhetoric have been mobilized in political culture, it is instructive to trace a longer nationalist undercurrent which has developed since the 1980s (Valluvan and Kalra 2019: 2394). Neoliberalism has been engaged in a concerted project of producing a society where community is increasingly depoliticized and subordinated to 'competitive' and atomistic logics of free-market economics (Gilbert et al. 2013: 9). Society is construed primarily as constructed of self-contained individuals and families, where community is increasingly understood only as homogenous cultural group formations based in race, ethnicity or religion, which combine in a vision of unified national community.

This process offers an important context for understanding the work of Jackie Kay, whose writing has been aligned with the multicultural national project with striking regularity. Identification of her work through reference to her biography has often restricted readings of her work, highlighting their compatibility with multicultural focus on plurality and hybridity at the expense of more disruptive and intransigent influences and orientations in her work. Kay's reference to the Black radical tradition, which was built through internationalist affinities in a postcolonial context, indicates a political orientation that was often critical of the European and American national projects. Likewise, her interest in figures of queer community that are incommensurable with state-sanctioned norms of kinship offer alternative directions for thinking the role of community in her work which exceed investment in the multicultural nation-state. This aligns Kay's work with thinkers who have sought to imagine community beyond its identification with nationalism and multiculturalism, unearthing more radical possibilities in its social function. For philosopher Jean-Luc Nancy, the task of thinking community in this context is to fundamentally 'dissociate the idea of "community" from all projection into a work that is made or to be made – a State, a Nation, a People, or The People' (2016: 72). Disentangling community from its instrumentalization in the neoliberal nation-state requires attention to forms of life historically excluded by it; these, existing outside its 'operativity', inhabit modes of disruptive relationality which offer new ways of thinking about community (Nancy 1991).

Daniel Loick (2021) has termed these disruptive communities 'counter-communities', which he argues can be found in 'queer and feminist movements that pose a fundamental challenge to the traditional family form, contesting the exclusivity and the conformism of conventional models of kinship' (2021: 16). Queer community is often compelled to guard its marginal forms of association and community against erasure in the wider social landscape, and queer literature can therefore have a vital role in preserving such possibilities for reimagining community. The final section of the chapter addresses how Kay's novel *Trumpet* (1998) offers in its depiction of a trans trumpeter and his relationship with his wife, a small but potent instance of 'counter-community' which produces a fragile vision of relationality beyond its use by the capitalist state. Foregrounding the symbolic illegibility of this relationship and its apparent incommensurability with the exclusionary function of the nation-state and its normative kinship apparatus, the chapter ends by arguing Kay's text is exploring transformative possibilities in communal possibility, gesturing to forms of human association beyond the historical limits of the neoliberal project.

## Between the national and the multicultural

In May 2015, less than a year before then prime minister David Cameron officially announced a referendum on the UK's membership to the European Union, Jackie Kay's poem 'Extinction' was published in the *Guardian*. Part of a series of original poems curated by Carol-Ann Duffy on the theme of climate change, Kay's text, originally titled 'Planet Farage', nevertheless combined its consideration of ecology with more sustained attention to a growing component of British political discourse during this period (Varty 2018: 137). The voice of Kay's poem animates a growing trend towards xenophobic nationalism, which takes climate change activism alongside many other subjects as enemies of its own imagined, national community. It is articulated through the tone of a triumphant 'we' which constitutes itself through variously stated exclusions: 'We closed the borders, folks, we nailed it. / No trees, no plants, no immigrants. / No foreign nurses, no Doctors; we smashed it' (Kay 2015: n.p.); these repeated negations effectively dramatize the rise of a powerful structure of feeling in Britain against signifiers of otherness which it celebrates having successfully excluded: 'We shut it down! No immigrants, no immigrants. / No sniveling-recycling-global-warming nutters' (n.p.).

The poem was publicly read by Kay as part of a poetry tour of Britain called 'Shore to Shore' that overlapped with the political campaigns which led up to the referendum itself. Its tone was intended to be largely satirical, dramatizing a comic incoherence and exclusionary fervour designed to produce criticism, but also enjoyment, in its expected reader. During this time, Kay's text would take on an altered significance. Anne Varty tracks how during the course of the tour Kay noted that reactions to the poem changed: '[n]ow that satire has become a reality, it suddenly isn't funny any more' (2018: 140). The triumphal tone of the piece began to lose its parodic hubris, rather tapping into a very real and newly bolstered 'nationalist turn' in political culture that would see its successful campaign to bind Britain to leaving the EU as its crowning achievement (Valluvan and Kalra 2019: 2394). In this context, the poem arguably takes on a more bitter, even abrasive style, channelling an emerging public confrontation around British identity encapsulated in its menacing final lines: 'Now, pour me a pint, dear. Get out of my fracking face.' Shifting its poetic voice from a nationally constituted 'we' to a more intimate, personalized scene of individual confrontation, the final lines resonate uncomfortably with a political situation where reports of threatening encounters with open misogyny, homophobia, racism and anti-European xenophobia were increasing (Albornoz et al. 2020).

This shift in reception around Kay's poem registers an important moment in recent British history that appeared to reignite nationalism as political force. In this moment, what is experienced is arguably the breaking of a political consensus: an 'interregnum' between one hegemonic way of understanding British society and another.[1] Various names are attributed to this previous consensus: 'late liberalism', which combines 'the twined formations of neoliberalism and liberal cultural recognition' (Povinelli 2013: 30–1); 'neoliberal cosmopolitanism', where 'neoliberal values ... undergird ... metropolitan diversity' (Johansen 2015: 296); and, more generally, 'multiculturalism', which Nathan Glazer notably declared in 1997 to have established hegemonic status across most political camps (1997: 3). Although for many a positive term which denotes crucial reforms in curtailing racism and promoting diversity, Stuart Hall argues 'multiculturalism' can reference 'a wild variety of political strategies', noting its increasing amenability to co-optation by 'conservative, 'corporate' and 'commercial' interests (2021: 410). Each term for this consensus describes a similar conjuncture whereby the exclusionary nationalism associated with the first iterations of neoliberalism in Chile, America and Britain in the 1970s and 1980s gives way to a political culture which accepts some aspects of plurality and diversity as part of a well-functioning neoliberal society. For Tony Blair in the 1990s, this would be expressed through reference to the new and exciting opportunities afforded by 'globalization': 'the driving force of economic change', necessitating that each 'country ... dismantle barriers to competition and accept the disciples of the international economy' (1996: 118–19). The reward for this supplication to global capitalist forces is the ability to take part in an 'internationalization of culture' where freer movement of capital, consumer goods and labour allows for a dynamic and visibly diverse national culture. New Labour advisor and director of Labour-aligned think tank *Demos* Geoff Mulgan similarly argues that

> as globalization dramatically recasts the landscape of the world's power, for the first time bringing billions into an open global market and rupturing and recasting traditionally enclosed cultures, it may well be that politics becomes far more, not less, important, as a way to solve problems and as a means of providing security and a stable sense of belonging. (1997: xii)

Engaged in a project to think 'after' or even 'beyond' the political, Mulgan echoes Blair's rhetoric on the exigencies of neoliberalism, arguing politics should be rethought in the wake of the establishment of a globalized, free-market consensus as the predicate, not subject, of political discussion. For cultural commentators of the time, not only did this economic ideology 'decimate ... the capacity of government and other democratic institutions to act upon the world' but it effectively produced a radically new political culture, where the British national project would be rethought in implicitly depoliticized and increasingly cultural terms (Bewes and Gilbert 2000: 233). This new political language can be captured by the term 'multiculturalism', but it is also characterized in its repeated and firm investment in building a unified sense of national community. This process of globalization is understood, as Mulgan notes, as 'rupturing and recasting traditionally enclosed cultures', indicating the way that communities might be radically displaced and transformed through their increased integration into the world economy. A language of multiculturalism therefore serves as a way of remaking such cultural and communal alliances, orientating them towards 'security and a stable sense of belonging' in a process invested in sustaining this new market-driven, globalized network of neoliberal nations. If neoliberalism has often been framed as a globalist project, working beyond the nation-state in ways that were seen to weaken the latter's power and significance, recent scholarship has demonstrated how in many cases the powers of the state, and a concomitant political nationalism, has grown since the late 1970s (Berger 2001). The history of neoliberalism has involved nationalism as a consistent, systemic factor in its political development, with Blairite multiculturalism arguably emerging as one of its most palatable iterations.[2]

The shift in political culture heralded by the New Labour years may be productively termed 'multicultural nationalism': the deployment of an optimistic investment in the neoliberal economy and the dynamism of its global consumer markets as the model for a new, reinvigorated and visibly diverse national identity. If some critics have argued that nationalism during the EU referendum regained a formerly diminished political confidence, many commentators have pointed out how this nationalism is not simply a novel or opportunistic 'attempt to fill the political void that a capitalist crisis engenders' but rather an 'amplification of the nationalism ... already ... deeply threaded through the capitalist restructuring' that has taken place through the past four decades (Valluvan and Kalra 2019: 2404). New Labour's use of multicultural nationalism was electorally successful in its ability to build constituencies across different social backgrounds, appealing to those with more conservative views, whilst packaging this alongside a more socially progressive agenda, embracing (limited) support for cultural plurality, feminism and support for

LGBTQIA* rights such as in new legislation for civil partnerships (Jessop 2003). Nonetheless, Labour's military adventures in Afghanistan and Iraq, growing hostility to asylum seekers, Islamophobia and lukewarm if not hostile attitudes to immigration reveal the limits to multicultural nationalism, demonstrating its capacity to subtly normalize nationalist ideologies in general political discourse.

In her poem 'Extinction', we may find Kay referencing this longer history of nationalism, combining growing concern over anti-European xenophobia and the demonization of immigrants with a wider perspective on the evolution of nationalist sentiment. Noting denunciations of 'lesbians', 'vegetarians' and 'HIV' as well as 'politically correct classes' and 'classes' as a concept at all, Kay's poem indexes a wide range of historical references (2015: n.p.). This exposes a deep vein of nationalist investments, encompassing the demonization of the gay community during the AIDS epidemic in the 1980s, anti-feminism and homophobia, the denigration of anti-discrimination legalization from the 1960s onwards, as well as the fate of 'class' in the Marxist tradition of understanding capitalist society. In so doing, Kay's poem combines xenophobia, homophobia and misogyny with climate change scepticism within a broad cultural nexus of 'otherness', demonstrating the way in which nationalist investment in traditional values of the family, social hierarchies and continuity have long identified a wide range of 'others' to its project of national unity. If the 1990s were seen to have eclipsed some of the most overt symptoms of the nationalist tendency through an ideology of multiculturalism, Kay's reference to the denying of 'class' is highly instructive, indicating broader shifts in political ideology away from class-based analyses of capitalist society. Class was not only disdained in the political rhetoric of the Thatcherite government but was renounced with renewed rigour by the New Labour governments led by Tony Blair and Gordon Brown.

New Labour marked a distinct move away from a politics based in worker solidarity, with Blair using an imaginary drawn from the corporate environment as a model for imagining a new, post-class society:

> The successful firm today works through partnership. Class distinctions are unhelpful and divisive. The good company invests in its people and takes them seriously. This is not kindness: this is good business. A country is not that different. (1996: 121)

The designation of class as 'divisive' is key to Blair's ideological investment in reorientating the political discourse of the Labour Party, admonishing the class-based notion of social antagonism between distinct economic classes towards a practical unity that is simply 'good business'. Reimagining the nation-state as a corporation accords with Blair's belief in the subordinate role states should play in relation to the global finance economy but also serves as a wider template through which he seeks to radically reimagine the political function of the national community itself. Through eschewing solidarities, affinities or communities based in shared class or political interests, Blair proposes a vision of national unity which necessitates a new basis for communal bonds. If a business is ultimately held together by a (usually hierarchical) investment in shared financial prosperity, this would serve as practical logic for society itself. This new vision of community is therefore effectively denuded of substantial political content, construing societal bonds through a purely practical, economic logic which deems class politics as an unnecessary and deleterious disruption of an otherwise unified and prosperous national destiny.

In 1997, Labour-aligned think tank *Demos* published an influential document which would take Blair's vision of a nation as a corporation to its limit, explicitly rethinking British national identity through an exercise in brand marketing. *Britain$^{TM}$: Renewing Our Identity* heralds a new multicultural identity that will indicate to the world that Britain is open for business, deploying language derived from the world of the burgeoning consultancy sector to reimagine politics with an optimistic, multicultural vision of national unity:

> Britain has always been open to immigration, more at ease with inward investment by German or Korean companies and open to cultural influences ranging from Indian food to Japanese manufacturing. The rich imagery of the sea has always been central to national identity – from the white cliffs of Dover to the great ports of Liverpool and Glasgow, from 'Heart of Oak' to Paul McCartney's folksy 'The Mull of Kintyre' or the imperial 'Rule Britannia'. (Leonard 1997: 44)

For Leonard it is Britain's identity as a 'hybrid nation' and as a 'silent revolutionary creating new models of organisation' that should demonstrate to the world 'our readiness to do business' (3). In this way, the performative 'we' of Leonard's experiment in reinventing the nation as a corporation implicitly aligns the social body with this singular market goal, cultivating and maintaining its successful financial outlook through proposing plural society as a unique, global brand. Different ethnic and cultural communities, queers and non-queers, immigrants and non-immigrants are integrated into a putatively harmonious history of integration, hospitality and unity, free from the divisive language of class, sexuality or race, or reference to colonialism, racism or homophobia. This imagined unity is for theorists of nationalism Benedict Anderson (1983) and Eric Hobsbawm (1990) the kernel of nationalist ideology, positing a highly selective or fictionalized account of history in order to cultivate nationalist investment in a population, where nationalism plays a distinctive role in building consent for prevailing economic systems and ideologies.

The community that emerges in the New Labour vision of the nation is, in the words of philosopher Jean-Luc Nancy, 'put to work': aggregating its members, construed either as individuals or as limited communities of identity, through the shared national project of fulfilling market goals (1991: 38). For Nancy, capitalism 'negates community because it places above it the identity and the generality of production and products: the operative communion and general communication of works' (75). When community is made operative in this way, and where human relationality works through a logic determined by an external force, Nancy claims we are not experiencing community but 'communion', a unity maintained through violent exclusions which ultimately destroy the community itself (12). In order for community to resist its reduction to a single work, something which Nancy sees as inevitably tied to authoritarianism, it is necessary to 'dissociate the idea of "community" from all projection into a work that is made or to be made – a State, a Nation, a People, or The People' (2016: 72). Community is greatly undermined by its identification with a nation or a state, and so too with its construal through self-contained cultural categories of ethnicity, religion or race. Against New Labour's redefining of community towards such restrictive goals, the task of many philosophers and writers has been to unearth and maintain alternative trajectories for community, imagining forms of association which exist outside or beyond imagined unities such as nations, states or bounded identity.

## The multicultural author and the international

The rest of this chapter will focus on the work of Jackie Kay, a poet, novelist and playwright whose early career overlapped with Blair's premiership, becoming emblematic of the multicultural vision that emerged during this period. Despite this identification, Kay's work exceeds this frame in its exploration of community, often implicitly questioning the way that nation-states contain or limit our understanding of human affinities and solidarities. Kay also explores how people living outside of norms of gender and sexuality who have been historically outlawed, punished or made invisible by the state have produced 'counter-communities' which call into question national community, whilst offering models for new ways of understanding and structuring sociality (Loick 2021). While Kay's use of biographical and autobiographical forms of writing in relation to questions of race, ethnicity, culture and sexuality have for many critics identified her work with multiculturalism, her work has been influenced by more radical ways of imagining community.

The critical reception of Kay exhibits a consistent trait. Introductions to chapters or articles on Kay almost invariably present her through an identification of her heritage, foregrounding her cultural persona and racial background before detailing her work or any cultural, literary or political framing device that might more ordinarily attend literary scholarship.[3] The primacy of the biographical in Kay's literary reception indicates a discursive matrix which always appears prior to it, where Kay's work is taken in a specific social context that inevitably orientates it to the multi-ethnic, the multicultural and the hybrid. Kay's status as a Black author of Nigerian descent, brought up by white Scottish parents, has been amenable to a multicultural framing, fitting her into the neat category of 'national poet' due to her tenure as Scottish Makar (Varty 2018). The effect of this is twofold: first, the literary status of Kay is iteratively diminished, subtly subordinated to a social significance of her background, and second, this multicultural framing is rarely itself given adequate critical attention, assumed as a consensus which does not itself require thorough interrogation or justification. Kay's compatibility with critical investments in the plural, hybrid and post-racial in this way have often obscured the heterogeneous political trajectories contained in her work, which in many ways exceed the broad investment in the multicultural across a wide range of sectors and political factions of British cultural life. Most noticeably, there are representations of queer life in Kay's work which draw attention to the exclusionary function of the nation-state and its investment in normative forms of kinship, which bring into question its compatibility with a radically queer or liberatory politics.

This tendency to identify Kay not primarily as a writer but as a social figure representing multicultural phenomena is expressed clearly in newspaper articles which frame Kay, who is Black, as having her adoption by two white Scottish parents to 'thank for her success' (Warwick 2014: n.p.). If Kay's own adoption is a complex subject in her literary works, biographical details about her life overtake her status as author, stripping her of the cultural currency and autonomy most public literary figures take for granted. Likewise, literary critics such as John McLeod demonstrate a similar tendency to foreground Kay's biographical status over the literary significance of her work, where her engagement with the poetic and semi-fictionalized personae in autobiographical texts is conflated directly with her own personhood. In his book *Life Lines: Writing Transcultural Adoption*, John McLeod sometimes abstains from close reading of texts by Kay, simply referring to her poem 'The Adoption Papers' as 'd[oing] much to bring into literature the postwar phenomenon of transcultural adoption' (2015: 210). Drafting Kay into his proposal of 'transcultural adoption' as a beneficial function of the multicultural state that gestures beyond the restrictive category of race itself, McLeod replicates a tendency of criticism to situate Kay as a manifestation of a social phenomenon, whilst uncritically investing in the nation-state as a site of reconciliation and benevolence.

McLeod's text elides direct questions of race by euphemistically collecting them within the term 'transcultural', but this pivot to the cultural nonetheless entails no close attention to concerns of sexuality or reference to queer theory and leaves the structural function of the multicultural nation-state largely uninterrogated. This is despite a long tradition of queer Black thought that has located the liberal state as 'a domain determined by racial difference and gender and sexual conformity' (Ferguson 2004: 3). In *Aberrations in Black; Towards a Queer of Color Critique* (2004), Roderick Ferguson points out that the reduction of political vectors such as race to issues of 'culture' 'compels identifications with … the normative ideals promoted by state and capital', demonstrating how a multicultural ideology can tacitly erode more radical trajectories in marginal communities (3). If 'liberal pluralism has traditionally constructed the home as the obvious site of accommodation and confirmation', Ferguson compiles a history of the capitalist state which demonstrates how it 'occludes the intersecting saliency of race, gender, sexuality, and class in forming social practices' (3).

Kay's work references a similar Black[4] tradition to that of Ferguson's account, where cultural and political affiliations necessarily exceed the nation-state, moving between global geographies still determined by colonialism, slavery and enduring asymmetries in global capitalism (Kay 2008, 2017). Her identification as a multicultural author belies a wider set of political commitments and influences, not least her adoptive parents' Communist convictions: a political tradition which has largely privileged an internationalist politics of class solidarity and criticized nationalist ideology. Kay's oeuvre demonstrates deep indebtedness to a wider range of radical political traditions, linking the Black Marxist tradition with the Highland clearances of the eighteenth and nineteenth centuries:

> I am learning about the Black Jacobins
> From CLR James and the memories of the
> Cheviot and the stag and the Highlanders
> Being forced oot of their crofts
> Came flooding back. (1988: 92)

Drawing on the Marxist anti-colonial work of C. L. R. James, whose influential 1938 book *Black Jacobins* detailed the Haitian revolution of 1791–1804, where former slaves drew on the principles of the French Revolution to overthrow French colonial rule, Kay puts this in dialogue with the broadly contemporaneous Highland clearances in Scotland. Referencing John McGrath's play on the topic, Kay combines two unexpected traditions, linking parallel processes of dispossession of African slaves, and Scottish peasants in the Highlands, whilst also invoking their respective resistance to this. In McGrath's play we see how in the Scottish context, colonialism was understood not simply as a process that took place overseas, in Africa, Asia and the Americas, but which developed practices of control and exploitation that were also deployed in the British mainland. The British Empire was not beneficial to the national community as a whole as it practiced techniques of exploitation and extraction against members of its lower social classes, regardless of their nationality, indicating bonds of potential 'anticolonial solidarity' between the oppressed peoples in England, Scotland and across the empire (Gopal 2019: 23):

> The highland exploitation chain-reacted around the world; in Australia the aborigines were hunted like animals; in Tasmania not one aborigine was left alive; all over Africa, black men were massacred and brought to heel. In America the plains were emptied of men and buffalo, and the seeds of the next century's imperialist power were firmly planted and at home the word went round that over there, things were getting better. (McGrath [1974] 2013: 29)

Likewise, Jackie Kay's 2017 text *Bantam*, her first poetry collection as Scottish Makar, indicates an internationalist tradition which exceeds any easy identification of her work with a nationally framed multicultural project. Invoking her adopted parents John and Helen Kay, who are the main objects of address in the collection's repeated use of the second person, Kay recalls their involvement in historical political demonstrations based in internationalist networks of solidarity:

> Nobody knew you greeted Madame Allende
> Or sang the songs of Victor Jara

Or loved Big Arthur's bravura 'Bandiera Rossa'
Or heard Paul Robeson at the May Day rally. (11)

Madame Allende was the wife of Chilean president Salvador Allende, who killed himself during the 1973 Chilean coup d'état when General Pinchot, with the backing of the Richard Nixon–led American administration, implemented the first neoliberal economic project after ousting Allende's democratically elected Socialist government (Taylor 2006). In exile, Madame Allende travelled the world building international opposition to Pinchot's brutal rule, becoming rector of the University of Glasgow in 1977 and returning to Chile in 1988. Kay also references Paul Robeson, an important internationalist figure, whose political activism in support of anti-fascist Republican forces in the Spanish Civil War, and support for the Soviet Union, saw the American government deny him a passport during the McCarthyite era (Goodman 2013). Such historical references foreground the internationalist anti-colonial struggles of the time, which often saw oppression as intrinsic to the nation-states that they opposed, building forms of political solidarity and community which sought to dislodge such structures. Based in scenes such as the 'May Day rally', spaces of communal joy in protest, song and political education, the basis of such collectivities is firmly rooted in an international outlook and shared political perspectives which defy containment within a national context. Writing that 'nobody knew' about her parent's political activities, something which 'The Adoption Papers' also confirms when her parents hide copies of Marxist literature as well as a 'poster of Paul Robeson' in order to be accepted as legal adopters, Kay notes how such political convictions and internationalist solidarities have often had to guard such allegiances from exposure in the capitalist state (1991: 15).

## Queer counter-community in *Trumpet*

Jackie Kay's account of her parents' concealing of their Communist politics demonstrates how communities that develop modes of solidarity or relationality which are incompatible with the state's projection of legitimate community must often guard themselves from exposure in a hostile or even dangerous sociality. Daniel Loick theorizes such communities through the paradigm of the 'counter-community', taking queer, migrant and feminist social movements as exemplary of this trend. Counter-communities are composed of 'subjugated' populations which exists at a necessary 'distanc[e] from dominant social structure' such as in 'oppositional subcultures and scenes, political movements and parties' or as alternative modes of 'kinship' (Loick 2021: 23). Despite their marginal status and fragility as communities, Loick draws on the work of queer theorists Michael Warner and Lauren Berlant to demonstrate how such communities are able to imaginatively recreate social bonds beyond was Nancy (1991) calls their 'operative' function which subordinates them to the logic of the state. Counter-communities can also, for Loick, engage in a form of 'world-making' that works beyond 'all forms of familial or national identity formation' (Berlant and Warner 1998: 558; Loick 2021: 19). This process of world-making is marked by 'an irreducible openness and a becoming', inventing alternative modes of sociality beyond the exclusions and normativity of the nation-state (Loick 2021: 19). Crucially, such inventive forms of community are 'neither compensatory nor deficient, but antagonistic and thus transcendent' in relation to the dominant mode of national community. They do not ask for 'integration to the existing order but its abolition' (4).

Given the tendencies in Kay's work which are critical of the restrictions of a nationalist, state multiculturalism, it is unsurprising that she turns to fiction as a form well suited to the process of radical world-making, offering a generative space where marginal forms of community can be explored and new modes of affinity can be captured. It is in her novel *Trumpet* (1998) that she offers her most incisive reimagining of community. *Trumpet* is a fictional rewriting of the life of jazz trumpeter Billy Tipton, who, upon his death, was revealed to have been born a woman. Likewise, this is the situation for the protagonist of Kay's novel Joss Moody, who is reimagined as a Black man living in Scotland, with the narrative told from the perspective of his ex-wife, son, mother, various officials (a registrar, doctor and funeral director), old friends and band members, as well as an unauthorized biographer and reporter named Sophie Stones. The novel navigates a social landscape where trans identities are not only unintelligible to many but provoke hostility, prejudice and misrecognition from the institutions of the state, necessitating retreat and secrecy in relation to broader sociality.

The starting passage is told from the perspective of Millie Moody, the wife of the recently departed Joss, who is hiding from reporters and photographer outside her window. Throughout the novel, an insidious 'they' of intrusive sociality is spectrally present, consistently confronting Millie with the difficulty of recognition in a landscape which wishes to instrumentalize her life with Joss Moody through sensationalist exposure: 'No doubt they will call me a lesbian. They will find words to fit onto me. Words that don't fit me. Words that don't fit Joss' (Kay 1998: 154). Millie's relationship with Joss in the novel is unintelligible for most people she encounters, rendered 'unreal' in the symbolic landscape of state kinship which does not recognize trans identities, and in so doing construes her relationship as 'lesbian' and therefore illegal and illegitimate: 'Each time I look at the photographs in the papers, I look unreal. I look unlike the memory of myself' (1). These 'photographs' are the visual markers of a general social misrecognition, circulated in an outside environment from which Millie can only retreat behind her 'curtain'. Subject to prurient investigation from reporters, and prejudice from many around her, it is only in her remembered relationship with Joss that she can understand her reality: 'It was real. We just got on and lived it' (125).

As we see in Loick, the 'counter-community' is constituted in its distance from the norms of the state to which they are sometimes illegible, producing modes of life and affinity which are incommensurable with its basic structure. The nation-state relies on its ability to 'reproduc[e] the dominant family ideology' where the domestic sphere serves the vital function of creating and sustaining new workers for the economy (10). Queer life therefore offers a vital repository for understanding ways of organizing and sustaining communities, relationships and affinities which exist outside of this. In their inability to be fully integrated with the nation-state, they are necessarily constituted as outside and beyond it, overlapping with Nancy's desire for a community that is 'inoperative' through being unbound by the work of the nation-state to reproduce itself as an identity (1991: 72). Although Joss and Millie's relationship is barely itself a community, it is what Bataille terms a 'community of lovers' which functions as a 'closed community' where lovers share in a bond which is forged through the exclusion of the community in general (Bataille 2009: 7). For Maurice Blanchot, who draws on Bataille, the community of lovers is constituted through the 'oblivion of the world: the affirmation of a relationship so singular' that it exceeds all social bonds as they are currently configured (Blanchot 1988: 34). If perhaps overstated and overly romantic in their articulation, Bataille and Blanchot's conception of love as a disruptive and transformative force takes on greater significance in the space of the counter-community, where marginal relationships disrupt the dominant order of relation, gesturing to potentially novel forms of relationality.

The representation of Joss and Millie's intimate closed community is presented by Kay as the only space in which the fragile and socially misrecognized category of 'trans' can be authentically understood. Only Millie has been present to Joss Moody's willed exposure as his body, the revelation of which on his death begins a process of violent social misrecognition. In an early scene of intimacy between the couple, Joss hesitates before exposing his body, faced with the possibility of rejection. Seeing the 'bandages' binding his chest, Millie at first assumes Joss is injured: 'to think all he is worried about is some scar he has. He should know my love goes deeper than a wound,' but as Joss 'keeps unwrapping endless rolls of bandage', Millie realizes the real reason for Joss's apprehension: 'I am still holding out my hands when the first of his breasts reveals itself to me. Small, firm' (Kay 1998: 21). Throughout the chapter, Kay engages in a careful pacing, slowly developing a compact prose of erotic tension produced through unexpected commas and short sentences: 'His breath is fast, excited' (19). Ending the chapter with the revelation of Joss's status as trans, Kay crucially curtails the development of the scene, leaving the couple's negotiation of Joss's trans identity suggested, but unrepresented. Evoking the structure of the counter-community which is liable to misrecognition and erasure in the national community, Kay replicates this at the level of her prose itself. The counter-community of Joss and Millie is here rendered through its constitutive unrepresentability, guarding its relationality from exposure. The scene is not fully developed because, in some crucial way, it is not representable. What ensues is the possibility of a relation which in many ways is utopian: unimaginable in the operative logics of relation and identity in which most of us live.

By foregrounding the community of lovers, who are closed off from wider society, Kay circumvents dominant conventions in categorizing and taxonomizing the gendered body. Essentialist constructions of the biological are entirely ignored by Millie, who does not dwell on the figure of the 'trans', a word which is not used in the novel, rather simply foregrounding his male identity as a given component of their shared lives. If state-sanctioned accounts of gender demand a stability and unity to gender identity, tying it to an origin-myth of biology and sex 'assignment' at birth, Moody's being as a man is nonetheless absolutely affirmed by Millie, who refuses any taxonomy but her own:

> I can't stare at these pictures and force myself to see '*this person who is obviously a woman, once you know*' – according to some reports. I can't see her. I don't know if I'll ever see her. The photographs of Joss on his album covers are the same to me. I can't change him. I can see his lips. His lips pursed when he played the trumpet. His lips open to talk. Him leaning over me, kissing me softly with his lips. All over my face. His dark full lips. (100, original emphasis)

In this passage, Kay subtly asserts gender identity not as part of social logic of enforced biological binarism but as the revelation of intimates. If 'some reports' wish to categorize Moody's gender, to assert its origin through reference to common recognition, where he is said to be '*obviously a woman once you know*', it is clear that many people, including all of Moody's close relations, experienced something very different to this. Rather than mirror the category prescription of the 'reports', we are offered the evocative memory of '[h]is dark lips', with the rhythmic repetition of short sentences preceded by masculine pronouns: '[h]is lips', 'him leaning', not asserting masculinity as a category to be stated as social reality but rather as a relation to be simply experienced. The careful pacing of the prose, which builds an almost poetic intensity with its short lines and repetitions, evokes the passionate rhythms of kissing, love-making and caress, where it is the meeting of skin: here, of 'lips', which produces the repeated affirmation of masculinity. In this sense gender is produced not through social categorization but through consistent uses of the masculine pronoun, denoting not 'man', but 'this man', 'here', whose meaning is not dependent on state-sanctioned structures of dominant sense but on a specific sensual encounter.

Through this mode of description, Kay eschews any attempt to reconcile her account with the dominant terms of gender as proposed by the state which regulates 'gender and sexuality' through its 'periodic reinvention of the family as an instrument for distributing wealth and income' (Cooper 2017: 17). She therefore follows José Esteban Muñoz in offering a form of 'disidentification' which distances itself from normative identity categories so they can be rethought and retooled towards their own purpose. This allows for dominant modes of kinship and operative norms to be exposed in their exclusionary function whilst also utilizing the 'code of the majority' 'as raw material for representing a disempowered politics or positionality that has been rendered unthinkable by the dominant culture' (Muñoz 1999: 5). To expose the 'unthinkable' is therefore to carve a place for a transformational politics that is not yet in existence, allowing forms of life which are not recognized by the state to exist at its margins, rerouting and transforming norms of kinship, community and sexuality. For trans theorist Gayle Salamon, 'trans' is a vital placeholder for a multiplicity of non-normative subject positions, and as such it must be asserted as a way of demanding recognition and rights at the same time as being understood as open to change and 'undecidability' (2010: 143). If forms of state-recognition ultimately underpin the ability of people to gain access to political rights, those communities who cannot receive this are 'condemn[ed] to placelessness' (144).

Muñoz and Salamon are interested in the ways in which queer and trans life has historically been condemned to a marginality, excluded from representations of the world and barred from proper legal or political recognition. Counter-communities of queer life which survive despite such erasures must work with current conceptions of gender, sexuality and community at the same time as reinventing them in creative ways, anticipating the possibility of alternative modes of community and kinship. Such possible futures are necessarily defined by an 'unrealizability' for Loick, who points out that counter-communities are not engaged simply in proposing concrete forms of community but in radically transforming the modes of power in the nation-state which define and regulate them towards their own ends (2021: 19). Similarly, in Salamon's account of 'trans', what is proposed is not simply reconciliation with the current system of gender-binarism, a desire for integration through the production of a new category or even the altering of existing ones. Trans life can also refuse inclusion, demanding a restructuring of society itself, calling into question the power of the state to regulate and determine our intimate lives, identities and communities. 'Trans' is therefore orientated towards an 'undecidability' which keeps the question of community and identity radically open (Salamon 2010: 144). If the multicultural state has been situated as the benevolent, hospitable and mutable grounds for such possibilities, the continuing history of exclusion and regulation also opens the possibility of rethinking such structures on a more fundamental level.

Kay points to this specific mode of 'undecidability' in the only section of the novel that focuses on Joss Moody's lived life, which she encapsulates through an evocative and experimental chapter centred on a description of his jazz improvisation. In this section, Joss inhabits an ambiguous relation to his body and gender norms, appearing to transcend in some ways social logics which confine and misrepresent him. For trans theorist Jay Prosser, the relation between the *actual* gendered body of trans people and the social logic which precedes and orders them is necessarily vexed. It demands understanding the potential 'fluidity' a trans body can have in relation to norms, at the same time asserting the absolute importance of their sexed embodiment as not only characterized by the fluid but also the 'flesh', and what Prosser privileges in terms of the body's 'materiality' (1998: 62). As has been seen with Muñoz, the process of 'disidentification' demanded by social marginalization and misrecognition demands not only distancing oneself from norms but also retooling and reclaiming their operative terms. In this section, music allows for Moody's body to retreat from the social landscape, taking on an embodied position of masculinity which is also elastic, experimental and fundamentally 'undecidable' (Salamon 2010: 143).

> When he gets down, and he doesn't always get down deep enough, he loses his sex, his race, his memory. He strips himself bare, takes everything off, till he's

> barely human. Then he brings himself back, out of this world. Back, from way. Getting there is painful. He has to get to the centre of the whirlwind, screwbaling in musical circles till he is very nearly out of his mind. (131)

In this intimate space of jazz improvisation, Joss 'loses his sex', his race disidentifying with social norms to find a liberated territory beyond them. Mirroring the music enveloping him, Joss appears fluid, disruptive and rhythmic in his own embodied being: 'he is bending in the wind, scooping pitch, growling', and if the music is 'fast' and 'speeding, crashing', this temporality proceeds from his 'fingers going like hammers, frenzied' and '[h]is leather lips. His satchelmouth' (131). The constantly shifting terms of this music move through and with his body in a manner akin to but '[b]etter than sex' (135). If music appears to 'transcend' the body, as some commentaries suggest, it is nonetheless located precisely within his body: 'There is music in his blood' and music proceeds from his bodily extremes: his 'leather lips' and his 'skin' (Byrne and Allen 2014: 94; Kay 1998: 134). Music does not simply transcend but presses at the limit of the possible: opening social categories of sex, gender and race to radical transformation. Moving freely through categories of gender and race: 'He is a girl. A man … Black, white' (Kay 1998: 136), Moody embodies the power of the counter-community to reorganize and reimagine dominant structures of sociality. Rendering the gendered and raced body as a space of undecidable and indefinite experimentation, Kay locates this rare liberatory moment in the novel through indifference to social norms and the possibility of radically transforming them. A world beyond restrictive and state-sanctioned gender roles, racism and exclusion may be imaginable in many ways, but by holding onto this potential, *Trumpet* insists on community as a project open to infinite, and even utopian, possibilities.

## Conclusion

Jackie Kay's critical reception is marked by a close identification of her work and biography with the multicultural, replicating forms of categorization which denude her work of its more disruptive and radical orientations. Her early career coincides with a period when Blair's government was attempting to reinvent Britain as an administrator of a globalized, neoliberal economy with a multicultural identity tacitly aligned with a strong investment in national community, subordinating communal bonds to a projected unity. At this time,

Kay was influenced not only by Marxist thought but also by the Black radical tradition, both of which have a long tradition of building political community, solidarity and affiliation beyond and against the structure of the nation-state. Internationalist solidarity, as evoked by Kay's referencing of figures such as Paul Robeson and Madame Allende, indicates a tradition of political thinking which highlights the enduring colonial legacy of Britain, as well as the importance of anti-colonial solidarity. Writing that if he was 'in Britain' he would 'feel a sense of oneness with the white working people', Robeson offers a vision of international community where 'common people are all nations are truly brothers in the great family of mankind' (1958: 48). A common reference point for Kay throughout her career, Kay's own evocation of community is influenced by Robeson's internationalist vision, imagining modes of community and affinity which are at times indifferent, antagonistic or transcendent of the nation-state itself.

This vision arguably finds its strongest articulation in Kay's attention to queer history of Billy Tipton, which she reinvents in the Scottish context in her novel *Trumpet*. Through its evocation of Joss and Millie Moody, the novel foregrounds the role the capitalist state can play in determining legitimate and illegitimate gender roles. This exposes how the state's promotion of the traditional nuclear family, which is the site where labour-power is reproduced, plays an exclusionary role for populations and kinship arrangements which do not conform to its structure. The figure of the 'trans' and its historical marginality demonstrates the ways in which queer communities and relationalities have long existed through modes of secrecy and social retreat, guarding communal arrangements unintelligible to the wider political landscape. Invoking Loick's recent proposal of the term 'counter-communities' to capture the political function of such communities, Kay's attention to the disruptive and unrepresentable function of the queer relationship at the heart of *Trumpet* demonstrates the possibility in her text of anticipating radical rearrangements of community and sociality beyond their restriction in the capitalist nation-state. If the articulation of such communities is marked by an indeterminacy and 'undecidability' that invoke a utopian register, such 'word-making' tendencies in imaginative fiction are arguably necessary to address the political challenges of the present (Berlant and Warner: 558). As the nationalist tendency in British society continues to grow apace, internationalist movements which attempted to reinvent political community beyond the nation-state and capitalism offer vital and still unrealized paths for political renewal.

## Notes

1 It has become common to use this Gramscian terminology to periodize neoliberalism's apparent demise since the financial crisis of 2008. For example, see Peck and Dawes (2020: 289–309).
2 Recent scholarship has decisively argued that far from abandoning the state, neoliberalism relied on nationalist support from a bolstered state for its survival. See Slobodian (2018).
3 A short review of recent articles on Kay confirms this. For example, Williams (2020); Elgezeery (2015) and Szuba (2017). Bettina Jansen's 2018 chapter on Jackie Kay in *Narratives of Community in the Black British Short Story* marks a refreshing departure from this trend.
4 Following Kwame Anthony Appiah, capitalizing the 'B' in 'Black' is a useful way to indicate it is not a 'natural category but a social one – a collective identity –with a particular history' (2020: n.p.).

## References

Albornoz, Facundo, Facundo Albornoz, Jake Bradley and Silvia Sonderegger (2020), 'The Brexit Referendum and the Rise in Hate Crime: Conforming to the New Norm', *Discussion Papers*, Nottingham: Nottingham Interdisciplinary Centre for Economic and Political Research.

Anderson, Benedict (1983), *Imagined Communities: Reflections on the Origin and Spread of Nationalism*, London: Verso.

Appiah, Kwame Anthony (2020), 'The Case for Capitalizing the B in Black', *Atlantic*, 18 June, https://www.theatlantic.com/ideas/archive/2020/06/time-to-capitalize-black-and-white/613159/.

Bataille, Georges (2009), *The Obsessions of Georges Bataille: Community and Communication*, New York: SUNY.

Berger, Mark (2001), 'The Nation-State and the Challenge of Global Capitalism', *Third World Quarterly*, 22 (6): 889–907.

Berlant, Lauren, and Michael Warner (1998), 'Sex in Public', *Critical Inquiry*, 24 (2): 547–66.

Bewes, Timothy, and Jeremy Gilbert (eds) (2000), *Cultural Capitalism: Politics after New Labour*, London: Lawrence & Wishart.

Blair, Tony (1996), *New Britain: My Vision of a Young Country*, London: Fourth Estate.

Blanchot, Maurice (1988), *The Unavowable Community*, New York: Station Hill.

Byrne, Aidan, and Nicola Allen (2014), 'Masculinity and Jazz in Jackie Kay's *Trumpet*, Jim Crace's *All That Follows*, and Alan Plater's *The Beiderbecke Trilogy*', in Erich Hertz and Jeffrey Roessner (eds), *Write in Tune: Contemporary Music in Fiction*, 85–98, New York: Bloomsbury Academic.

Cooper, Melinda (2017), *Family Values: Between Neoliberalism and the New Social Conservatism*, New York: Zone.

Elgezeery, Gamal (2015), 'Fluid Identity of the Daughter in Jackie Kay's "The Adoption Papers"', *International Journal of Applied Linguistics and English Literature*, 4 (4): 125–6.

Ferguson, Roderick (2004), *Aberrations in Black: Toward a Queer of Color Critique*, Minneapolis: University of Minnesota Press.

Gilbert, Jeremy (2013), *Neoliberal Culture*, London: Lawrence & Wishart.

Glazer, Nathan (1997), *We Are All Multiculturalists Now*, Cambridge, MA: Harvard University Press.

Goodman, Jordan (2013), *Paul Robeson: A Watched Man*, London: Verso.

Gopal, Priyamvada (2019), *Insurgent Empire: Anticolonial Resistance and British Dissent*, London: Verso.

Hall, Stuart (2021), 'The Multicultural Question', in Paul Gilroy and Ruth Wilson Gilmore (eds), *Selected Writings on Race and Difference: Stuart Hall*, Durham, NC: Duke University Press.

Hobsbawm, Eric (1990), *Nations and Nationalism since 1780: Programme, Myth, Reality*, Cambridge: Cambridge University Press.

Jansen, Bettina (2018), *Narratives of Community in the Black British Short Story*, Basingstoke: Palgrave Macmillan.

Jessop, Robert (2003), 'From Thatcherism to New Labour: Neo-Liberalism, Workfarism, and Labour Market Regulation', in Overbeek Henk (ed.), *The Political Economy of European Employment: European Integration and the Transnationalization of the (Un)Employment Question*, 137–53, London: Routledge.

Johansen, Emily (2015), 'The Banal Conviviality of Neoliberal Cosmopolitanism', *Textual Practice*, 29 (2): 295–314.

Kay, Jackie (1988), 'Kail and Callaloo', in Shabnam Grewal, Jackie Kay, Liliane Landor, Gail Lewis and Pratibha Parmar (eds), *Charting the Journey: Writings by Black and Third World Women*, 90–2, London: Sheba.

Kay, Jackie (1991), *The Adoption Papers*, Newcastle upon Tyne: Bloodaxe.

Kay, Jackie (1998), *Trumpet*, London: Picador.

Kay, Jackie (2008), *The Lamplighter*, Tarset: Bloodaxe.

Kay, Jackie (2015), 'Extinction', *Guardian Online*, 15 May, https://www.theguardian.com/environment/2015/may/15/a-climate-change-poem-for-today-extinction-by-jackie-kay?CMP=share_btn_tw.

Kay, Jackie (2017), *Bantam*, London: Picador.

Leonard, Mark (1997), 'Britain™: Renewing Our Identity', *Demos*, London, https://www.demos.co.uk/files/britaintm.pdf.

Loick, Daniel (2021), 'The Ethical Life of Counter-Communities', *Critical Times*, 4 (1): 1–28.

McGrath, John ([1974] 2013), *The Cheviot, the Stag and the Black, Black Oil*, London: Bloomsbury.

McLeod, John (2015), *Life Lines: Writing Transcultural Adoption*, London: Bloomsbury Academic.

Moosavi, Leon (2015), 'Orientalism at Home: Islamophobia in the Representations of Islam and Muslims by the New Labour Government', *Ethnicities*, 15 (5): 652–74.

Mulgan, Geoff (ed.) (1997), *Life after Politics: New Thinking for the Twenty-First*, London: Fortana.

Muñoz, José Esteban (1999), *Disidentifications: Queers of Color and the Performance of Politics*, Minneapolis: University of Minnesota Press.

Nancy, Jean-Luc (1991), *The Inoperative Community*, Minneapolis: University of Minnesota Press.

Nancy, Jean-Luc (2016), *The Disavowed Community*, New York: Fordham University Press.

Peck, Jamie, and Simon Dawes (2020), 'Contextualizing Neoliberalism: An Interview with Jamie Peck', in Simon Dawes and Marc Lenormand (eds), *Neoliberalism in Context: Governance, Subjectivity and Knowledge*, 289–309, London: Palgrave Macmillan.

Povinelli, Elizabeth A. (2013), 'Defining Security in Late Liberalism: A Comment on Pedersen and Holbraad', in Martin Holbraad and Morten Axel Pedersen (eds), *Times of Security: Ethnographies of Fear, Protest and the Future*, 28–32, Abingdon: Routledge.

Prosser, Jay (1998), *Second Skins: The Body Narratives of Transsexuality*, New York: Columbia University Press.

Robeson, Paul (1958), *Here I Stand*, London: Cassell.

Salamon, Gayle (2010), *Assuming a Body: Transgender and Rhetorics of Materiality*, New York: Columbia University Press.

Slobodian, Quinn (2018), *Globalists: The End of Empire and the Birth of Neoliberalism*, Cambridge, MA: Harvard University Press.

Szuba, Monika (2017), 'From the Adoption Papers to Fiere: Jackie Kay's Writing and Scottish Multiculturalism', *Tekstualia*, 4 (51): 75–86.

Taylor, Marcus (2006), *From Pinochet to the 'Third Way': Neoliberalism and Social Transformation in Chile*, London: Pluto.

Valluvan, Sivamohan, and Virinder S. Kalra (2019), 'Racial Nationalisms: Brexit, Borders and Little Englander Contradictions', *Ethnic and Racial Studies*, 42 (142): 2393–412.

Varty, Anne (2018), 'National Poets on Tour in June 2016: "Shore to Shore" and Brexit', *Review of English Studies*, New Series, 70 (293): 135–57.

Warwick, Norman (2014), 'Literature Festival Poet Jackie Kay Has Adoption to Thank for Her Success', *Manchester Evening News*, 5 June, https://www.manchestereveningnews.co.uk/news/local-news/adopted-child-poet-jackie-kay-7324061.

Williams, Nerys (2020), 'Jackie Kay', in Richard Bradford, Madelena Gonzalez, Stephen Butler, James Ward and Kevin De Ornellas (eds), *The Wiley Blackwell Companion to Contemporary British and Irish Literature*, 431–40, Newark: Wiley-Blackwell.

# 5

# Community versus commodity: Neoliberalism and (sub)urban identities in twenty-first-century London novels

Caroline Lusin

I wander thro' each charter'd street,
Near where the charter'd Thames does flow.
And mark in every face I meet
Marks of weakness, marks of woe.

– Blake ([1794] 2008)

The myth of the individual
Has left us disconnected   lost
and pitiful.

– Tempest ([2016] 2017)

## London literature and the concept of community

From William Blake's *Songs of Innocence and Experience* (1789/1794) to Kae Tempest's *Let Them Eat Chaos* (2016), London has served as a yardstick for many notable figures in British literature in judging the status quo of their society. Both Blake and Tempest depict the society of their time as fractured and unequal by tracing the stories of several lives profoundly blighted by a system bent solely on profit. Blake's emphasis in 'London' on how everything and everyone is hired out for profit is strikingly in line with the focus adopted in a whole range of contemporary London novels. In the novel form, Alex Preston (2012: n.p.) traces this preoccupation back to Anthony Trollope's *The Way We Live Now* (1875), whose 'shifting viewpoints, keen engagement with contemporary themes, and use of London as a microcosm' recur in recent 'Neo-Trollopian' (2012: n.p.) fiction such as Amanda Craig's *Hearts and Minds* (2009), Justin Cartwright's *Other People's Money* (2011) and John Lanchester's *Capital* (2012). In contemporary fiction, the effects of today's financialization, privatization and commodification have swapped places with the negative repercussions of the industrialization haunting late-eighteenth- and nineteenth-century literature. These effects originate in the same neoliberal 'myth of the individual' (Tempest [2016] 2017: 72) Tempest identifies in *Let Them Eat Chaos* as the source of a worrying degree of disconnection. Based on the notion that 'each individual is held responsible and accountable for his or her wellbeing' (Harvey 2005: 65), neoliberalism 'proposes that human well-being can best be advanced by liberating individual entrepreneurial freedoms and skills within an institutional framework characterized by strong private property rights, free markets, and free trade' (2). In the perception of its critics, this ideology has created a world characterized by social atomization, exploitation and a ruthless commodification of all spheres of life, not unlike the picture of the city Blake creates in 'London'.

Focusing once more on the metropolis, Kae Tempest and Fiona Mozley explore the effects of neoliberalism on contemporary society in two recent additions to their oeuvre, *The Bricks That Built the Houses* (2016) and *Hot Stew* (2021). Set in south London and in Soho, respectively, *The Bricks That Built the Houses* and *Hot Stew* explore the repercussions of neoliberalism's emphasis on competition and individual responsibility for personal as well as collective identities and communal cohesion. Contemporary British fiction has spawned detailed portrayals of circumscribed London communities like these, be it the Fitzrovia and Bloomsbury of Ian McEwan's *Saturday* (2005), the Hounslow of Gautam Malkani's *Londonstani* (2006), the Willesden of Zadie Smith's *NW* (2012), the Chelsea of Jonathan Coe's *Number 11* (2015) or the Neasden of Guy Gunaratne's *In Our Mad and Furious City* (2018). While all these novels critically interrogate the idealizing notion that 'community is a "warm" place, a cosy and comfortable place' (Bauman 2001: 3), Tempest and Mozley emphasize the negative impact of neoliberalism on (sub)urban communities and identities unusually clearly. In *The Bricks That Built the Houses*, Tempest traces the interconnected stories of four young adults struggling to carve out their place in life: Becky, a talented dancer with a thwarted career making a living as an erotic masseuse; Pete, who holds a degree in international relations but aimlessly drifts through assorted low short-term jobs; and Harry and her best mate Leon, who have been dealing drugs since their schooldays so as to be ultimately able to finance a better existence. Much like the seven young Londoners of *Let Them Eat Chaos*, these are depicted as characters 'who, under neoliberal conditions, blame themselves for their failures when blame should be sought within the system' (Schuhmaier 2021: 104). The economic and social system of neoliberalism also has a decisive impact on the lives of the characters in Mozley's *Hot Stew*, which shifts her poignant critique of Thatcherism in her debut novel *Elmet* (2017) from the countryside to an urban setting. Adopting a more comprehensive point of view in terms of class and social status than *The Bricks That Built the Houses*, *Hot Stew* focuses on a conflict between a group of sex workers and a super-rich owner of multiple estates threatening to evict them from their Soho residence. The central focus in terms of plot is on sex worker Precious and her partner Tabitha, who set up a protest against the eviction, on the one hand, and the estate owner Agatha Howard on the other. This plot line is closely entwined with the stories of various other characters from altogether different backgrounds, including a group of homeless people, all of whom are in some way connected.

What is at stake in *The Bricks That Built the Houses* and *Hot Stew* is the search for meaningful communal connection in a world in which everyone is fending for themselves. Sociologically, community represents 'a particular form of social organization based on small groups, such as neighbourhoods, the small town, or a spatially bounded locality' (Delanty 2003: 2), which the specific local focus of the novels seems to endorse; but community is much more than that. As Gerard Delanty explains, community is neither simply a social group nor an idea, but both – it 'does in fact designate both an idea about belonging and a particular social phenomenon, such as expressions of longing for community, the search for meaning and solidarity, and collective identities' (3). It is both localized and spatial, and abstract and symbolic; at any rate, it is 'related to the search for belonging in the insecure conditions of modernity' (1), and associated with safety, trust and understanding (see Bauman 2001: 1–2). While both novels endorse Zygmunt Bauman's argument that what the word community 'evokes is everything we miss and we lack to be secure, confident and trusting' (3), both concomitantly project different localized forms of community and communal solidarity, counteracting the increasing fragmentation, urban destruction, displacement and loss of community associated with the global neoliberal city from the 1980s onwards (see Delanty 2003: 56–7).

The issue of gentrification in particular, a 'process of capitalist renewal of cities that involves massive changes in the urban fabric' (Di Masso et al. 2021: 221), is featured in *The Bricks That Built the Houses* and *Hot Stew* as a crucial, even violent obstacle to achieving a feeling of communal cohesion, belonging and a meaningful identity.¹ This is in line with the results of studies that have linked gentrification 'to anxiety, stress … a sense of weakening social and community bonds … and a questioning of self-identity' (222). In his essay on American gentrification fiction, James Peacock emphasizes how literature facilitates depicting individual, divergent perspectives, serving as 'an antidote to the homogenization – of consumption, class, ethnicity, sexuality – inherent to gentrification' (2021: 103). Written in a similar vein, *The Bricks That Built the Houses* and *Hot Stew* critically interrogate the 'capacity of local community to provide an alternative to the social fragmentation brought about by global capitalism' (Delanty 2003: 69) – remaining painfully aware of the limitations to communal connectedness. In the following, I will explore their approach to community in close conjunction with their critique of neoliberal ideology and policy.

## From community to 'heroic individualism'

'It gets into your bones', declares the narrator in the first sentence of *The Bricks That Built the Houses*. 'You don't even realise it, until you're driving through it, watching all the things you've always known and leaving them behind' (Tempest 2016: 3). What at first seems a vague statement refers to London – Leon, Harry and Becky are driving through London as they are fleeing the country after a drug deal gone badly wrong. But what has got into their bones is not just London, but life – victuals consumed, the physical features of the city, people defined by their roles in the social system and the general facts of existence: 'It's in their bones. Bread and booze and concrete. The beauty of it. All the tiny moments blazing. Preachers, parents, workers. Empty-eyed romantics going nowhere. Street lights and traffic and bodies to bury and babies to make. A job. Just a job' (3). The metaphor signals the characters' inextricable connection to this city, but the entire section also subtly echoes the second stanza of William Blake's 'Freedom and Captivity', which serves as a poignant motto for the second part of the novel, adding a jarring note to the bitter-sweet nostalgia of the prologue: 'The souls of men are bought and sold/ In milk-fed infancy for gold, / And youth to slaughter-houses led; / And beauty, for a bit of bread' (Blake qtd from Tempest 2016: 181). This foil identifies Tempest's preachers and parents as guilty of selling out their protégés to a ruthlessly exploitative system; in contrast to Blake, the romantic visionary, Tempest's failed romantics are aimless and 'empty-eyed', lacking a vision of how things could be different. This position is reminiscent in more than one way of Mark Fisher's idea of 'capitalist realism'. According to Fisher, the ideology of capitalism (or neoliberalism) has become so pervasive that 'it is now impossible even to *imagine* a coherent alternative to it' (2009: 1, original emphasis), and Tempest's bone metaphor echoes Fisher's argument that neoliberalism has come to operate even 'at the level of the cultural unconscious' (6). On an aesthetic level, the almost imperceptible incorporation of Blake's poem into the novel's beginning thus mirrors the way neoliberalism operates today. As George Monbiot puts it in the *Guardian*: 'So pervasive has neoliberalism become that we seldom even recognise it as an ideology' (2016: n.p.).

In the lines to follow, *The Bricks That Built the Houses* indeed leaves no doubt that it seeks to foreground the repercussions of a system in which everything is geared towards making profit in the sense of economic, but also social and cultural, capital. Writing in the *Guardian*, Monbiot identifies Britain as 'the loneliness capital of Europe' because '[w]e are all neoliberals now' (2014: n.p.). In *The Bricks That Built the Houses*, the narrator chimes in with this critique:

> People are killing for Gods again. Money is killing us all. They live under a loneliness so total it has become the fabric of their friendships. Their days are spent staring at things. They exist in the mass and feel part of the picture. The most that they can hope for is a night out smashed to pieces, sloppy-faced from booze and drugs that hate them in the morning. (Tempest 2016: 3–4)

In a world dominated by money in which neoliberalism, according to David Harvey, 'has pervasive effects on ways of thought to the point where it has been incorporated into the common-sense way many of us interpret, live in, and understand the world' (2005: 3), loneliness is ubiquitous, Tempest suggests. According to *The Bricks That Build the Houses*, this loneliness derives from an (a)social meritocratic system positioning competition as a universal principle and 'primary virtue' (Harvey 2005: 65), which creates self-centred individuals blighted by a fundamental lack of empathy and thus defies human connection: 'Everybody's talking about themselves. *I'm doing this*, says everyone. *It's going great. And have you heard about this that I do, and this other thing as well, have you heard about that?* Questioning postures and emphatic responses' (14, original emphases). Social interaction is degraded to a one-man show and people reduced to 'props' (14). From this point of view, *The Bricks That Built the*

*Houses* clearly agrees with Monbiot, who depicts neoliberalism as 'a life-denying ideology, which enforces and celebrates our social isolation' (2014: n.p.) echoing Hobbes's *Leviathan* (1651):

> The war of every man against every man – competition and individualism, in other words – is the religion of our time, justified by a mythology of lone rangers, sole traders, self-starters, self-made men and women, going it alone. For the most social of creatures, who cannot prosper without love, there is no such thing as society, only heroic individualism. (Monbiot 2014: n.p.)

It stands to reason that this state of things is, in the words of Belgian psychologist Paul Verhaeghe, 'fatal for society as a community' (2012: 57).

*The Bricks That Built the Houses* is devastating in its critique of a social, political and economic system that, while allegedly championing the freedom of the individual, in fact represses any true individuality, again an idea indebted to the works of William Blake. Within the highly competitive neoliberal system, which reduces everything and everyone to their market value (see Harvey 2005: 3), people are compelled to extract the maximum of profit – literally and figuratively, the novel argues – from their own talents:

> Chase your talent. Corner it, lock it in a cage, give the key to someone rich and tell yourself you're staying brave ... Nothing's for you but it's all for sale, give until your strength is frail and when it's at its weakest, burden it with hurt and secrets. It's all around you screaming paradise until there's nothing left to feel. Suck it up, gob it, double-drop it. Pin it deep into your vein and try for ever to get off it. Now close your eyes and stop it.
>
> But it never stops. (4)

The compelling rap rhythms of Tempest's narrator lend this section a sense of urgency that underlines the force of these social imperatives. From this point of view, the system creates a 'fiction of systematic effectiveness' which, as Paul Verhaeghe argues drawing on the ideas of Scottish philosopher Alasdair McIntyre, is 'nothing more than a mask for excessive social control' (2012: 58). The narrator's drug references not only highlight Harry's and Leon's own implication in that system as drug dealers, but they also function as the epitome of consumption, gesturing towards the primacy of enjoyment which, according to Verhaeghe, has turned into life's overall purpose:

> Today our primary duty is enjoyment, to 'benefit' as much as we can whether for cash or increasingly on credit ... Enjoyment in the true meaning of the word has become an important medical commercial goal ... The result is that people

fall ill from an excess of 'enjoyment', from an addiction to everything from sex to shopping. (58)

Tempest's cage metaphor recalls the novel's motto, taken from William Blake's political allegory 'Visions of the Daughters of Albion' (1793), where Oothoon describes her feeling of social and epistemological confinement as follows:

They told me that the night and day were all that I could see;
They told me that I had five senses to inclose me up;
And they inclosed my infinite brain into a narrow circle,
And sunk my heart into the abyss, a red round globe hot burning.

(qtd in Tempest)

Evocative of Oothoon's 'cultural conditioning', these lines, Kevin Hutchings illustrates, are not unlike Tempest's in that they reveal 'a political intention, a methodical denial of other (non-empirical, non-European) modes of knowledge carried out in order to subjugate and imprison ("to inclose … up") enslaved peoples' (2001: 14). Significantly, though, the novel withholds from readers Oothoon's conclusion, 'Till all from life I was obliterated and erased' (Blake 2008: 60), reinforcing the narrator's own conclusion: 'But it never stops'.

Money and enjoyment are also inscribed into the very setting in *Hot Stew*, which traces the stories of people belonging to different social strata in Soho, an urban microcosm increasingly shaped by the tenets of neoliberalism. Traditionally 'a place "built around enjoyment and entertainment" as well as exploitation and excess' (Tyler 2019: 1), Soho affords the opportunity to introduce a broad spectrum of characters in terms of class and social status. All their lives are determined by the ideals of competition and individual responsibility in one way or the other. At the bottom of the scale, Cheryl Lavery, a homeless, apathetic drug addict ironically nicknamed Debbie McGee, has been almost literally 'obliterated and erased from life' (Blake 2008: 60). Forced to feed on the scraps left over from consumption, Cheryl represents a character whom the market has stripped of her individuality, even her humanity, as she has lost the capacity to feel:

There was once a time when she took pleasure in many things … There was once a time when she was saddened by other things … There was also a period in her life when nothing but heroin made her happy or sad … That time also passed. For the woman they call Debbie McGee, there is nothing left to feel. (13)

Along with her feelings, she has also lost her name, and to some degree even the ability to speak – in short, Cheryl has become devoid of her identity as human being and is lacking a voice in the system (see 57). By evoking the fairy-tale phrase 'once upon a time', the description identifies a more human existence as almost unreal. In the logic of the novel, Cheryl flaunts the de-individualizing tendencies of a system viewing individuals chiefly as a factor of production:

> Individuals enter the labour market as persons of character, as individuals embedded in networks of social relations and socialized in various ways, as physical beings identifiable by certain characteristics (phenotype and gender), as individuals who have accumulated various skills … and as living beings endowed with dreams, desires, ambitions, hopes, doubts, and fears. For capitalists, however, such individuals are a mere factor of production. (Harvey 2005: 168)

Foregrounding the flipside of prosperity, Cheryl is the character in *Hot Stew* most seriously affected by a world in which the system of stately protections has been largely demolished in favour of individual responsibility (168). Instead of subscribing to the neoliberal idea of eliminating poverty through wealth 'trickling down',[2] the novel supports Glenda's argument that '[c]harity is inherently reactionary, isn't it? It puts the onus on individuals rather than on the collective. It relies on certain individuals having large amounts of disposable income' (Mozley 2021: 120). In making a case for collective rather than individual responsibility, *Hot Stew* powerful indicts a society lacking a sense of community.

Not unlike *The Bricks That Built the Houses*, *Hot Stew* shows most of its characters confined by the tenets of neoliberalism, whose effects range from a feeling of being creatively stunted to a condition of emotional and moral myopia. There seems to be no space for the aesthetic and political ambitions of characters such as Glenda, Laura and Lorenzo in a market in which 'only short-term contracts are offered on a customary basis' to the 'individualized and relatively powerless worker' (Harvey 2005: 168). Glenda, who really wants to be a theatre director, has a job with an estate agent that is 'just a short-term thing' (45), and actor Lorenzo has to rely on 'two part-time jobs … to earn money between roles' (46). Reduced to merely chasing their dreams in the manner described by Tempest, theirs is a precarious existence. But even those who personify the conscientious, successful neoliberal individual and prosper economically, such as Rebecca, display the cost of neoliberalism's 'heroic individualism'. From the first, Rebecca, with her 'catalogue of accoutrements' (21) for personal improvement, is associated with consumption; in the morning, she emerges from the bathroom 'as a pristine facsimile of herself from the day before' (22), and she puts up a 'performance' (73) even in front of her friends. Ambitious and competitive, she has imbibed the monetary value system of neoliberalism to a degree where she even conceives of her relationship to Bastian 'as a sound investment' (80) due to its solid economic value: 'They are from similarly wealthy backgrounds; they are likely to have similarly successful careers' (80). Apart from thus appearing emotionally stunted, Rebecca showcases the damage constant competition inflicts on the individual, as the narrator observes:

> Rebecca looks stressed. Bastian has started to appreciate what a deeply anxious person she is. She worries about everything: about work, whether or not she is working hard enough, whether she is doing well, whether the people at her work like her or whether they are only pretending to like her. (115)

She is a case in point for Verhaeghe's (2021) observation regarding a value system where professional success is constantly monitored, '[i]ndividualism, profiteering and the "me-culture" are becoming quasi-endemic' and '[s]trong social bonds between colleagues are virtually excluded' (60). Rebecca's perfect façade cannot conceal how 'social angst', according to Verhaeghe, represents 'the hallmark of the new identity': '[b]elow the surface, there is fear, ranging from a fear of failure to wider social angst' (60).[3] There is a certain irony to the fact that the most economically successful character in *Hot Stew* – estate owner Agatha Howard – is most strongly affected by social angst and a pronounced obsession with and fear of revolution. Thoroughly shaped by money – 'Wealth does not simply determine the external: the life the document set out for Agatha built her from the inside out' (153) – Agatha is keeping a luxury yacht ironically named 'Versailles' moored in London and fully provisioned in case of an insurrection.

The critique of the damaging effects of the market on social bonds and coherence is couched in both *Hot Stew* and *The Bricks That Built the Houses* in the discourse of gentrification, which 'reflects one form of territorialisation of current capitalist logics' (Di Masso et al. 2021: 221) and has a crucial impact on questions of community.

## Gentrification, urban change and the struggle for space

*Hot Stew* opens with a sweeping panorama of the history of Soho, a brief tour de force highlighting urban change that may well turn into one of the more iconic fictional representations of London. It is anchored in a seventeenth-century building encapsulating stability, diversity, but also fragility in the face of a changing, commodified cityscape:

> On the corner of the street, there is an old French restaurant with red-and-white chequered tablecloths. Des Sables has been there for decades and has changed very little in that time. It has served the same dishes, with ingredients sourced from the same suppliers, and wines from the same vineyards … The restaurant serves escargots. The restaurant has served escargots since it opened. (Mozley 2021: 3)

Gesturing towards Soho's traditional character as a multicultural community (see Tyler 2019: 19), this description emphasizes historical continuity, with the old vineyards evoking deep roots in the past. Its signature dish of escargots positions the restaurant firmly in opposition to neoliberal values because they are literally 'slow' food: the narrator goes to great lengths to describe meticulously how one of the snails escapes from the kitchen, slowly making its way outside. In his essay 'Eating the Future', Robert Albritton observes how food production and consumption have developed into 'a highly concentrated form of capitalist production' whose emphasis on profit 'results in increasingly spectacular threats to the health of humans and their environment' (2010: 51). Fast food 'fits well in with a faster pace of life, with more demanding jobs and less sleep time' (54); slow food, in contrast, and by extension the restaurant, in more than one way represents the antithesis of a capitalist lifestyle.

In the plot of *Hot Stew*, the building turns into the focus of a contest between a capitalist conception of space as 'something to be altered at will and to maximize profit' (Albritton 2010: 47) on the one hand and space as historically grown, as a meaningful source of community and a feeling of belonging, on the other. The former is represented by Agatha, who subscribes to the capitalist point of view that 'space is simply stuff for profit-making' (47) and aims at redeveloping Des Sables, arguing that '[r]estaurants like this are quaint, but they aren't profitable' (9). The latter position is that of the sex workers around Precious and Tabitha living in the upper stories of the building, who organize a protest against the eviction. Their stance on the issue corresponds to neo-Marxist political geography, seeing 'gentrification … as a historically situated expression of capitalist investments in the cityspace, expropriating basic democratic rights such as the right to the city, the right to housing and the "right to stay put" in one's neighbourhood' (Di Masso et al. 2021: 222).[4] In housing the French restaurant as well as the sex workers from a variety of cultural backgrounds and sheltering homeless people in the cellar, the building represents a more integrative approach to community beyond the sphere of mere profit: The fact that the restaurant is French nods to 'successive waves and generations of French Huguenots ... [who] made Soho their place of work and home' (Tyler 2019: 19) over several centuries, becoming integrated into a community 'inextricably connected with, and indebted to, migration' (19). Originally from Nigeria, Precious is a case in point for this, too, as the novel repeatedly highlights how she has developed a deeper, reciprocal relationship to Soho. While she does acknowledge the dark and seedy sides of it, Precious feels deeply attached to this part of the city:

> And it's home. She doesn't totally know what a home is but she guesses it's got something to do with being in a place that's left its mark on you, for better or for worse, and also being in a place that you've left your own mark upon, for better or for worse. A place that remembers you've been there, that bears your imprint, like a squashy chair you've sat in a bunch of times. (165)

This vision is one of continuity and growth, of being rooted in the place, a notion encapsulated by the secret garden Precious and Tabitha have established on the roof.

Such reciprocal relationships between person and place also feature prominently in *The Bricks That Built the Houses*, a novel that repeatedly personifies London to the effect that the city appears almost like another character: 'The city yawns and cracks the bones in her knuckles' (Tempest 2016: 123), '[s]harp buildings rise like fangs in the city's creaming mouth' (20) and the street is 'packed like a clogged artery' (26). Vice versa, Harry is identified with the city, as the narrator states that '[s]he is all London: cocksure, alert to danger, charming, and it flows through her' (27). In the south London communities the characters navigate in this novel, Deptford, Lewisham and Peckham, the city and its people are inextricably connected from Harry's point of view, as 'she feels the hum of all the endless houses she has lived amongst since she was born. She holds on to the comfort of this road, this wall, this corner. Hers. She looks around. The houses are filled with people. The people are filled with houses' (123). The city has virtually become part of them, an experience Harry also shares with Pete as they are walking to their mother's new house: 'The grime that clings to the walls is the same grime they've lived with all their lives' (125). Sam Byers hence comments in the *New York Times* that London, 'for better or for worse, makes these people who they are, and they in turn make London the city Tempest unflinchingly evokes: cold, gray, profoundly lonely, but shot through with homely chatter and rare warmth' (2016: n.p.).

Against the backdrop of this close connection of people and place, *The Bricks That Built the Houses* foregrounds how '[u]rban capitalism materially and socially takes place, reshaping the urban scene and its embedded forms of cultural and social life in ways that renew capitalist logics' (Di Masso et al. 2021: 221), a development the novel associates with the death of the city and, to some degree, also the death of community, as Harry reflects:

> Could be perfect. But Peckham's changed. It's unrecognizable now ... She thought south London would hold its own for ever. But her home town is dying, it's half dead already. All that she knows to be true is suddenly false. Communities flattened to make room for commuters. (122)

The changes in the gentrified city perceived by the characters illustrate how gentrification 'tends to alter and recreate symbolic representations of urban space and residents' subjective relationships with places' (221). After Becky and Harry have returned from their stint abroad, '[t]he streets are as busy as ever, but it feels empty' (391). The houses and flats previously alive and identified with people 'stand empty and black-eyed. Their windows smashed, their fronts ripped off. Their insides on display' (391). Life, in other words, has gone. This metaphor of the death of the city is closely associated not just with actual spatial change but perhaps even more so with a change in the characters' perception of and emotional connection with the city:

> Becky looks around for all the things she has missed so much, but nothing is the same. The snooker hall has gone; its foundations are wrapped in construction hoardings and it stands four stories taller than it used to, rapidly becoming another block of luxury apartments. The half-derelict bridal store and beauty bar where she used to get her nails done and pick up weed – the one that had the mournful mannequin in the window, dressed in the same peacock-blue sequin gown for years – is now a glass fronted café with exposed brickwork and low-hanging lamps. She wonders what's happened to Naima, the woman who used to run the shop. (390)

Becky's failure to reconnect with the familiar landmarks charged with detailed and intimate memories poignantly illustrates how gentrification 'challenges and reshapes senses of place, in the two senses of "sense": past and present ways of perceiving (that is, making sense) and feeling (that is, sensing) one's neighbourhood and the broader urban scene' (221).

## Making connections

It is precisely such a notion of 'sense of place' in which *The Bricks That Built the Houses* and *Hot Stew* locate the experience of community. In exploring different approaches to community, Gerard Delanty argues that considering community as 'shaped by cognitive and symbolic structures that are not underpinned by "lived" spaces and immediate forms of social intimacy' (2003: 3) had a detrimental effect on debates about the concept. The cognitive perspective 'inevitably led to a view of community as shaped by what separates people rather than what they have in common' (3). Both *The Bricks That Built the Houses* and *Hot Stew* strongly advocate the opposite perspective, suggesting the need 'to reinsert the social into community and recover the sense of place that was displaced by the cultural turn in the theory of community' (3). In both novels, the notion of community is closely linked to the experience of lived and shared space, which crucially depends on both making sense of and feeling it.

In *The Bricks That Built the Houses*, the experience of community revolves around and takes place in actual spaces that become the site of shared experience, highlighting 'the capacity of local community to provide an alternative to the social fragmentation brought about by global capitalism' (69). The key site for such experience in *The Bricks That Built the Houses* is the Deptford pub to which Becky returns from abroad, the Hanging Basket, a meeting place for various different people:

> People shelter here. People who wear colourful clothes and have half-shaved heads and leather jackets and live in squats or on old boats or in vans. Or grey-haired, square-shouldered men who work all day and sit with paint-flecked jeans, tip the Guinness and talk it over. Or sensitive young artists reading alone with pints of ale. Or wreck heads ready for anything ... Modern punks and ancient drunks ... If you need love, you can come here. You can find it where it hangs. (348–9)

Described later in the novel as 'the jewel in south London's shackles' (395), the pub provides an experience of commonality creating a feeling of community as belonging while still acknowledging diversity. The fact that many of the visitors to the pub lack a fixed place of residence highlights the idea of providing a shared, secure, inclusive space functioning like the ideal community outlined by Zygmunt Bauman as

> a 'warm' place, a cosy and comfortable place. It is like a roof under which we shelter in heavy rain, like a fireplace at which we warm our hands on a frosty

day. Out there, in the street, all sorts of dangers lie in ambush … In here, in the community, we can relax – we are safe … In a community, we all understand each other well, we may trust what we hear, we are safe most of the time and hardly ever puzzled or taken aback. We are never strangers to each other. We may quarrel – but these are friendly quarrels. (2001: 1–2)

It is exactly such a place which Harry strives to create herself. As she describes her plans to Becky: 'It'll be a restaurant and café and a bar, so that it pays for itself. But also it will be, like, a community centre. There'll be a workshop space. You know, it'll be a place for people to go. To relax and hang out and learn things' (43). The place Harry envisions is exactly the opposite of the fashionable venues striving for exclusivity and geared towards making profit that are part of the city's gentrification (see 45–6); but she fails to acknowledge that besides being still just a dream and hence purely speculative, her community centre would originate in the same neoliberal system she is struggling against, paid for with the money made from dealing drugs.

If *The Bricks That Built the Houses* imagines an apparent alternative to the effects of heroic individualism still relying fundamentally on the same system, the characters in *Hot Stew* forge community out of protest against the system. Organized as a community of purpose in the first place, the sex workers manage to mobilize support for their struggle against eviction that unites them in a carnivalesque protest against social hierarchies. According to Bakhtin, carnival subverts everyday hierarchies by facilitating a different kind of interaction that is 'frank and free, … liberating from norms of etiquette and decency imposed at other times' (1984: 10); crucially, it involves 'the lowering of all that is high, spiritual, ideal, abstract; it is a transfer to the material level, to the sphere of earth and body in their indissoluble unity' (19–20). It thus creates 'a reversal of the hierarchic levels' (81) through parody, humiliation, profanation, travesty and role-play. The novel clearly marks the street protest as carnival, as Precious wears 'a carnival mask she bought in Venice' (160), and the other sex workers are masked, too. Explicit sexual references on cardboard signs, such as 'OCCUPY MY VAGINA' and 'NO TO BANKING | YES TO BONKING' (161), violate norms of decency in a carnivalesque manner. In a final twist, Precious's colleague Candy humiliates representatives of key institutions by shouting at a policeman, 'I piss on men like you every day … I've pissed on police officers. I've pissed on judges. I've pissed on politicians' (168); she concludes by actually urinating against one of the policemen who have closed in around the protesters, thus turning the power balance on its head. This protest shows the sex workers and their allies experiencing community as '*communitas*' in the sense expressed in Victor Turner's *The Ritual Process* (1969), which draws on Arnold Van Gennep's concept of liminality (see Delanty 2003: 44). Just as liminality 'refers to those "between" moments, such as carnivals, pilgrimages, rites of passage or rituals in which normality is suspended' (44), *communitas* 'is sustained by anti-structure, when 'structures' are resisted' (44–5). This is what happens in the protest, as the protesters resist both the police and neoliberal structures of urban planning. In staging the protest, the novel thus gestures towards how, according to Turner, '[c]ommunitas breaks in through the interstices of structure, in liminality; at the edges of structure, in marginality, and from beneath structure, in inferiority' (Turner qtd from Delanty 2003: 45).

*Hot Stew* positions such *communitas*, grown at the edges and from beneath structure, as an antidote to and protest against the hierarchical world of individual consumers. The notion of subverting and perhaps overthrowing hierarchies is inscribed into Agatha's Russian background and shows in her anxious obsession with revolution; significantly, her mother shares her name with Grand Duchess Anastasia Nikolaevna of Russia, youngest daughter of the last of the tsars, Nikolai II, whom the Bolsheviks deposed and killed with all his family in 1918. While this parallel highlights the oppressiveness and exploitation at the core of Agatha's 'regime' as an estate owner, it gestures towards the possibility of overcoming such hierarchies.[5] In terms of rebelling against hierarchies, the regenerative potential of carnivalesque transgression comes to the fore in the almost miraculous transformation of Cheryl, which takes place underground. Having walked into a vast hole on a Soho building site, Cheryl, at this point more dead than alive, makes her way through a network of tunnels until she illicitly enters a luxurious underground bunker, where she 'cocoon[s] herself' (Mozley 2021: 195) to emerge rejuvenated six months later. Fully provisioned and complete with swimming pool, sauna, cinema, library, lounge and kitchenette, the bunker facilitates her healing. Part of a '"new billionaires" craze for building elaborate subterranean extensions' (Wainwright 2012: n.p.), it represents hyper-capitalist excess and indicates what Mike Davis calls an 'ecology of fear' (see Delanty 2003: 62).[6] Built as a highly exclusive means of individual salvation from social or environmental hazards, it signals the very opposite of 'community trust and solidarity' (62). The final collapse of the restaurant building, with its old structure undermined by underground excavations, foregrounds how capitalism has undermined the type of integrative community the building represents. However, in forging new life from her liminal existence in the bunker, Cheryl in turn exploits the exploiters transgressively.

Finally, both *The Bricks That Built the Houses* and *Hot Stew* open up imaginative ways of resistance on the level of their discourse. In explaining capitalist realism, Mark Fisher quotes from the *Communist Manifesto* that capital 'has drowned the most heavenly ecstasies of religious fervor, of chivalrous enthusiasm, of philistine sentimentalism, in the icy water of egotistical calculation. It has resolved personal worth into exchange value' (2009: 4). In their essay *On Connection* (2020), Kae Tempest introduces an antidote to this coldly disconnected state of egotistical calculation. According to Tempest, we have internalized competition and exploitation so strongly that they shape our personal interactions: 'When we are fixated on what we can get from an exchange, or how we can benefit, instead of considering what we can offer, we are being exploitative' (n.p.). The solution to this is empathy, an ability based on 'remembering that everybody has a story. Multiple stories. And remembering to make space to hear someone else's story before immediately telling your own' (n.p.). In facilitating a connection to someone else or someone else's story, empathy is an important step in forging a sense of true togetherness, and from there, community. Studies have long acknowledged that reading fiction 'cultivates empathy' (n.p.), and this principle is also at the core of the characters' stories in *The Bricks That Built the Houses*. As Sam Byers puts it, '[i]n Tempest's London, no one is insignificant; everyone has a story. The devotion and care with which she recounts these tales … is deeply … touching in its empathic humanity' (2016: n.p.). Imaginatively engaging with the stories of others offers a way of resisting and escaping the shackles of competitive individualism and egotistical calculation. A similar kind of imaginative resistance is also at work in *Hot Stew*. Gentrification fiction usually has 'a strong realist line, befitting stories concerned with the material aspects of urban change … – [but] it is a realism often inflected by magical *ostranenie*, fabulism, hauntings and comically exaggerated picturesque' (Peacock 2021: 106). While *Hot Stew* does not include straightforward fantasy, Cheryl's sojourn underground is certainly not realistic in a colloquial sense. In thus transcending the boundaries of realism, *Hot Stew* asks us to make a leap – and imagine how things could be different after all.

## Notes

1 The term 'gentrification' was coined by British sociologist Ruth Glass in 1964 to denote 'the displacement of "working class occupiers" by the middle classes in areas of inner London' (Peacock 2021: 104).

2 This notion is represented in *Hot Stew* by Bastian. As the narrator explains, 'Tipping generously gives Bastian a pleasant feeling of his own largesse. Wealth, after all, is meant to trickle down' (Mozley 2021: 25). For the metaphor of wealth 'trickling down' see Harvey, who illustrates how '[u]nder the assumption that "a rising tide lifts all boats", or of "trickle down", neoliberal theory holds that the elimination of poverty (both domestically and worldwide) can best be secured through free markets and free trade' (2005: 64–5).

3 In *The Bricks That Built the Houses*, Pete with his belief in conspiracy theories is another representative of this kind of vague social angst (see Tempest 2016: 170–1).

4 In view of the novel's neo-Marxist approach to gentrification, it is certainly fitting that it should be set in Soho, since Soho is where Marx and Engels first drafted their *Communist Manifesto* (see Tyler 2019: 18). In real life, the sex workers' concerted protest against their eviction has an equivalent in Save Soho, a coalition got together by Tim Arnold and Stephen Fry 'with the aim of protecting and nurturing iconic venues that are disappearing' (https://www.facebook.com/savesoho). Like the sex workers' protest in *Hot Stew*, it was founded in reaction to urban redevelopment, 'after a Soho property company called Soho Estates closed and repossessed world renown club Madame Jojo's' (https://savesoho.com/about/).

5 Where Agatha herself is concerned, her dog Fedor, being a Borzoj, confirms her association with the Russian aristocracy. Owning huge estates and exploiting their dehumanized and disenfranchised tenants was a hallmark of the Tsarist Russian ruling class. However, the fact that the Soviet regime following the revolution was at least as repressive as the Tsarist one, and deadly to its opponents on a far greater scale, remains unacknowledged in the novel.

6 Vast underground extensions representing hypercapitalism and exploitation also feature prominently in Jonathan Coe's *Number 11* (see Lusin 2018: 254–8).

# References

Albritton, Robert (2010), 'Eating the Future: Capitalism Out of Joint', in Robert Albritton, Robert Jessop, and Richard Westra (eds), *Political Economy and Global Capitalism: The 21st Century, Present and Future*, 43–66, London: Anthem.

Bakhtin, Mikhail (1984), *Rabelais and His World*, trans. Hélène Iswolsky, Bloomington: Indiana University Press.

Bauman, Zygmunt (2001), *Community: Seeking Safety in an Insecure World*, Cambridge: Polity.

Blake, William ([1794] 2008), *Blake's Poetry and Designs: Illuminated Works. Other Writings. Criticism. A Norton Critical Edition*, ed. Mary Lynn Johnson and John E. Grant, 2nd ed., New York: W. W. Norton.

Byers, Sam (2016), '"The Bricks That Built the Houses", by Kate Tempest', *New York Times*, 1 June, https://www.nytimes.com/2016/06/05/books/review/the-bricks-that-built-the-houses-by-kate-tempest.html.
Coe, Jonathan (2015), *Number 11, or, Tales That Witness Madness*, London: Viking.
Davis, Mike (1998), *Ecology of Fear: Los Angeles and the Imagination of Disaster*, New York: Metropolitan.
Delanty, Gerard (2003), *Community*, London: Routledge.
Di Masso, Andrés, Viktor Jorquera, Teresa Ropert and Tomeu Vidal (2021), 'Gentrification and the Creative Destruction of Sense of Place: A Psychosocial Exploration of Urban Transformations in Barcelona', in Christopher M. Raymond, Lynn C. Manzo, Daniel R. Williams, Andrés Di Masso and Timo von Wirth (eds), *Changing Senses of Place: Navigating Global Challenges*, 221–33, Cambridge: Cambridge University Press.
Fisher, Mark (2009), *Capitalist Realism: Is There No Alternative?*, Ebook, Winchester: O. Books.
Harvey, David (2005), *A Brief History of Neoliberalism*, Oxford: Oxford University Press.
Hutchings, Kevin (2001), 'Gender, Environment, and Imperialism in William Blake's Visions of the Daughters of Albion', https://romantic-circles.org/praxis/ecology/hutchings/hutchings.html.
Lusin, Caroline (2018), 'The Condition of England Novel in the Twenty-First Century: Zadie Smith's *NW* (2012) and Jonathan Coe's *Number 11, Or Tales That Witness Madness* (2015)', in Vera Nünning and Ansgar Nünning (eds), *The British Novel in the Twenty-First Century: Cultural Concerns – Literary Developments – Model Interpretations*, 247–63, Trier: Wissenschaftlicher Verlag Trier.
Monbiot, George (2014), 'The Age of Loneliness Is Killing Us', *Guardian*, 14 October, https://www.theguardian.com/commentisfree/2014/oct/14/age-of-loneliness-killing-us.
Monbiot, George (2016), 'Neoliberalism – the Ideology at the Root of All Our Problems', *Guardian Online*, 15 April, https://www.theguardian.com/books/2016/apr/15/neoliberalism-ideology-problem-george-monbiot.
Mozley, Fiona (2021), *Hot Stew*, London: John Murray.
Peacock, James (2021), 'Gentrification', in Kevin R. McNamara (ed.), *The City in American Literature and Culture*, 103–17, Cambridge: Cambridge University Press.
Preston, Alex (2012), 'The Way We Live Now? Follow the Money Trail Back to Anthony Trollope …', *Observer Online*, 12 February, https://www.theguardian.com/books/2012/feb/12/trollope-state-nation-london-novel.
Save Soho (2014), *Save Soho*, https://savesoho.com/about/.
Save Soho Facebook (n.d.), https://www.facebook.com/savesoho.
Schuhmaier, Sina (2021), 'Singing the Nation: The Condition of Englishness in the Lyrics of PJ Harvey and Kate Tempest', in Sandra Dinter and Johanna Marquardt (eds), *Nationalism and the Postcolonial*, 92–108, Leiden: Brill Rodopi.
Tempest, Kae (2016), *The Bricks That Built the Houses*, London: Bloomsbury.

Tempest, Kae ([2016] 2017), *Let Them Eat Chaos: A Poem*, New York: Bloomsbury.
Tempest, Kae (2020), *On Connection*, Ebook, London: Faber.
Turner, V. (1969), *The Ritual Process: Structure and Anti-Structure*, London: Routledge & Kegan Paul.
Tyler, Melissa (2019), *Soho at Work: Pleasure and Place in Contemporary London*, Cambridge: Cambridge University Press.
Verhaeghe, Paul (2012), 'Capitalism and Psychology – Identity and Angst: On Civilisation's New Discontent', in Wim Vermeersch (ed.), *Belgian Society and Politics: The Crisis Comes in Many Guises*, 55–63, Ghent: Gerrit Kreveld Foundationn, https://paulverhaeghe.psychoanalysis.be/artikels/Identity%20and%20Angst.pdf.
Wainwright, Oliver (2012), 'Billionaires' Basements: The Luxury Bunkers Making Holes in London Streets', *Guardian Online*, 9 November, https://www.theguardian.com/artanddesign/2012/nov/09/billionaires-basements-london-houses-architecture.

# 6

# Writing othered Asian British skins: Interrogating racism in fictional Asian British communities

Devon Campbell-Hall

The late 1980s gave rise to a new generation of young British writers, from both inside and outside Asian British communities, whose creative outputs represent various aspects of first- and second-generation Asian British migrant experiences. Many scholars have examined the significance of such artefacts as noteworthy cultural products both *by* and *about* Asian British communities (Campbell-Hall 2009; Hand 1995, 2001; Kumar 2000, 2002, 2004; Nasta 2002; Upstone 2010) and of fiction produced *by* writers from *within* the wider BAME communities in Britain (Bromley 2000; Innes 2002; McLeod 2004; Procter 2000, 2003; Sandhu 2003; Stein 2004; Wisker 2004). I am more interested, however, in exploring how Asian British communities are represented fictionally by British writers whose ethnic backgrounds are not of central importance to the creative texts they produce. Courttia Newland and Jacob Ross ask: 'Does the writer have a responsibility to their community?' (2004: 3). In the case of the texts under consideration here, a sense of community – for both the writers and the fictionally represented Asian British characters under consideration – is based on a self-constructed sense of where one fits into the fabric of a multicultural, multiracial, postmodern, postcolonial Britain, deeply influenced by a social and historical context of racial difference. Amit Chaudhuri argues in the Introduction to *The Picador Book of Modern Indian Literature* that 'to be interested in a canon, you have to be interested in how a nation or community sees itself' (2001: xviii). Arguably, in this context nation denotes a unity between different ethnic communities based on citizenship, whereas community suggests the relative coherence and self-identity of an ethnic community. For the sake of this piece, I will consider this 'nation' or 'community' to be one of writers who fictionally represent Asians in Britain, regardless of their own ethnic status. These writers are all Britons, yet the most obvious shared community they inhabit is one of writers who share subject matter. Literature that represents Asian British communities is helpful for gaining insight into how these writers perceive the fluid identities of Asian Britons as British and Asian, as well as a fusion of the two. Writing that interrogates how othered skins are perceived as 'not quite British' arguably plays a potentially educative role as it challenges readers – regardless of race or ethnicity – to question their own cultural positioning. Of course, writers often represent characters from ethnic groups/genders/religious groups/social categories they do not themselves inhabit; if we only write of own experiences, most works of fiction would be tedious in their univocality. Thus, both writers and readers are presented with the opportunity of temporarily 'getting into another's skin' via such texts.

This chapter considers how British writers Raman Mundair (*Lovers, Liars, Conjurers and Thieves*, 2003), Ravinder Randhawa (*A Wicked Old Woman*, 1987), Zadie Smith (*White Teeth*, 2000) and Meera Syal (*Anita and Me*, 1996) fictionally confront scenes of racism and interrogate the possibility of genuinely multicultural communities through representations of racism as faced by first- and second-generation South Asian migrants to the UK. I am considering a selection of texts published between 1987 and 2003, a period that gave rise to several critically acclaimed novels that represent a Britain in the throes of a post-imperial identity crisis, in which multi-ethnic Britons continually contend with issues of who rightfully maintains a stronghold in the centre of British culture and who or what is relegated to the margins. It is useful here to consider Dhooleka Raj's argument that '[a]ssimilation is assessed in two dominant measurements of cultural change premised on the nostalgia for culture – intergenerational culture clash and integration pressure' (2003: 5). If we consider the fictional Asian British communities within these texts, these are but two of the cultural phenomena that highlight how the Asian British presence within wider multi-ethnic communities is changing. Paul Gilroy argues that we are required 'to be alert to the workings of political racism and able to apprehend "race" as a process of relation, imaginary kinship, and real narration rather than some badge worn on or lodged deep inside the body' (2004: 163). Within celebratory acknowledgements of multiculturalism as a possibility, this serves as a warning against depoliticizing community action. All the communities under consideration here portray varying levels of South Asian cultural integration into mainstream British society, and, arguably, all challenge traditional hegemonic constructions of an unnaturally white Britishness.

Most of these texts place the brown skins of Asian Britons in direct conflict with the white skins of Anglo-Britons, subverting the hegemonic colonial binaries of us and them. Rather than falling seamlessly into the roles written for them by colonialist historical narratives of European domination/subcontinental subordination, the Asian British characters within these texts destabilize these unhelpful categories. It is only when the brown characters resist the Orientalist discourse that threatens to exoticize their visible difference from mainstream Anglo-Britishness that real empowerment is textually possible. Thus, it becomes crucial for these Asian Britons to reject the exotic to gain any subversive potential. Crucially, brown skin that resists fetishization serves as a signifier of resistance within these novels.

Mundair, Randhawa, Smith and Syal are amongst those writers who portray diverse aspects of Asian British communities, in which the Asian British characters subvert the outdated Orientalist, colonial binary of white over non-white. From the platform of their fiction and poetry, these writers explode the myth of Asian Britons as nice, well-behaved members of society. Their work interrogates depoliticized, sentimental portrayals of Asian Britons, as does Felicity Hand when she considers how '[h]ard working, law-abiding, locked into their own culture but harmless is the description that comes to mind to many white British people about the Asian community in the United Kingdom' (2001: 109). Laura Moss's (2003) arguments towards the normalization of an 'everyday hybridity' are supported within some examples of this writing, but others interrogate the idealistic, neoliberal notion of a Britain made up of genuinely multicultural communities.

My focus on the significance of fictional representations of Asian British communities is supported by Paul Ricoeur's argument that 'just as narrative fiction does not lack reference, the reference proper to history is not unrelated to the "productive" reference of fictional narrative' (in Kearney and Rainwater 1996: 143). Ricoeur's suggestion indicates that events are more likely to be remembered as a part of ongoing life if they are written down – or represented – even if this is documented via fiction rather than direct reportage. He appears to recognize that although fiction does not replace sociological or historical study, it can have important moments of intersection with culture, thus providing a valuable narrative of alternative 'truths'. Using Ricoeur's notions of the validity of fictional representations, I would like to examine how fiction and poetry can be read as culturally significant indicators of the movement of visibly non-white Britons from the margins to the centre of the communities in which they live.

In her article for *Wasafiri*, 'How British Are the Asians?', Felicity Hand argues that

> In spite of Farrukh Dhondy's insistence that Britain is probably the least racist society in the world and that the number of people who express their objections to black people in a violent manner are only a small percentage of a liberal-minded majority, his optimism is not typical of British Asian writers in general. (1995: 12)

Dhondy's conviction arguably supports Tariq Modood's notion that multiculturalism is both normative and relatively unproblematic in late-twentieth-century British communities. Modood suggests that genuine multiculturalism would allow 'communities and individuals the right to be culturally different from their neighbours and to be understood in their own terms rather than in the terms of racist and anti-racist stereotypes' (1992: 6). This stands in direct contrast to multiculturalism as portrayed in the texts under consideration in this chapter, which arguably align more closely with Hall's notion of multiculturalism as an example of 'sheer facticity', where 'things *are* just what is seen on the surface' (in Chen and Morley 2006: 136, original emphasis). Meera Syal and Ravinder Randhawa appear to share Hand's scepticism, as does Zadie Smith, a non-Asian British writer who represents the problematic nature of idealizing multiculturalism within a contemporary Britain still coming to terms with its own postcolonial, postmodern identity.

Stuart Hall's suggestion that identity is fluid and constructed 'within, not outside of, representation' (1990: 222) indicates how literature plays a potentially significant role in the public perception of communal identities. I suggest that these fictional representations of Asian Britishness portray the domestic and everyday as inherently political, and that these works both encourage and challenge popular notions of how such communities can be both British and Asian, as well as a merging of the two. However, these texts also represent some Asian Britons as alienated from disparate cultural elements of their fictionally constructed communities. A clear example of this is when Raj (2003) describes the response of one young Hindu Punjabi man to the unhelpful question 'Where are you from?' 'He states, "I go back to India, and I'm a stranger, and I accept that. But I'm still a stranger here too"'. Raj suggests that '[t]hese words provide insight into how South Asian minorities in Britain experience alterity in both locations they could potentially claim' (2, as qtd in *Observer* magazine, 19 September 1999, 17).

I am specifically interested in issues raised within these texts that reflect tensions created when fictional Britons of varying skin tones – along with the historically informed expectations of characters with brown skin and those with white skin – interact within their communities. Within these texts, visual differences in skin colour become benchmarks against which self-identity is constructed as an imagined cultural and social trope; skin becomes a powerful and destructive metaphor for difference, with reference to the brown skins of South Asian immigrants and the white skins of those Anglo-Britons with varying levels of tolerance towards visible ethnic diversity. Hall argues that 'Identity is formed at the unstable point where the unspeakable stories of subjectivity meet the narratives of history, of a culture' (1986: 44). The exploitative colonialist relationship between Britain and the Indian subcontinent inescapably informs the construction of a post-imperial Britishness, in which whiteness no longer holds the dominant reins within the ethnic power struggle characterizing contemporary British society. The discrepancies between subjective perceptions of one's own experience and the grand narratives which historically inform culture on a larger scale are central to the formation of the identity of those who do not visibly spring from the centre of the dominant elements of community.

Skin itself becomes an important location of cultural confrontation within these texts. It serves as a crucial point of contact between those relegated to the margins and those supposedly inhabiting the centre. I am using Claudia Benthien's definition of the racist practice of 'othering', which she describes as the 'demarcation and devaluation of the other' (2002: 145), to interrogate the notion of skin's role in the racist practice of othering. I will apply Benthien's notion of coloured skin, as opposed to supposedly 'light' skin, as a culturally 'marked epidermis; ... a skin that departs from the neutral norm' (148) to examine the brownness of Asian British skins in directly marked contrast to the predominantly white Anglo-British skins of the represented dominant community. I argue that brown skins within these novels act as signifiers of resistance to the dominant cultural hegemony, supporting Benthien's point that personal identity is profoundly affected by history and 'subject to continuous change and cultural interpretation' (9). This aligns with Stuart Hall's suggestion that fluid identity is constructed 'within, not without, representation' (1990: 222).

By focusing this discussion on fictional representations of skin – brown skin, white skin and the tensions arising from community confrontations between the two – I am suggesting that ignoring the cultural codifications of skin, as portrayed within these novels, could become a dangerous racist practice. Three aspects of skin within these texts particularly interest me. Firstly, I will reflect Dyer's conceptualization of 'whiteness' to interrogate the racist community confrontations within Meera Syal's *Anita and Me* (1996) and examine these fictional conflicts as cultural barriers that define self from other. Dyer argues that 'to apply the colour white to white people is to ascribe a visual property to a group that thrives … on invisibility' (1997: 42). Yet it is the visibility of the white characters within these novels that provides a framework for understanding the Asian British characters. The skin of these characters becomes the outwardly visible signifier of their ethnic – as well as their personal – identity.

Secondly, I will discuss how the skins of Asian Britons are represented as eroticized expressions of an exoticized 'other' within Zadie Smith's *White Teeth* and Ravinder Randhawa's *A Wicked Old Woman*. Codell and MacLeod's (1998) concept of the 'Easternization of Britain' will be used to consider the representations of the fetishized obsession that Smith's Poppy Burt-Jones has for the dark-skinned British Bangladeshi Samad Iqbal, as well as Michael the Archangel's passion for Kulwant's 'dusky' complexion in Randhawa's novel. Codell and MacLeod argue that this Easternization of Britain concerns the ways in which South Asians intervene 'in the hegemonic colonial or Orientalist discourse' and that they 'negotiated, revised, subverted and reinvented it to serve their own cultural expressions, political resistance and self-representations' (1). Arguably, the fictional Asian Britons under consideration do indeed subvert the notion of Orientalist discourse, particularly in the multicultural, multiracial community environment of postcolonial London.

The final area under consideration is how the notion of a second skin can be applied to the fictional Asian Britons in these texts, and how this might relate to a reverse version of cultural appropriation. From the idea of costume as a temporary second skin, to the notion of passing as another race, this concept will be analysed using Fanon's ([1967] 1986) idea of 'Black Skin, White Masks'. Fanon's thesis provides the conceptual framework for examining both the ways in which these Asian Britons are depicted as 'more English than the English' and, conversely, the way in which some of the white Britons are portrayed as 'more Indian than the Indians', suggesting fluidity of racial identity within these fictional British communities. The texts to be considered in this section are Raman Mundair's poetry collection *Lovers, Liars, Conjurers and Thieves* and Ravinder Randhawa's *A Wicked Old Woman*.

## Defining self and other through skin colour in
## *Anita and Me*

It is not simply the misrecognized visibility of skin that renders it essential to identity formation. Skin is vulnerable and soft and requires protection from the elements and from potential onslaughts such as burning, scarring, cutting or bruising. American artist Jenny Holzer 'conjures the theme of skin as a boundary, a fragile parchment unable to protect against violence' (in Benthien 2002: 3). The violence to which Holzer refers could just as easily suggest aggressive physical attacks as the insidious, subtle violence of racism in which the colonialist binaries of us and them are clearly defined through the colour of one's skin. Benthien argues that skin is 'continually read and interpreted in all social situations, that human beings have understood and misunderstood it as an expression of depth, of soul, of inner character' (11). How helpful is it, however, for skin to be considered an accurate vessel from which we can interpret the depth of human experience? Is it not inherently problematic for the physical, visible and external to be considered a truthful indicator of what lies inside? By nature of its very visibility and universality, skin becomes a form of public community property, open to the inept, ignorant interpretations of those for whom skin colour is inseparable from colonialist history and a more generalized discourse of white supremacy. Skin is so powerfully – and dangerously – received as a guarantor of interiority that individuals who wish to free themselves from the historical implications of their skin colour necessarily enter a battleground in which cultural loyalty and community identity come under intense scrutiny.

It is the permanence and immutability of the brownness of Meena Kumar's 'othered' skin that threatens to destabilize the established hierarchy within the community of 'Tollington Wenches' in Meera Syal's *Anita and Me*. For the fictional child with 'othered skin', mimicry of the dominant white cultural norm seems to be the favoured survival mechanism. As her chosen technique for social survival, Meena adapts a Lacanian camouflage for most of the novel, when she recognizes that the only way for a plump brown girl to fit into white, working-class Tollington is to mimic slim, pale and brassy Anita Rutter's lifestyle choices. Jacques Lacan suggest that 'The effect of mimicry is camouflage ... It is not a question of harmonizing with the background, but against a mottled background, of being mottled' ([1949] in Bhabha 1994: 85). Rejecting one's physicality necessarily confuses the sense of self. What Meena neglects to consider is that the dominant whiteness of the Tollington community is profoundly affected by other issues such as class, educational levels and unemployment. When considered against the whiteness of her local community, Meena's brownness becomes an obstacle to full belonging within the dominant culture. Yet rather than enabling Meena to inhabit the centre, her uneasy mimicry brings about more cultural confusion than cohesion.

These stabs at imitating the other result in a rejection of self at the level of the epidermis:

> I wanted to shed my body like a snake slithering out of its skin and emerge reborn, pink and unrecognisable. I began avoiding mirrors. I refused to put on the Indian suits my mother laid out for me ... I took to walking several paces behind or in front of my parents when we went on a shopping trip, checking my reflection in shop windows, bitterly disappointed it was still there. (Syal 1996: 146)

Meena's adoption of what she perceives as whiteness acts as what Fanon terms 'lactification' ([1967] 1986: 47) – the unspoken urge to whiten dark skin. Yet rather than visibly blending in with the dominant culture, Meena's rejection of her brownness and what she feels it represents merely fractures her fragile sense of personal identity. This supports Fanon's suggestion that the internalization of an inferiority complex – in this instance, what is perceived as cultural inadequacy – is an 'epidermalization of this inferiority' (13). Meena believes that her brown skin is the marginalizing factor that renders her unable to be fully accepted into the community of Tollington youth culture. James Procter argues that Syal's focus on 'white communities and cultures allow ... Syal to provincialize Englishness' (2003: 128). He suggests that it is the specific whiteness of the community that allows Syal to 'poke fun at and distance [herself] from "native" white culture' (128). Interestingly, the whiteness within Tollington is characterized by what Meena and her parents are not: poorly educated, working-class, unemployed and with little hope for a better future. Within this context, whiteness indicates a lack of those very signifiers of Indianness so valued by Meena's parents – a respect for education and a subtle sense of cultural superiority.

This is clearly shown in the passage in which the mystery of the Big House and its inhabitants is revealed – not only are the owners of the house *not* white, but Mr Singh is undeniably Indian:

> My miracle was complete. The Big House boss was an Indian man, as Indian as my father, and he spoke Punjabi with a village twang to his dog. He was as brown as a nut and possessed that typical North Indian Roman nose, and the gold signet ring on his little finger sported the Hindu symbol 'OM'. (1996: 317)

Harinder Singh's brown skin and defiantly Indian ways provide Meena with a tangible role model for brown Britishness that clearly delineates for her how resistant he and his French wife are to the racist happenings within the small community. Whereas previously Anita Rutter's brash whiteness served as an unlikely role model for the impressionable Meena, a growing awareness of the value of her Indianness and her visible difference from the white Tollington Wenches – along with their class differences – renders this untenable. This is reflected in Fanon's argument that 'the *eye* is not merely a mirror, but a correcting mirror. The *eye* should make it possible for us to correct cultural errors' (1986: 202, original emphases). Meena's growing awareness of her own education-/class-enabled agency serves to reconstruct her sense of self. It is specifically her conscious acknowledgement of the benefits of her brownness that readjusts her misconceptions about Anita's problematic brand of Englishness. Throughout this process, Meena's brown skin becomes a symbol of motion, of the possibility of escape from the working-class whiteness of the small community. Her visible otherness is not only a barrier to full acceptance into the sexually experimental white adolescence of her schoolmates but it provides her with a way out. Arguably, Syal's representations of both brown and white skins within this novel support Benthien's suggestion that 'the physiognomic readability of skin colours is fundamentally put into question, reflected on the narrative level in contradictions and on the level of the characters in mutual misinterpretations' (2002: 157). Due to the destabilizing influence of class and education within this novel, traditional colonial assumptions about the significance of brown and white skins are inverted, and it is predominantly the brown-skinned characters that are textually represented as having both choice and agency. Improved ability to undertake professional employment, access to grammar-school education and the cultural understanding enabled by travel together allow the Kumar family opportunities largely unavailable to the indigenous inhabitants of Tollington.

## Fetishizing brown skin in *White Teeth* and *A Wicked Old Woman*

I would now like to explore what Codell and MacLeod describe as an underexamined dimension of 'the coloniser's desire for the exotic or erotic, the dangerously sublime ... for visual and experiential novelty' (1998: 3). Their study predates Huggan's pioneering *The Postcolonial Exotic* (2001), which discusses, amongst other issues, the depoliticizing of 'otherness' within a largely culturally materialist arena. Codell and MacLeod's statement arguably reflects a colonial geography in which the exoticized other stems from outside the supposedly ethnically homogenous Britain. Interestingly, both novels are indeed set in multicultural, multiracial, postcolonial communities within London. In this consideration of exotic brown Britain within fiction, the idea of the dangerously sublime indicates an element of the forbidden in which the objects of the colonizing gaze are brown Britons. This is reflected in the blatantly eroticized desire the white, middle-class and unmarried music teacher Poppy Burt-Jones has for the Asian, working-class and married Samad Iqbal in Zadie Smith's *White Teeth*. For Poppy, the idea of Indianness is more fundamental to her colonialist fantasies than the realities of geography and history:

> 'I'm not actually from India, you know', said Samad ... Poppy Burt-Jones looked surprised and disappointed.
> You're not?'
> 'No, I'm from Bangladesh.'
> 'Bangladesh ...'
> 'Previously Pakistan. Previous to that, Bengal.'
> 'Oh, right. Same sort of ball-park, then.'
> 'Just about the same stadium, yes.' (Smith 2001: 133)

That Samad as a symbol of eroticized, exoticized brownness is physically located upon British soil does not lessen the extent to which his skin inspires a complicated internal monologue within Poppy's imagination, further evidencing the transplantation emphasized by Codell and MacLeod. To her, he embodies the East. Samad's Britishness is largely depoliticized as Smith portrays him as falling into the role of Poppy's colonial desire. Smith ironically interrogates within her novel the problematic and often all-too-limited decisions of immigrant families, as she describes that the 'tragedy of the Iqbals – [is] that they can't help but re-enact the dash they once made from one land to another, from one faith to another, from one brown mother country into the pale, freckled arms of an Imperial Sovereign' (2001: 162).

It is specifically the brownness of Samad's skin and what Poppy believes it to represent that ensure her attachment to the short-lived affair resulting from this mutual fascination with visible difference. An imagined list of brown characteristics forms in Poppy's mind as she insists, 'We just don't have that in the West – that sense of sacrifice – I just have so much admiration for the sense your people have of abstinence, of *self-restraint*' (160). With a delightful rejection of this assertion, Samad's act of 'meeting the loquacious lips of Poppy

Burt-Jones with his own feverish pair' (160) hints at his potential to reject the colonial gaze and subvert expectations to 'serve [his] own cultural expression' (1), in the words of Codell and MacLeod.

However, it is arguably the youthfulness rather than the whiteness of Poppy's skin that makes it irresistible to Samad. She does indeed stand for what he is not – a representative of young, predominantly white, educated and middle-class Britain. Poppy's lack of both history and encumbrances renders her a safe object of erotic obsession to fuel the actions of Samad's midlife crisis. When Poppy attempts to flatter Samad with her suggestion that 'dark skins wrinkle less', his response is simply, 'Do they?' as he '[forces] himself to imagine her taut, pink skin, folder over in layer after layer of dead epidermis' (Smith 2001: 136). The cultural and social space between Poppy's whiteness and Samad's brownness supports Codell and MacLeod's description of a 'charged distance between colonized and colonizer that is constantly inscribed and re-inscribed by the inherent instability in the imperialist project' (1998: 3).

Smith portrays their relationship as a continuous power struggle that constantly flounders on the edge of subverting colonial binaries. Arguably, there is a radical resolution to this battle, as it is brown-skinned Samad who declares the end of the affair; the colonized inverting the power binary to assert control over the white-skinned colonizer. Samad's fellow waiter Shiva contends with this as he insists:

> I told you not to fuck with that business, didn't I? Too much history there, man; it ain't just you she's angry with, is it? ... It's all brown man leaving English woman, it's all Nehru saying See-Ya to Madam Britannia ... Ten quid says she wanted you as a servant boy, as a wallah peeling grapes. (Smith 2001: 202)

Samad exhibits a developing sense of community solidarity forged with other brown men based on a shared experiences of unwelcomed exoticization. This is clarified as the reader is subjected to his internal monologue. As Samad waits upon yet another drunken table of obnoxious white Britons at the Indian Palace, he considers: 'the pink faces that strike [him] now as pith-helmet-wearing gentlemen, feet up on the table with guns across their legs; as tea-slurping ladies on verandas cooling themselves under the breeze of the brown boys who beat the ostrich feathers' (206).

This passage represents whiteness as what Hall terms 'a politically and culturally constructed category' (1996: 443); yet, interestingly, Samad's brownness comes across as fluid and volatile. It is precisely the growing awareness of the Britishness of his brownness that acts as a catalyst for Samad to reject the dominant discourse and claim some element of agency. When Samad himself recognizes the patronizingly reductive perception Poppy has of his 'Indianness', he is empowered into renegotiating the power dynamics of skin colour. He can then disallow the continuance of the colonialist hegemonic discourse that reduces his brown skin to an object of desire within his London community.

The problematic process of fetishizing brown skin is similarly interrogated within the characterization of Michael the Archangel in Ravinder Randhawa's *A Wicked Old Woman*. The brown-skinned Kulwant's rejection of Michael's offer of marriage arguably launches him into a mentally unbalanced state as he insists that 'The kiss of a wogess is addictory ... Her blackness was my blindfold' (1987: 85). Kulwant's brown skin cannot be separated from the colonial past that has fashioned its otherness into an exotic commodity. By refusing his proposal, the dominant discourse of white skin maintaining power over brown skin is challenged. It is Michael's perception of his own whiteness that is most offended by Kulwant's rejection. The cultural climate of Randhawa's fictionalized representation of a 1960s British community does not easily allow a brown-skinned migrant's refusal of the romantic attentions of an eligible, white British bachelor. Michael's reductive eroticization of brownness instigates a blurring of the colonial binaries of insider and outsider as he is blinded to the larger cultural implications of any imagined future they might have had together. It is arguably the discrepancies between her perceptions of skin colour and the exigent nature of a dual-cultural identity that give rise to Kulwant's determination to reject her suitor, where 'She'd messed it all up because she had wanted everything, wanted to be Indian and English, wanted to choose for herself what she wanted out of both ... She rubbed the colour of her skin, which wasn't ever going to rub off, and made her decision' (29). This surprisingly fixed 1980s representation of cultural and ethnic identity renders problematic the notion of the fluidity of identity, as suggested by Hall when he points out the importance of a 'new conception of ethnicity as a kind of counter to the old discourses of nationalism or national identity' (1986: 46). Kulwant craves the fixedness of an identity which is equally Indian and British, but the reality of her brownness renders her forever in the blurred regions between worlds. Although she largely functions as an individual Asian Briton within a multi-ethnic London community, Kulwant's attempts to reject an exoticized, individually assigned identity suggests her desire to fade into the safety and cultural invisibility of a larger Asian British community. Her position appears to more neatly support Connolly's assertion that 'identity is what I am and how I am recognised rather than what I choose, want or consent to' (1991: 64) than that of Hall.

Randhawa's novel interrogates the fetishization of brown skin as problematizing the individual. Kulwant recalls how

> He turned her differentness inside out, creaming her as his 'Indian Princess', 'the mysterious oriental woman', and the 'Mata Hari of his heart'. She feigned nonchalance though every pore of her loved every syllable and not till later did the memory cringe at these borrowings from schoolboy comics. (1987: 6)

Even as she swoons at his 'flattering' comparisons, Kulwant begins the process of rebelling against an identity imposed upon her by others instead of an identity whose origin is in the self. I have discussed Kulwant's second-skin transformation from youthful object of exoticized desire to an unthreatening, elderly Asian British woman in 'Desexing the Crone': 'In the chaotic, unstructured [community] space in between stereotypes, [her] decision to appear invisible is powerful, dangerous, and profoundly political' (2016: 283). These reductive associations with exotic stereotypes support the idea of skin as a powerful and destructive metaphor for difference, as they depoliticize representations of Asian Britons as merely cosmetic accessories whose brownness complements white Britishness. The inversion of the status quo is nearly complete when Kulwant is able to ask, 'Was I your contribution to anti-racism? Not only can you say, "some of my best friends are black", but also "some of my best lovers"?' (Randhawa 1987: 143). With this, she arguably subverts Orientalism by refusing to submit to the passive Asian woman stereotype. Instead, she renders Michael the subjugated party, thus challenging the expectations of their shared community.

In a lucid moment of revisionism, an example of Hall's notion of the 'immense process of historical relativization which is just beginning to make the British … feel just marginally "marginal"' (1986: 46), Randhawa introduces an acid critique of the multicultural project and the British tendency to commodify Indianness by asking: 'How come we never learned about the Indian soldiers who fought with the Brits? Looks like a deliberate suppression of the facts to me. I mean that's what a multicultural education should be about, not Diwalis and sari parties' (1987: 156). Interestingly, this reflects the concerns raised by Samad Iqbal in *White Teeth*, as he demands of his fellow British soldier in the belly of their shared tank: 'Is it so complex, is it so impossible, that you and I, stuck together in this British machine, could find it in ourselves to fight together as British subjects?' (Smith 2001: 86). Smith, like Randhawa, identifies the inability of many white Britons to accept the multicultural and multi-ethnic nature of twentieth-century Britishness.

## Second skin or cultural appropriation in *Lovers, Liars, Conjurers and Thieves* and *A Wicked Old Woman*

I have so far attempted to support Hall's notion that the construction of identity is characterized by fluidity, and that migrant identity is necessarily subject to multiple cultural influences that problematize the idea of a cohesively constructed community identity. For the fictional Asian Britons within this discussion, everyday cultural confrontations between Britishness and Asianness both fragment and inform a sense of self. If we are to recall Connolly's definition, it appears we have no real control over how our identities are assigned, as the traditional colonial power structures in which those with agency inevitably define the perceived identity of those who have none.

For the brown-skinned Asian Britons within these texts, identity is not simply how one is recognized by dominant society but is formed through a developing awareness of the 'otherness' of his/her own brownness in relation to the dominant whiteness surrounding them. Fanon argues that 'in the white world the man of colour encounters difficulties in the development of his bodily schema. Consciousness of the body is solely a negating activity. It is a third-person consciousness' (1986: 110). Through becoming aware of the self, one is automatically taken outside the self to become an observer of one's own actions. Rather than experiencing life within the expected position of the first person, an awareness of one's own otherness distances the subject from the essential self. Fanon's argument that this awareness is a 'negating activity' suggests that to become aware of the otherness of self prohibits full participation in a first-person relationship to everyday life.

Is it not ironic that an awareness of one's skin in relation to the skins of others is precisely what leads us into the adoption of what I call a 'second skin'? Second skin is differentiated from primary skin – that with which we are born – by its provisionality. The choice to assume the disguise of a second skin that temporarily camouflages our natural epidermis manipulates how we are perceived by others. An example of this is putting on costumes that act as disguises or even wearing 'ethnic' clothes from a culture not one's own to *appear* connected with the community these garments represent. The act of putting on this 'second skin' is arguably a form of cultural appropriation as second-generation migrants working between different cultures are necessarily creative and elective in the way they comport their appearance and identity. This can be seen as the subject adopts what Lacan refers to as the 'identification' of the mirror stage. He describes this as 'the transformation that takes place in the subject when he assumes an image' ([1949] 1995: 328) – I argue that this image could be that of the 'other' – to hide what is felt to be lacking in the self.

Zadie Smith takes a rather cynical view of the tokenistic attempt to embrace British multiculturalism in *White Teeth*, as she describes Marcus and Joyce Chalfen, 'an ageing hippy couple both dressed in pseudo-Indian garb' (2001: 131). These second skins are imbued with cultural codifications and clues to identity formation. With these second skins comes a set of packaged assumptions: the wearers are liberal minded, they are sensitive to cultural differences, they appreciate the 'otherness' of multicultural society and, most importantly (to the Chalfens, at least), they are not mainstream Britons. Smith uses this description to critique the adoption of the temporary second skin of an exoticized other to inflate one's own sense of cultural superiority. These temporary skins provide the location for libidinous community encounters – such as that of Samad, who adopts the second skin of a restaurateur rather than a waiter during his brief liaison with Poppy – and an identity that is clumsily chosen rather than culturally assigned.

In *A Wicked Old Woman*, Randhawa similarly uses the trope of her character adopting a second skin to provide an alibi. The eccentric protagonist, Kulwant, 'masquerades behind her old woman's disguises of NHS spectacles and an Oxfam coat, taking life or leaving it as she feels inclined, seeking new adventures or venturing back into her past' (1987: back cover). Kulwant is a forty-something Asian British woman who chooses to costume herself with the second-hand clothes of an elderly matriarch – complete with an unnecessary walking-stick. I have written earlier about Kulwant's deliberate use of second-skin cast-offs as a tool for resisting her 'patriarchal objectification as [an] exoticized commodit[y] ripe for Western sexual consumption' (2016: 279). Rather than accept the cultural vulnerability of her assigned identity as a desirable Asian British woman, Kulwant's self-manufactured exterior successfully interrogates both oppression and exploitation and serves as what Fanon calls 'a dialectic between [her] body and the world' (1986: 111). Second skins arguably serve as a bridge of unspoken communication between the subject who has deliberately chosen this disguise and the society which receives and interprets the message it sends out. Susheila Nasta suggests that 'Kulwant's disguise as the wicked old woman of the novel's title … is employed by Randhawa both as a literary device … and the literal sign of her need to deconstruct any predetermined notions of her authenticity as a representative "Asian" voice' (2002: 192). Nasta has identified one of the traps that ethnic British writers can easily fall into – that of producing exotic prose that hints towards a genuine insight into the vagaries of non-Anglo British lives. Instead, Randhawa presents a character who inverts the expected dialectic between mainstream British culture and second-generation Asian British migrant by adopting a rebellious persona who chooses a disguising second skin to further her own aims.

The manipulative potential of the second skin should not be underestimated. In an example of reverse cultural appropriation, Kulwant temporarily rejects the outward appearance of her own exotic Indianness to adopt the second skin of a homeless British pensioner, 'Going out, and making her way to the public loos; casting a cautious look to check that no one she knew would know that she'd gone into the Ladies' Convenience for a character change for the she that emerged up the urine stairs could be an old bag or a smelly old hag whose address was a patch under the Charing Cross bridge' (1987: 3–4). Randhawa's decision to represent Kulwant as choosing to pass as an unattractive, homeless pensioner as opposed to the cultured, educationally sophisticated and elegant woman she is subverts the notion of mimicry. In a scathing textual response to the stereotypical pressure to become either an exotic, 'dusky doe-eyed maiden from the East' or a 'nice immigrant who has gratefully adapted to British ways', Randhawa describes how 'The sweet-smile ladies thought it strange … to see an Asian lady trying and choosing cast-offs and rejects of who knows who for it was said they were particular about second-hand skins' (3). It is only when she is adequately armoured with her 'othering' second skins that Kulwant truly comes into her own as a woman. She liberates herself from perceptions of 'acceptable' femininity within her community through her rebellious actions. In denying the sexual attractiveness of a young woman, she is freed from the burdens of others' cultural expectations. This supports Fanon's suggestion that 'it is the wreckage of what surrounds me that provides the foundation for my virility' (1986: 211). By destabilizing the perceptions of the Oxfam shop ladies, Kulwant asserts agency.

Kulwant's actions evidence an active rejection of the undesirable role of the exoticized Asian woman; she chooses instead temporary empowerment by manipulating the way in which others can visually construct her identity. She provides the window and thus successfully inverts the colonial power structures alluded to by Huggan when he argues that 'The exoticist rhetoric of fetishized otherness and sympathetic identification masks the inequality of the power relations without which the discourse could not function' (2001: 14). Kulwant claims the ground of identity back from her oppressors – those well-meaning white British ladies in the Oxfam shop. Within this scene, Kulwant successfully uses her second skins not as accurate guarantors of her identity but as cunning commodities of power within her wider community.

It is this interrogation of how communities are constructed that is clearly addressed by Raman Mundair, whose use of poetry successfully addresses the alienating aspects of visual identity based on sociocultural perceptions of skin and second skins in her poetry collection, *Lovers, Liars, Conjurers and Thieves*. She introduces the notion of skin (in this case, a second-hand skin) as the originating location of shame in the poem 'Charity': 'your tall, skinny boy's frame // suited in the shame // of a Salvation Army // shop-bought suit' (2003: 45).

For the migrant child described in Mundair's poem, the second skin of his visibly second-hand – though undoubtedly British – suit is unable to mask the visible 'otherness' of chromatically non-white skin and his sense of feeling profoundly outside his community. Within this context, no second skin can successfully enable the non-white Briton to appear visibly neutral, as the politicized otherness inherent in his brownness overshadows any attempts to pass as white. Arguably, the neutral space desired by the child within the poem could be characterized by what Fanon describes as 'a zone of nonbeing, an extraordinarily sterile and arid region, an utterly naked declivity where an authentic upheaval can be born' (1986: 10). The inability of the child to adopt what is perceived as a neutral skin, coupled with the shame introduced by the second-hand suit, perfectly prepares him to enter a zone where anger and a lack of agency naturally give rise to cultural rebellion.

Although it is ostensibly the second-hand suit that introduces otherness into this piece, it is the migrant child's lack of agency that most poignantly reflects Connolly's definition of identity as mentioned earlier. Mundair writes of how she, a 'Punjabi Alice', was 'transplanted to England to struggle with the rough musicality of Mancunian vowels … she found no true reflection of herself … but mirrors which dissolved, shrank and obscured her size' (2003: back cover). This directly reflects the power balance she writes into the little boy in 'Charity', who was also unlikely to have any say in the matter of being uprooted and transplanted into a strange land, where he had no sense of belonging to any community as an insider.

Mundair continues her critical examination of the defiant potential of adopting second skins in her poem 'Light Relief'. In a blatant rejection of an unwanted persona thrust upon her by an insensitive lover, she writes of how

> The women of your fantasy are as diverse as you are inconsistent. // There is the woman who dances like a courtesan // but whose modesty is as dark as a hijab …

// There is the woman who slips effortlessly into the dead // woman's clothes that hang in your wardrobe ... // The women of your fantasy are as diverse as you are inconsistent, // and you demand me to wear them, like the dead woman's clothes // in your wardrobe. But did I not mention: last season's look // has never been my style, and crushing my esteem // so that it fits into your rhythmic, lubricated palm, // never my desire, fantasy or fashion. (49–50)

Completely unlike Kulwant, this woman sees the costumed potential of adopting another character through the medium of garments as disempowering and degrading. The woman in 'Light Relief' adopts a position of power as she resists objectification. This woman subverts the Orientalist discourse that would render her obedient, submissive and, above all, unquestioning.

## Conclusion

This chapter has considered the role of skin in the construction of Asian British community identity within a selection of works of British writing. I have discussed how visual differences become benchmarks against which self-identity is constructed, keeping in mind Stuart Hall's idea of identity forming at the unstable point where personal subjectivity meets with the grand narratives of both history and culture (1986: 4). While examining the fictional tensions between chosen and assigned identities, I have found textual examples that both support and critique Connolly's idea of identity being more socially constructed than personally chosen by the subject. Through the process of 'demarcating and devaluing the other' (Benthien 2002: 3) through a judgement of skin itself, I have attempted to deconstruct the racist myth of an impossibly pure Britain. Most importantly, this chapter has shown that exoticizing brown skin disempowers non-white Britons and dangerously depoliticizes the racist behaviours within these texts, as if communal identities were not constructed largely through a sense of belonging. An examination of these texts has revealed how brown and white characters define themselves within their communities and how these serve as constructors of identity in relation to those others around them, reflecting Lacan's argument that all mimicry is a form of camouflage that mottles both the self and the background. Brown skin is a signifier of resistance to the mentality of colonial domination within these representations, as the characters initially submerge their Asianness, then feel they have lost it and only later do they renegotiate the empowering potential of their visible otherness within a predominantly white mainstream Britain. The rejection of white skin by brown skin subverts the hegemonic discourse, shifts the grand colonialist narrative and optimistically points towards a new concept of Britishness.

Writers such as Raman Mundair, Ravinder Randhawa, Zadie Smith and Meera Syal interrogate tokenistic attempts towards multiculturalism in contemporary Britain through fiction and poetry, and their writings evidence a changing trend within British cultural anatomy. Although many of their characters at first appear to fall into the trap of fetishized Asian immigrant, these writers at once acknowledge and critique the reductive depoliticization of the issues surrounding racist behaviour and cultural ignorance. Fiction and poetry prove to be apposite fora for analysing racist responses to cultural difference as well as idealistic contentions of scholars such as Modood that multiculturalism is relatively unproblematic within contemporary British communities.

## References

Benthien, Claudia (2002), *Skin: On the Cultural Border between Self and World*, New York: Columbia University Press.
Bhabha, Homi (1994), *The Location of Culture*, London: Routledge.
Bromley, Roger (2000), *Narratives for a New Belonging: Diasporic Cultural Fictions*, Edinburgh: Edinburgh University Press.
Campbell-Hall, Devon (2009), 'Renegotiating the Asian-British Domestic Community in Recent Fiction', *Journal of Postcolonial Writing*, 45 (2): 171–9.
Campbell-Hall, Devon (2016), 'Desexing the Crone: Intentional Invisibility as Postcolonial Retaliation in Ravinder Randhawa's *A Wicked Old Woman* and Chitra Banerjee Divakaruni's *The Mistress of Spices*', in Daria Tunca and Janet Wilson (eds), *Postcolonial Gateways and Walls: Under Construction*, 279–91, Amsterdam: Rodopi.
Chaudhuri, Amit (2001), *The Picador Book of Modern Indian Literature*, London: Picador.
Chen, Kuan-Hsing, and David Morley (2006), *Stuart Hall: Critical Dialogues in Cultural Studies*, London: Routledge.
Codell, Julie F., and Dianne Sachko MacLeod (1998), *Orientalism Transposed: The Impact of the Colonies on British Culture*, Aldershot: Ashgate.
Connolly, William (1991), *Identity/Difference: Democratic Negotiations of Political Paradox*, Ithaca, NY: Cornell University Press.
Dyer, Richard (1997), *White*, London: Routledge.
Fanon, Frantz ([1967] 1986), *Black Skin, White Masks*, London: Pluto.
Gilroy, Paul (2004), *After Empire: Melancholia or Convivial Culture?*, London: Routledge.

Hall, Stuart (1986), 'Minimal Selves', in *Identity: The Real Me*, 44–6, ICA Identity Documents 6, London: ICA.
Hall, Stuart (1990), 'Cultural Identity and Diaspora', in Jonathan Rutherford (ed.), *Identity: Community, Culture, Difference*, 222–37, London: Lawrence & Wishart.
Hall, Stuart (1996), 'New Ethnicities', in David Morley and Kuan-Hsing Chen (eds), *Stuart Hall: Critical Dialogues in Cultural Studies*, 441–8, London: Routledge.
Hand, Felicity (1995), 'How British Are the Asians?', *Wasafiri*, 21: 9–13.
Hand, Felicity (2001), 'Forget India, We're British!', in Kathleen Firth and Felicity Hand (eds), *India Fifty Years after Independence: Images in Literature, Film and the Media*, 109–20, Leeds: Peepaltree.
Huggan, Graham (2001), *The Postcolonial Exotic: Marketing the Margins*, London: Routledge.
Innes, Catherine Lyn (2002), *A History of Black and Asian Writing in Britain, 1700–2000*, Cambridge: Cambridge University Press.
Kumar, Amitava (2000), *Passport Photos*, Berkeley: University of California Press.
Kumar, Amitava (2002), *Bombay-London-New York*, London: Routledge.
Kumar, Amitava (2004), *Away: The Indian Writer as Expatriate*, London: Routledge.
Lacan, Jacques ([1949] 1995), 'The Mirror Stage as Formative of the Function of the I as Revealed in the Psychoanalytical Experience', in Richard Kearney and Mara Rainwater (eds), *The Continental Philosophy Reader*, 330–5, London: Routledge.
McLeod, John (2004), *Postcolonial London: Rewriting the Metropolis*, London: Routledge.
Modood, Tariq (1992), *Not Easy Being British*, Stoke-on-Trent: Trentham.
Moss, Laura (2003), 'The Politics of Everyday Hybridity: Zadie Smith's *White Teeth*', *Wasafiri*, 18 (39): 11–17.
Mundair, Raman (2003), *Lovers, Liars, Conjurers and Thieves*, Leeds: Peepal Tree.
Nasta, Susheila (2002), *Home Truths: Fictions of the South Asian Diaspora in Britain*, Basingstoke: Palgrave.
Newland, Courttia, and Jacob Ross (2004), 'Does the Writer Have a Responsibility to Their Community?', *Wasafiri*, 41: 3–7.
Procter, James (2000), *Writing Black Britain: 1948–1998*, Manchester: Manchester University Press.
Procter, James (2003), *Dwelling Places: Postwar Black British Writing*, Manchester: Manchester University Press.
Raj, Dhooleka S. (2003), *Where Are You From? Middle-Class Migrants in the Modern World*, Berkeley: University of California Press.
Randhawa, Ravinder (1987), *A Wicked Old Woman*, London: Women's Press.
Ricoeur, Paul (1995), 'On Interpretation', in Richard Kearney and Mara Rainwater (eds), *The Continental Philosophy Reader*, 136–58, London: Routledge.
Sandhu, Sukhdev (2003), *London Calling: How Black and Asian Writers Imagined a City*, London: HarperCollins.
Smith, Zadie (2000), *White Teeth*, London: Penguin.

Stein, Mark (2004), *Black British Literature: Novels of Transformation*, Columbus: Ohio State University Press.
Syal, Meera (1996), *Anita and Me*, London: Flamingo.
Upstone, Sara (2010), *British Asian Fiction: Twenty-First Century Voices*, Manchester: Manchester University Press.
Wisker, Gina (2004), 'Negotiating Passages: Asian and Black Women's Writing in Britain', *Hecate*, 30 (1): 10–30.

# Part 3
# Precarious Community

7

# Performing the nation: A disunited kingdom in Jonathan Coe's *Middle England*

Kristian Shaw

On 6 July 2005, the IOC (International Olympic Committee) announced London had been awarded the 2012 Summer Olympics. For Charles Kennedy, former leader of the Liberal Democrats, the decision would 'unite the country just as it united the three main political parties in its support' (qtd in Bowcott 2005). Yet the 2012 London Olympic Games were hosted during a crucial moment of political upheaval: the severe effects of the 2008 financial crisis were sending shockwaves across the world; the politics of austerity were already underway following a shift from New Labour to a Tory-led coalition; in 2011 English cities witnessed some of the worst riots for decades; the approaching 2014 Scottish independence referendum threatened the bonds of unionism; and Britain's membership of the European Union continued to divide parties and communities. Moreover, the morning after London won its bid the capital was rocked by coordinated terrorist attacks which immediately countered any national jubilation. The so-called *United* Kingdom was not a territory at ease with itself in the twenty-first century but rather still suffering the post-war effects of economic and cultural decline; repeated blows to its self-confidence and tensions surrounding devolutionary dispensations were damaging the prospect of intra-UK coherence. The fallout of the financial crisis in particular was responsible for dampening the enthusiasm for Olympics preparations; by 2007, the estimated cost of conducting the Games rose from £2.4 billion to £9.3 billion with the burden increasingly placed on public sector funding rather than private sector contributions. A poll in August 2008 revealed only '15% of the public at large thought that hosting the games would be "good for the country's international reputation"' (Beard 2008).

As Alan Tomlinson reminds us, 'the messages of Olympism are interpreted anew according to the interests and priorities of the host city' (2014: 248). London's bidding process for the 2012 Games involved a desire to capture a cohesive British national identity, while promoting the capital as an empathetic and tolerant city, reflecting the complex interplay between nationalist and cosmopolitan discourses.[1] Mark Pope et al. (2017) note the IOC often draws on cosmopolitan language to advance 'universal fundamental ethical principles' and the 'harmonious development of humankind', yet naturally couch such ideals in national contexts by drawing on the symbols of flags and anthems to maintain a competitive spirit (IOC 2011). The cosmopolitan nationalism which emerges thus complicates sources of allegiance and identification and arguably limits the potential for positive cultural recognition across communities. The 2012 Games, keeping the spotlight firmly on London, also reinforced emergent tensions between constituent nations of the UK and weakened claims for unionism. During the Olympics, the London-centric media framed Scottish athletes as unpatriotic for their refusal to sing the national anthem and their resistance to the 'Team GB' tag, which seemingly prioritized English interests in a moment of Scottish nationalism. The Team GB name invited further controversy for its symbolic neglect of Northern Ireland, demonstrating that the UK was a political entity beset by bitter disputes and internal imbalances.

Major sporting events and spectacles have long been manipulated and influenced by political ideologies to improve public moods. As Alan Tomlinson and Christopher Young state, a global sports spectacle 'foregrounds the sculptured and commodified body and orchestrates a physical display of the body politic' (2006: 3). Such events allow countries to 'add to their national status and identity' and also their 'national narratives' (Roche 2006: 267). In the context of establishing a *British* national community representative of the present, Michael Silk notes that '[s]porting contexts have served as spaces through which assertions of devolved multicultural "Britishness" have been played out', but 'these post-imperial re-anchorings are not necessarily more inclusive and egalitarian; they are frequently underscored by myopic and jingoistic xenophobia' (2011: 741). For several commentators, the forthcoming Games would not only be a vital distraction from an increasingly fractured society but help to redefine the parameters of Britishness and highlight Britain's continued dominance on the world stage. London's opening ceremony on 27 July 2012 registered this attempt to project Britain as an inclusive, outward-facing nation comfortable with its own identity.

However, this chapter will argue that rather than demonstrating sport's unique ability to serve as an equalizing force, the ceremony encapsulated the tensions and contradictions between two Britains – one inward-looking and conservative, the other outward-facing and cosmopolitan – as well as concealing the widespread inequalities scarring the face of the nation. Drawing on Jonathan Coe's state-of-the-nation novel *Middle England* (2018), which contains a detailed deconstruction of the opening ceremony, it will be suggested that the jingoistic spectacle of the Games was an elegant façade masking the ingrained divisions affecting the body politic: divisions which would come to the fore during the EU referendum campaign. Documenting events between 2010 and 2018, Coe's social satire forges crucial links between the London Games and post-Brexit Britain, marking a crucial literary engagement with the debates surrounding Britishness and national belonging that would go on to characterize the post-Olympic moment. For Coe, the rancorous events of 2016 clearly serve as revisionary lessons to the celebratory mood of 2012, revealing that the roots of nationalist fervour were already well planted.

## Imagined nation

Watched by approximately 90 per cent of the UK population, the London 2012 opening ceremony was directed by Danny Boyle and scripted by novelist Frank Cottrell Boyce, both cultural figures well versed in delivering powerful and dramatic narratives. As Jackie Hogan identifies, Olympics opening ceremonies often serve as 'elaborately staged and commercialized narratives of nation', comprised of historical events, national practices, symbols and rituals to strengthen the illusion of a stable and united imagined community (2003: 102). Olympics minister Tessa Jowell appreciated the opportunity the 2012 Olympics represented, stating that the Games must promote the UK as an 'inclusive' and 'welcoming place to live in' (DCMS 2012: 4). Boris Johnson, then mayor of London, used his welcoming remarks to suggest London was *already* the image of a tolerant cosmopolis, claiming the capital 'enjoys a diversity unrivalled anywhere in the world. This diversity ... is now thoroughly twined into London's DNA, both cause and effect of its phenomenal success and much-envied reputation' (LOCOG 2012: 7). As Coe's deconstruction of London's opening ceremony will suggest, however, the spectacle gave rise to latent feelings of nationalism amongst citizens opposed to the diversity and heterogeneity of the present.

It is clear why Coe has chosen to mark the 2012 Games as a moment of national concern, given the opening ceremony was noted for its Anglocentric portrayal of British history and heritage, and was accused of conflating Britishness and Englishness to depict a stable UK and promote Team GB. His various characters, watching the spectacle 'alone' in their separate homes but united by the same imagined sense of community, are fundamental to the novel's commentary on nationhood; indeed, Coe's repetition of the word 'alone' across this chapter not only captures their social and political alienation from one another but reinforces that what defines a nation's history and culture is esoteric and subject to individual interpretation (2018: 129). As the countdown footage begins with the 'Journey Along the Thames' sequence, the divergent perspectives of what constitutes or defines Britishness, and what is seemingly integral to the popular cultural imaginary, become clear. Philip Chase and his wife Carol, for example, argue over whether viewers will identify Pink Floyd references, with such innocuous arguments within households beginning to assume greater importance when located within the context of nationhood and cultural inheritance.

The opening chronological prologue of the ceremony begins with scenes of a bucolic, prelapsarian Britain. This Blakean 'Green and Pleasant Land' sequence features a cappella performances of the UK's unofficial national anthems by youth choirs – Danny Boy for Northern Ireland, Flower of Scotland for Scotland, Bread of Heaven for Wales and Jerusalem for England – to reflect intra-UK unity. Yet Boyle's overriding message of the ceremony, 'This is for everyone', is clearly at odds with that of the viewing public (LOCOG 2012: 10). For Helena Coleman, the 'Green and Pleasant Land' sequence performed in the arena is closer to her ideal of quintessential Englishness: a narrow conception of nationhood which is dependent on a quasi-mythical imaginary in place of lived experience and is often mistakenly considered to serve as a wider representation of Britishness. Boyle himself inadvertently reinforces this perspective, describing these idyllic pastoral scenes in the media guide, taken from Kenneth Graham's *The Wind in the Willows* (1908), as 'the countryside we all believed existed once' (LOCOG 2012: 20). For Boyle, England's green and pleasant land is 'embedded' in the British consciousness, crying out 'to all of us like a childhood memory' (qtd in Harvey 2012). As Jason Whittaker argues, the decision to draw on Blake's poem for the title of the opening sequence can 'be read as some not-so-hidden indication of the special importance of England in the union'; but if Jerusalem remains applicable to twenty-first-century England, it is only through the idea 'of a fallen Albion at war with itself, engaged in the bitterest of mental fights'

(2018: 391).¹ While the sequence stops short of dramatizing national *myths*, the cultural performance still focuses intently on antiquated notions of nationhood, becoming a spectacle of paralysis which merely manufactures a false sense of unity. The ceremony's minute of silence in remembrance for those lost in the two world wars reinforces this agenda, serving as a cherished visual source of identification for a beleaguered and anxious national community aware of their diminished position on the global stage. These featured icons of cultural conservatism exude a sense of cultural superiority, opening the national sensory pathways to more *traditional* times when Britain was a major global power.

The subsequent 'Pandemonium' sequence, with Kenneth Branagh's iconic depiction of Isambard Kingdom Brunel delivering Caliban's 'Be not afeard' speech from *The Tempest* on Glastonbury Tor, continues this supposed chronological history, marking the beginnings of the Industrial Revolution. As the ceremony moves closer to the contemporary moment, though, cracks appear in cultural perceptions of Britishness. Having praised the opening sequence for its Anglocentric focus, Helena grows increasingly disturbed at the inclusion of Black actors for the 'Pandemonium' sequence as Britain transitions from a rural economy to a period of industrialization: 'Why did they have to *do* that? Why? Did people have no respect for history any more?' (Coe 2018: 131, original emphasis). Her reaction demonstrates how historical representations often remain fixed within the national imaginary; attempts to refashion what Eric Hobsbawm and Terence Ranger (1983) would term Britain's 'invented traditions' are not well received. Helena's aggressive refusal to allow a more inclusive Britishness to define her identity signals an ideological retreat to the safety of the *English sublime*: 'a nationalist fable founded on a haunting and destructive jingoism which aggressively mourns the illustrious past, offers redemptive traces of former imperial glories and laments the cultural heterogeneities of the inferior present' (Shaw 2021: 72). Boyle certainly conjures key elements of the English sublime in the opening sequence, stitching quintessential symbols of nationhood into the cultural imaginary to establish a coherent imagined community; however, his overriding effort to mobilize and unite the British community around contemporary sociocultural developments is interpreted as an act of sabotage by some characters, rewriting an alternative narrative of nation which clashes uncomfortably with prevailing ethnonationalist sentiments.

In Coe's fictional rendering, left-leaning political journalist Doug Anderton approaches the ceremony in a sceptical mood but is soon caught up in Boyle's 'eccentric hymn to Britain's industrial heritage':

there was something hugely affecting and persuasive about it ... Something fundamentally *truthful*, in fact. And what he felt while watching it were the stirrings of an emotion he hadn't experienced for years – had never really experienced at all, perhaps, having grown up in a household where all expressions of patriotism had been considered suspect: national pride. (2018: 131)

Sophie, a liberal art history lecturer radically opposed to any form of patriotism engendered by sporting events, shares Doug's initial reservations. She plans to ignore the television coverage, feeling 'instinctively repelled' by the nationalistic or monarchistic scenes about to unfold, but is soon swayed by Boyle's use of intertextual references to explore and deconstruct youthful versions of Britishness (129). On the other hand, her partner Ian, who had been instinctively drawn to the prospect of a major sporting event, begins to lose interest in the historical references of the opening sequences; rather, it is the more overt symbols of nationhood within the 'Happy and Glorious' sequence – 'the Queen! James Bond! The Union Jack!' – which induce in Ian 'an almost orgasmic surge of patriotic excitement', exposing emergent fault lines within their already fractious relationship (133).

Boyle's inclusion of the woman's suffrage movement, the Jarrow Crusade and the Empire Windrush in this sequence was designed to suggest the power of 'trade unionism and protest to solve many of the problems' faced by Britain, the so-called workshop of the world (LOCOG 2012: 22). Yet these gender, class-based and racial divisions were amplified and performed in the present as 'mere historical artifacts' within 'a common, fixed and concretely grounded past that centred on an Anglicized, simple, stable, safe and pure fantasy' (Silk 2014: 68). For retiree Colin even the reference to the HMT Windrush (not just a pivotal historical moment but a fraught ethnopolitical crisis continuing to affect the nation) sparks a defensive reaction, directing his ire at the BBC for permitting a soft liberal to creep into this moment of national celebration: 'bloody political correctness brigade are at it again' (Coe 2018: 132). Colin perceives the intrusion of recent events into the cultural imaginary as a purposeful destabilization of England's monocultural foundations, interpreting their presence as an unwelcome development in his nation's narrative.

The following sequence, 'Second to the right, and straight on till morning' – its title taken from J. M. Barrie's *Peter Pan* (1904) – exacerbates this perceived attack on cultural conservatism. Boyle utilizes literary narratives (featuring characters from children's works by authors such as J. K. Rowling and Lewis Carroll) to negotiate tensions surrounding citizenship, community and identification within Britain and expose the fictional basis of our national heritage. He aimed for this sequence to instil a sense of civic pride in public institutions such as the NHS. The ceremony's inclusion of real NHS staff (who would go on to hold the country together during the Covid-19 pandemic) is particularly relevant to this discussion as the official media programme describes the NHS as 'the institution which more than any other unites our nation' (LOCOG 2012: 26). Boyle faced pressure from the Coalition government to cut this section of the ceremony, and its defiant presence is thus a veiled critique of creeping Tory privatization threats and a response to the Coalition government's announcement of substantial cuts to the public sector in the run-up to the Games (qtd in Osborne 2016). Whereas Coe's other characters are invigorated by the ceremony – Sophie and Ian make love for the first time that week while Doug's Corbynista daughter Coriander is energized by the reference to Brookside's first lesbian kiss on national television – Helena shares Colin's reservations about the British media. She becomes so depressed by perceived cultural intrusions into her national imaginary that she stays up long after the coverage has finished to compose a letter to the *Telegraph* attacking the ceremony for its 'left-wing bias' (Coe 2018: 138). The insertion of recent changes to the demographics of Britain's body politic ruptures Helena's inviolable belief that she is a communicant of an 'essentially incommunicable deep nation' that remains suspended in a form of cultural stasis and is impervious to external threats (Wright 1985: 81). As Hogan reminds us, 'Nations are more than geopolitical entities; they are discursive constructs – constructions of the character, the culture, and the historical trajectory of a people. Such constructions, by their very nature, are acts of inclusion and exclusion' (2003: 100). Colin and Helena thus give voice to many on the political right, for whom the ceremony was a betrayal of Britain's cultural history and an act of national rebranding. Peter Hitchens (2012), for example, claimed 'Leftists' would view the ceremony as 'a triumph for their version of truth', bemoaning the ways by which 'our proud past is ridiculed and our history rewritten'. Hitchens, of course, fails to recognize that similar sentiments were shared by many on the left, and that such debates had destabilized established political lines. The reaction to the ceremony reveals the intricate symbiotic relationship between, and treatment of, political and cultural forms of nationalism in the media: a relationship which would become more pronounced during the EU referendum campaign.

Coe's depiction of the subsequent 'Frankie and June Say … Thanks Tim' section reveals the latent sociopolitical fault lines within his fictional British society, creating a clear juxtaposition between more traditional notions of national heritage and emergent forms of nationhood. Whereas the opening sequence adheres to the symbolism of the English sublime, evoking a decidedly monocultural depiction of a mythical Albion, the 'Frankie and June' section offers a reinscription of a broader, more inclusive *British* identity based on a contemporary civic multiculturalism. The sequence depicts a burgeoning relationship between a young mixed-heritage couple across the last decades of the twentieth century, projecting the spectacle of a nation comfortable with both its heritage and multicultural composition, as opposed to a nation bitterly divided by both deep-rooted trauma and recent political events.[2] For Silk, however, the inclusion of the 'Frankie and June' section fails to depict a Britain undergoing progressive change; rather, the 'natural' hierarchy was 'threatened, but undisturbed, by the demands of cosmopolitan mores':

> the noises of the past became amplified in the present: plastic multi-ethnic performances in this Olympic post-museum represented acquiescence to – commonality with – selected British histories, making it all the easier, with a subtle sleight of hand, to reassert a utopic abstraction of nation and assimilation to core British values. (2014: 73, 76)

By beginning the national narrative with the 'Green and Pleasant Land' and 'Pandemonium' sequences, the ceremony draws upon culturally conservative icons and 'concrete historically entrenched signifiers that define those rooted in Boyle's British past as *unconditionally belonging* to, and the *rightful managers* of, nation' (79, original emphases). Multi-ethnic Britain was consequently denied a past in the ceremony as 'differential legitimating discourses, histories, belongings and identities were simply absent or silenced', ensuring 'there was no opportunity to travel through history together' (76). Rather than positioning London as a harmonious cosmopolis, 'a plural space of opportunity devoid of antagonisms – a space of elective belonging', the ceremony 'performs a terrifying and fetishistic politics' in which cosmopolitan ideals can only be tolerated within a rigid national frame which elides the cultural and racial inequalities continuing into the contemporary moment (74). For Silk, a 'utopic multi-ethnic *national fantasy*' emerges which exposes the continued centrality of 'privilege and hierarchy within a postcolonial heterophilic Britain' and requires that citizens toe the line as 'appropriate national subjects' (69, 75, original emphasis). As a result, the Games functioned as 'a highly affective, and extremely public, political, pedagogic, corporate and powerful media spectacle though which to define the parameters of *the* "sanctioned" nation', demonstrating how histories of 'corporeal recollection and embodiment become ingrained with the discourses of nation, subjectivity, fear, regulation and consumption' (69, 78, original emphasis). Boyle's production, despite its best intentions, shows the socio-historical battles being played out across the nation, revealing 'the very selective historical noises which "we" can "belong to"' (78). Coe's deconstruction of the ceremony in *Middle England* aligns itself with Silk's reading, gesturing to the underlying tensions surrounding incompatible contemporary visions of Englishness and Britishness. However, Coe's satirical take on Britain's cultural imaginary not only continues his tendency towards excruciating national introspection – evident in *What A Carve Up!* (1994) and *Number 11* (2015), which explored the influence of powerful interest groups under Thatcherite rule and Tory spending cuts within London, respectively – but his own bitterness towards the referendum result, with the novel occasionally lacking his nuanced acerbic acuity as a result.

According to Stuart Hall, when it comes to social constructions of belonging: 'National cultures construct identities by producing meanings about "the nation" with which we can identify; these are contained in the stories which are told about it, memories which connect its present with its past, and memories which are constructed of it' (2000: 613). Coe's detailed engagement with the opening ceremony, and his diagnosis of the English identity crisis throughout *Middle England*, suggests the lingering presence of what Paul Gilroy terms a 'postcolonial melancholia' in the national psyche, which continues to shape debates surrounding nationhood and multicultural belonging (2004: 109). Gilroy critiques Britain's reliance on its venerated history which is constructed around 'an obsessive repetition of invasion, war, contamination, loss of identity' and ensures 'an anxious, melancholic mood [becomes] part of the cultural infrastructure' of the nation (15). Britain's inability 'to face, never mind actually mourn, the profound change in circumstances and moods that followed the end of the Empire and consequent loss of imperial prestige' results in certain citizens retreating to ideas of racial purity in order to locate and justify their national identity' (98).[2] The wider public attacks on athletes who came to be pejoratively termed 'plastic Brits' – on account of being born abroad – such as Mo Farah, were part of an anti-multicultural agenda reflected in Colin and Helena's responses to the opening ceremony. For Poulton and Maguire, when it came to celebrating and defining contemporary values and icons of nationalism in reference to Team GB, there were clearly 'complex mediated patriot games at play' (2012: 19). Governments often utilize a form of soft power, which John Hoberman (1993) terms 'sportive nationalism', celebrating Olympians as 'living, breathing representations of national or racial characteristics' to demonstrate the health and prestige of the body politic (Clarke and Clarke 1982: 62). The initial cynical framing of Farah in the British press immediately changed following his gold-medal success in the 5,000 m and 10,000 m events, with his Somali heritage downplayed in favour of a progressive national narrative of multi-ethnic accomplishment and pluralization. Farah's acceptance by the British community was also dependent on a personal demonstration of attachment to his nation, suggesting that 'hegemonic models of racialized nationhood' continued to dominate discussions of citizenship and belonging (Burdsey 2016: 14).[4] Silk anticipated this aesthetic manipulation in the run-up to the 2012 Games, arguing the foregrounding of Black British and British Asian athletes in the Olympic bid process asserted a 'multiculturalist nationalism' in which citizens are not only 'let in' but redefined as integral to the self-image of the nation as 'tolerant' and 'inclusive' (Fortier 2005: 560; Silk 2011: 742).

The tension between the opening sequence and the 'Frankie and June' sequence recalls Littler and Naidoo's (2004) proposed formation of a 'white past, multicultural present'. Littler and Naidoo's alignment operates 'simultaneously as a lament and a celebration – a celebration of our nation being modern, young, hip and in tune with the globalized economy as well as harbouring a nostalgia and lament for a bygone contained, safe and monocultural world' (338). For Colin and Helena, the impulse to defend their white past and sacred sources of national memory triggers a resultant fear that they must resist more recent changes which threaten what they consider more *legitimate* forms of heritage and cultural identification. The broader narrative of *Middle England* oscillates between those English citizens who lament a 'lost' national past and those who hold a fragile faith in the present. Such oscillation also aligns with June Edmunds and Bryan Turner's (2001) comparison of 'benign and malign' nationalism as two competing models of Englishness. Whereas benign Englishness is more inclusive and tolerant, open to the idea of European integration and multiculturalism, malign Englishness is more insular and operates in a similar manner to ethnonationalist tendencies, perceiving national identity to be 'in the blood' and at risk of infection from European bureaucracy, devolutionary reform and globalizing processes. While Edmunds and Turner's model may create a false dichotomy, simplifying the more complex emotional attachments that underpin nationalism, it is undoubtedly a rather useful litmus test in reflecting the intergenerational and ideological divides between the characters of *Middle England* and their subsequent position on the EU referendum; particularly those characters who 'don't appreciate Johnny Foreigner coming over to the land of Dickens and Shakespeare and telling them how it should be done' (Coe 2018: 27).

Boyle's remark, 'if you believe in something, you carry people with you', would prove to be rather prescient but not for reasons he would have envisaged. As Jonathan Freedland (2013) notes, the ceremony was swiftly seized upon by political commentators as representative of a 'new approach, not only to British culture but to Britishness itself … shorthand for a new kind of patriotism that does not lament a vanished Britain but loves the country that has changed'. The ceremony arguably provided

> a nation that had grown used to mocking its myriad flaws with a new, unfamiliarly positive view of itself … It was, perhaps, this lack of cynicism that people responded to … So used to British irony and detachment, it felt refreshing to witness an unembarrassed, positive case for this country. (Freedland 2013)

The waning of Doug's liberal cynicism and uncharacteristic, tentative embrace of a patriotic stance encapsulates this very point, 'at this moment he felt proud, proud to be British, proud to be part of a nation which had not only achieved great things but could now celebrate them with such confidence and irony and lack of self-importance' (Coe 2018: 131). Nonetheless, in their social study Pope et al. find that the self-congratulatory tone adopted by the British press did not circulate in international media and the more archaic visions of British heritage retained their salient edge in the public's imagination, ensuring 'the transmission of emotions operated more through nationalist than cosmopolitan discourses': a finding that was to prove rather intuitive in the subsequent years (2017: 427).

For historian Simon Schama (2012), the London Games was a successful demonstration of the belief that 'All colours and classes turn out to belong to the same family … Britain is, after all, a *community*'. It would, however, be more accurate to suggest the Games served as an early indicator of a culture war emerging within the nation and the continued dominance of England within the British hierarchy. The closing footage of British athletes, draped in the treasured Union flag, symbolizes an attempt to safeguard the UK's structural integrity and mask the internal frailties of our fractious union. Coe's lengthy dissection of the opening ceremony – a performative theatrical space for antagonistic, opposing versions of national identity – thus reveals the ceremony encapsulated divisions which would come to define the EU referendum: a globalized Great Britain versus an endangered Little England. The glossing over of regional differences, particularly between constituent nations, signalled an attempt to narrate the nation: the affirmation of a false coherence which elided the socio-economic and cultural contestations affecting a disunited kingdom. As Coe's novel goes on to demonstrate, when it came to Brexit, the ceremony's archaic vision of a monocultural, pastoral Little England won out over the vibrant multiculturalism of a modern Great Britain.³

## Dreams of England past

Coe's positioning of the Games, immediately before the 'Deep England' section of the novel, is also structurally revealing. Patrick Wright's notion of a 'Deep England', predicated on 'ceremonies of remembrance and recollection', is reflected in the anxieties of his older or more conservative characters, for whom the more multicultural and globalized aspects of the ceremony endangered a safe and legitimate source of national identification, rewriting and undermining established narratives of nation (1985: 85). The performance of national identity as embodied practice, after all, engenders firmer emotional attachments to nationhood, and any refashioning of British identity threatens the privileged place certain rituals, practices and symbols hold in the popular cultural imagination. Boyle's opening sequence even leads liberal Sohan to abandon his current literary research and examine the source of this 'Deep England' aesthetic: 'Was it a psychogeographical phenomenon, to do with village greens, the thatched roof of the local pub, the red telephone box and the subtle thwack of cricket ball against willow?' (Coe 2018: 202). Despite his best efforts, he fails to define the term adequately, or explain where it can be located, gesturing to the intangible, elusive nature of an archaic Englishness which nevertheless continues to reside in the hearts and minds of its populace.⁴

Coe's purposeful utilization of Wright's term reinforces the novel's suggestion that inaccurate representations of national past and heritage can be manipulated and mobilized to respond to the contemporary political situation, operating in relation to racialized discourses and responding to fears surrounding Britain's decline on the world stage.⁵ In the process, a distorted invocation of the cultural imaginary emerges, which merely simplifies the tenebrous corners of our national history and fails to address contemporary anxieties. As Doug insightfully notes, nostalgia very much remains 'the English disease', with the EU referendum result confirming how 'a simplifying nostalgia can replace any principled democratic consideration' (Coe 2018: 391; Wright 1985: 244). In the EU referendum campaign, Vote Leave utilized an emotional restorative nostalgia, drawing on the ideals and practices of an imagined past to reorder and redefine the present. For Linda Hutcheon:

It is the very pastness of the past, its inaccessibility, that likely account for a large part of nostalgia's power ... This is rarely the past as actually experienced, of course; it is the past as imagined, as idealized through memory and desire. In this sense, however, nostalgia is less about the past than about the present. (1988: 20)

The various reactions of Coe's characters to the Olympic opening ceremony anticipate dormant fissures in the national community that were to (re-) awaken during the EU referendum campaign. The 'Deep England' section of *Middle England* goes on to consider the early motivations for the fateful Leave vote, suggesting how modes of remembrance and the deferential treatment of national heritage in the British press transfigured the discourses surrounding the referendum.[6] The novel's attempt to diagnose the psychopathology behind Brexit necessitates this examination of England's febrile landscape where 'Years of anger, years of bitter, rancorous, resentful co-existence were rising up and coming to the boil' (Coe 2018: 83). Reviving characters from his earlier works, such as *The Rotters' Club* (2001) and *The Closed Circle* (2004), Coe gestures to the legacy of Thatcherite social policy as a contributing factor in shaping our turbulent times, establishing fault lines within communities and unravelling the potential for a cohesive and tolerant society to emerge from the ruins of deindustrialization. Writing for the *New Statesman*, Coe jokes that the subtitle for his novel could have been 'Britain: Where Did It All Go Wrong?' as he locates the ideological 'trigger points' for citizens of England-without-London (Coe 2019).

The rest of the novel retains a close concentration on Benjamin Trotter, who quits London and relocates to a quiet mill house near Shrewsbury – an area saturated with English Heritage and National Trust sites – to finally complete his overwrought novel on Britain's accession to the Common Market. Benjamin cerebrates on how the impact of the opening ceremony, uniting 'millions of disparate people' under the banner of nationhood, is reflected in the 'silence of England' as it sinks 'into a deep, satisfied sleep ... a country at ease with itself' (Coe 2018: 139). The River Severn outside his mill house, 'proceeding on its timeless course ... merrily, merrily, merrily, merrily', seems to reflect this moment of national calm (139). Indeed, the river (which, rather tellingly, flows across the Anglo-Welsh border – the two nations to return a defiant Leave vote) assumes a psychogeographical power; its quiet, slumbering murmur is soon amplified and threatens to spill over as the British public forget the events of 2012 and turn their attention to the forthcoming referendum campaign: 'supposing the river were to abandon its quiescent and reasonable habits … What form might that anger take?' (22). Middle-class citizens who 'had grown used to comfort and prosperity and now saw those things slipping out of their reach' would soon, like the river, abandon their 'quiescent and reasonable habits' (19–20, 22).

Benjamin finds his Middle England landscape to be an unhappy site of simmering disaffection and quiet rage, with its communities determined to hold on to outdated national symbols and ways of life as acts of resistance against cosmopolitan London and rapid cultural developments. The Woodlands Garden Centre located near his house recalls the aesthetic of Boyle's 'Green and Pleasant Land' sequence, encapsulating a quintessential Englishness and serving as a sanctuary for citizens fearful of foreign influences diluting their nation's sacred essence. This 'mighty empire' trades in nostalgic items such as jigsaw puzzles 'depicting farmyard scenes from pre-industrial days, Spitfire and Hurricane aircraft in mid-flight [and] scenes of traditional English village life' and serves classic English cuisine to customers who resist any internationalization of the menu (58, 59). The centre, much like the opening scenes of the 2012 ceremony, provides a form of cultural protection by rejecting the encroachment of cultural diversity and projecting a monocultural representation of the body politic. Operating almost as a National Heritage site, the centre offers 'that momentary experience of utopian gratification in which the grey torpor of everyday life in contemporary Britain lifts and the simpler, more radiant measures of Albion declare themselves again' (Wright 1985: 76).

The novel's final section, appropriately titled 'Old England', opens with Jo Cox's poignant plea for greater unity in her maiden speech to the House of Commons but captures the feverish and polarized atmosphere of a post-Brexit Britain still defined by its backward-looking impulses. Coe utilizes his Dickensian cast of friends and relations to comment on the intergenerational and class-based divides scarring the nation. As the discussion of the Olympic opening ceremony revealed, resistance to multiculturalism and immigration retains its salience as the 'subject that divided people more than any other' (Coe 2018: 90). Doug laments the means by which Leave supporters have been manipulated by anti-immigration scare tactics and post-truth populist rhetoric while his own articles are dismissed as naive think-pieces by a metropolitan spectator. Nonetheless, he comes to acknowledge how his complicity with the 'self-satisfied cosmopolitanism' of London, writing from behind the confines of his multimillion-pound pad, prevents him from identifying with vast swathes of the populace: 'There can't be more than about twelve people in the country who understand how the EU works … This campaign is going to be won on slogans and soundbites, and instincts and emotions' (269). Coe documents the galvanizing effect of xenophobic rhetoric during the final weeks of the referendum campaign, encouraging citizens to give voice to their simmering resentment and reinforce their defences 'built out of fear and suspicion and … those most English of all qualities, shame and embarrassment' (90). Colin resents hearing other languages spoken on English streets while Helena fails to defend her Lithuanian cleaner from post-Brexit racial abuse, struggles to understand how Sophie's PhD dissertation can examine *Black* Europeans and cites Enoch Powell's 'rivers of blood' speech as an unappreciated, prophetic vision for her country. Even Sohan, with his scepticism towards the notion of a conservative 'Deep England', concedes foreign affluence has ruined London, which no longer *feels* like a British city.

The symbolic appeal of Brexit also concerns a (specifically English) nostalgic desire to restore a form of imperial greatness and repair a contemporary landscape which, for certain sections of the electorate, has been defaced and marred by widespread multiculturalism, rising immigration levels and structural inequality. For Colin, the promise of Brexit supplies a form of personal and communal salvation; his Leave vote is a final act of defiance against creeping multiculturalism. Colin's aggressive mourning for the decline of his old workplace, the British Leyland car plant, symbolizes a more general lament for the decline of working-class communities in the Midlands and their wartime pluck: 'What a spirit, eh? What a country we were back then!' (Coe 2018: 262). His granddaughter Sophie, a staunch Remainer, laments this blatant xenophobia endorsed by the older generation, believing a part of her 'modern, layered, multiple identity' has been irrevocably damaged by the vote (326). Reflecting on the London Olympics with post-Brexit hindsight, Sophie registers her own melancholy nostalgia for 'that week in the summer of 2012 and the missed opportunity' that it represented, as the celebratory, cosmopolitan energies of the opening ceremony were unable to maintain their optimistic momentum (411).[7] While visiting Hartlepool for a potential job, which returned a defiant 69.5 per cent Leave vote, Sophie (like Doug) recognizes her London-centric complacency contributes to the sense of estrangement she feels from her fellow countrymen: 'She considered herself a Londoner, now, and from London she could not only travel by train to Paris or Brussels more quickly than she could come here, but she would probably feel far more at home on the Boulevard Saint-Michel or Grand-Place' (24, 369). She soon realizes this ideological estrangement extends to her partner Ian, who begins to espouse Leave sentiments and internalize his mother's xenophobia after losing out on a promotion to Naheed, his junior Asian female colleague, resulting in the swift breakdown of their marriage. Sophie and Ian's subsequent 'Post-Brexit counselling' sessions allow Coe to gesture towards the deep-rooted causal factors of the EU referendum, as the couple acknowledge their conflicting perspectives 'weren't about Europe at all … something much more fundamental and personal was going on' (327). Although the couple's eventual reconciliation and the arrival of their 'beautiful Brexit baby' may intimate Coe's 'tentative gesture of faith' that British society can heal the poisonous scars disfiguring the face of the nation, Benjamin's decision to relocate to France to open his creative writing school in the closing scenes of the novel signals a symbolic retreat from a national community which has failed to remedy its internal divisions (421). As the Olympic opening ceremony brought so arrestingly to light, perceived deficits within the European project function as a convenient and misguided proxy for pre-existing structural imbalances haunting our United Kingdom.

Billings et al. rightly argue that the 'patriotism, nationalism, and smugness' evident during the Games 'did not translate into a sense of global kinship' (2015: 81). The self-congratulatory mood merely allowed neoliberal and exclusionary policies to be developed in its wake. As Freedland (2012) recognizes, the Olympics failed to effect a paradigm shift when it came to public attitudes towards immigration in particular: 'Somali-born asylum seekers unblessed by Mo Farah's gifts will not be applauded as they walk into the pub. Our problems haven't gone away just because the news bulletins have barely mentioned them for two weeks.' In 2018, Theresa May's government began plans for a £120 million Festival of Brexit to re-establish a sense of national kinship and community evident during the 2012 Games. The proposed celebration, redolent of the Great Exhibition of 1851 and the 1951 Festival of Britain, was to be spear-headed by Martin Green, the organizer of the London 2012 opening ceremony, who hoped it would rekindle a sense of patriotism in the wake of Brexit. May announced the festival with typical post-Brexit hyperbole:

> Almost 70 years ago, the Festival of Britain stood as a symbol of change. Britain once again stands on the cusp of a new future as an outward-facing, global trading nation … just as millions of Britons celebrated their nation's great achievements in 1951, we want to showcase what makes our country great today. (qtd in Buchan 2018)

Her announcement failed to mention that the festival would cost at least £120 million of public money and depend on the work of figures in the creative arts who overwhelmingly voted against EU withdrawal. Coinciding with the queen's platinum jubilee, the festival would likely do little to bridge social divides or heal an ailing union but simply provide a brief respite from the fallout of the Covid-19 pandemic. Indeed, its formal working title, Festival UK, continues the governmental effort to promote a United Kingdom of shared interests. The SNP has since called for UK to be dropped from the title, while pro-EU groups are already planning an alternative event to offset the national isolationism and buccaneering spirit implied by the festival's remit.

In gesturing to the valid narrative links that exist between the events of 2012 and 2016, *Middle England* emerges as a key work of *Brexlit*: literature that responds to the 'nostalgic appetite for (an admittedly false) national heritage' identifies 'anxieties surrounding cultural infiltration' and 'a mourning for the imperial past' and 'engage[s] with the subsequent sociocultural, economic, racial or cosmopolitical consequences of Britain's withdrawal' from Europe (Shaw 2018: 18). Both the London Games and the EU referendum amplified England's lingering identity crisis and the internal tensions threatening the future of the UK. As Fintan O'Toole remarks, post-Brexit negotiations themselves became 'one long closing ceremony for games that refuse to end' (2020: 356). David Cameron's confident claim that the Olympics provided 'a boost for the Union' proved to be as misguided as his faith in the Europhilic sentiments of the British public (qtd in Shipman 2012: 8). Vote Remain was unable to sustain the soft power of London 2012 to aid in the promotion of a multicultural, inclusive ethos and Boris Johnson, utilizing the popularity he attracted on the back of the Games, became the bumbling juggernaut that delivered a Leave victory. Speaking with post-Brexit hindsight, Stuart Heritage (2019) argues the fleeting halcyon spectacle of 2012 contained such a 'focused optimism' that it lulled Remainers into 'a false sense of security' where 'nothing bad [would] ever happen again'; as a result, 'they sleepwalked into a referendum they were convinced they'd win, and then couldn't understand why they lost'.

Boyle's juxtaposition of a nostalgic Albion with contemporary visions of a multicultural Britain symbolizes an effort to confront: 'where have we come from, what is the heritage, the historical, what are we now and where are we going; and on that journey what are the values that we hold up as being valuable?' By constructing a microcosmic spectacle of Britain's national heritage (in the vein of Nora's *lieux de memoire*), narrating and negotiating complex and differing conceptions of Britishness across history, Boyle's ceremony challenges essentialist forms of cultural identification and interrogates who belongs in our cultural imaginary (Nora 1998: 1). According to Roshi Naidoo, 'the more readily we accept the idea of the nation as a fiction, the easier it is to write new ones' (2005: 43). Yet, Coe himself is guilty of unintentionally embracing and reproducing outdated paradigms, behaviours and caricatures associated with England's cultural imaginary. As *Middle England* so acutely reveals, then, attempts to build an island story which incorporates visions of the globalized present into the treasured national fantasy of Britain's hegemonic past, utilizing communal memories alongside mythical and discursive histories, are always going to invite criticism and unwittingly expose the fault lines within our trembling union. With this in mind, the development of a Britain 'which can admit the myths and fictions upon which it is built' may prove to be the most pressing task for our post-Brexit moment (Naidoo 2005: 43).

## Notes

1 Blake's words were to be utilized once again on the morning of the referendum result; the *Telegraph* announced 'England! Awake! Awake! Awake!' to assert that the country was waking from a slumber having been subservient to EU law for too long (Whittaker 2018).
2 The 2012 opening ceremony was described as being reminiscent of the Festival of Britain, a national exhibition in the summer of 1951, which aimed to install a sense of national recovery and renewal following the devastation of the Second World War, promoting the best of British technology, science and the arts.
3 An Ashcroft (2016) poll revealed two-thirds of those who defined themselves as 'more English than British' voted Leave; in comparison, two-thirds of those who considered themselves 'more British than English' voted Remain.
4 Sohan's effort to capture the master signifier of incommunicable nationhood echoes Jack Pitman's attempt to define the '50 Quintessences of Englishness' in Julian Barnes's *England, England* (1998). As Jacob Torfing identifies (and as would prove to be the case in the Brexit debate) dominant nationalisms can come to 'provide the empty signifier of the nation, which symbolizes an empty fullness, with a precise substantive content that people can identify with' (1999: 194).
5 In 2015, just a year before the EU referendum, market research organization Ipsos MORI (2015) found that fewer than 10 per cent of British voters cited the EU as a 'top three' issue affecting their lives.
6 A similar consideration of Britain's past in relation to the EU referendum can be found in other Brexlit novels such as *Missing Fay* (2017) by Adam Thorpe, *Ghost Wall* (2018) by Sarah Moss, *All Among the Barley* (2018) by Melissa Harrison and *Broken Ghost* (2019) by Niall Griffiths.

7 Ali Smith's *Autumn* contains a more subtle allusion to the London 2012 Olympics, placing the reader in a febrile post-Brexit landscape where the celebratory memory of the Games has been eroded and the inward-looking cultural melancholia once again shines through the outward-facing façade: 'now you couldn't tell that any of these summer things had ever happened. There was just empty field. The sports track had faded and gone' (2016: 115).

# References

Ashcroft (2016), 'How the United Kingdom Voted on Thursday … and Why', *Lord Ashcroft Polls*, 24 June.
Beard, Matthew (2008), 'Only 15% Say 2012 Will Lift Britain's Reputation', *Evening Standard*, 14 August.
Billings, Andrew C., Natalie A. Brown, Kenon A. Brown, Guoqing, Mark A. Leeman, Simon Ličen, David R. Novak and David Rowe (2015), 'From Pride to Smugness and the Nationalism Between: Olympic Media Consumption Effects on Nationalism Across the Globe', in Andrew C. Billings and Marie C. Hardin (eds), *The Global Impact of Olympic Media at London 2012*, 64–86, London: Routledge.
Bowcott, Owen (2005), 'London 2012: "Fantastic … It Will Unite the Country"', *Guardian*, 7 July.
Boyle, Danny (2012), 'Boyle Reveals Opening Ceremony', *Daily Telegraph*, 12 June.
Buchan, Lizzy (2018), 'Britain to Hold Post-Brexit Festival Celebrating Culture, Sport and Innovation, Theresa May Announces', *Independent*, 29 September.
Burdsey, Daniel (2016), 'One Guy Named Mo: Nation and the London 2012 Olympic Games', *Sociology of Sport Journal*, 33 (1): 14–25.
Clarke, Alan, and John Clarke (1982), 'Highlights and Action Replays: Ideology, Sport, and the Media', in Jennifer Hargreaves (ed.), *Sport, Culture, and Ideology*, 62–87, London: Routledge.
Coe, Jonathan (2018), *Middle England*, London: Viking.
Coe, Jonathan (2019), 'The Brexit Referendum Tells the Story of the Radicalisation of Middle England', *New Statesman*, 20 March.
Department for Culture, Media and Sport (2012), 'Our Promise for 2012: How the UK will Benefit from the Olympic and Paralympic Games', DCMS.
Edmunds, June, and Bryan S. Turner (2001), 'The Re-invention of a National Identity?: Women and Cosmopolitan Englishness', *Ethnicities*, 1 (1): 83–108.
Fortier, Anne-Marie (2005), 'Pride Politics and Multiculturalist Citizenship', *Ethnic and Racial Studies*, 28 (3): 559–78.
Freedland, Jonathan (2012), 'London 2012: We've Glimpsed Another Kind of Britain So Let's Work for It', *Guardian*, 10 August.
Freedland, Jonathan (2013), 'Danny Boyle: Champion of the People', *Guardian*, 9 March.

Gilroy, Paul (2004), *After Empire: Melancholia or Convivial Culture?*, Abingdon: Routledge.

Hall, Stuart (2000), 'Modernity: An Introduction to Modern Societies', in Stuart Hall, David Held, Don Hubert and Kenneth Thompson (eds), *The Question of Cultural Identity*, 596–632, Oxford: Blackwell.

Harvey, Oliver (2012), 'Pageantry, Parody and Pistols … It Was Perfect', *Sun*, 28 July.

Heritage, Stuart (2019), 'The London Olympics Opening Ceremony: A Moment of Optimism that Destroyed the Decade', *Guardian*, 26 December.

Hitchens, Peter (2012), 'Am I an "Animal" or a "Cow" – or Just Another Victim of BBC Bias?', *Mail on Sunday*, 4 August.

Hoberman, John (1993), 'Sport and Ideology in the Post-Communist Age', in Lincoln Allison (ed.), *The Changing Politics of Sport*, 15–36, Manchester: Manchester University Press.

Hobsbawm, Eric, and Terence Ranger (1983), *The Invention of Tradition*, Cambridge: Cambridge University Press.

Hogan, Jackie (2003), 'Staging the Nation: Gendered and Ethnicized Discourse of National identity in Olympic Opening Ceremonies', *Journal of Sport & Social Issues*, 27 (2): 100–23.

Hutcheon, Linda (1988), *Irony, Nostalgia and the Postmodern*, Toronto: University of Toronto Press.

IOC (2011), Olympic Charter, The International Olympic Committee, http://www.olympic.org/Documents/olympic_charter_en.pdf.

Ipsos MORI (2015), April 2015 Issues Index, *Ipsos MORI*.

Littler, Jo, and Roshi Naidoo (2004), 'White Past, Multicultural Present: Heritage and National Stories', in Robert Phillips and Helen Brocklehurst (eds), *History, Nationhood and the Question of Britain*, 330–41, Basingstoke: Palgrave.

LOCOG (2012), *London 2012 Olympic Games Opening Ceremony Media Guide*, London: LOCOG.

Naidoo, Roshi (2005), 'Never Mind the Buzzwords: "Race", Heritage and the Liberal Agenda', in Jo Littler and Roshi Naidoo (eds), *The Politics of Heritage: The Legacies of 'Race'*, 36–48, London: Routledge.

Nora, Pierre (ed.) (1998), *Realms of Memory: Rethinking the French Past*, Chicago, IL: University of Chicago Press.

Osborne, Samuel (2016), 'Danny Boyle Claims Tories Tried to Axe NHS Celebration in London 2012 Olympics Opening Ceremony', *Independent*, 10 July.

O'Toole, Fintan (2020), *Three Years in Hell: The Brexit Chronicles*, London: Head of Zeus.

Pope, Mark, Niklas Rolf and Nora Siklodi (2017), 'Special Affects: Nationalist and Cosmopolitan Discourses through the Transmission of Emotions: Empirical Evidence from London 2012', *British Politics*, 12 (3): 409–32.

Poulton, Emma, and Joseph Maguire (2012), 'Plastic or Fantastic Brits?: Identity Politics and English Media Representations of "Team GB" during London 2012', *JOMEC Journal*, 1 (2): 1–30.

Roche, Maurice (2006), 'Nations, Mega-Events and International Culture', in Gerard Delanty and Krishan Kumar (eds), *The SAGE Handbook of Nations and Nationalism*, 260–72, London: SAGE.

Schama, Simon (2012), 'A Letter from America to Beatific Olympic Britain', *Financial Times*, 11 August.

Shaw, Kristian (2018), 'BrexLit', in Robert Eaglestone (ed.), *Brexit and Literature: Critical and Cultural Responses*, 15–30, London: Routledge.

Shaw, Kristian (2021), *Brexlit: British Literature and the European Project*. London: Bloomsbury.

Shipman, Tim (2012), 'Cameron: Games Have Brought UK Closer Together', *Daily Mail*, 13 August.

Silk, Michael (2011), 'Towards a Sociological Analysis of London 2012', *Sociology*, 45 (5): 733–48.

Silk, Michael (2014), '"Isles of Wonder": Performing the Mythopoeia of Utopic Multi-ethnic Britain', *Media, Culture & Society*, 37 (1): 68–84.

Smith, Ali (2016), *Autumn*, London: Hamish Hamilton.

Tomlinson, Alan (2014), 'Seizing the Olympic Platform: 6.6 Million and Counting', in Vassil Girginov (ed.), *Handbook of the London 2012 Olympic and Paralympic Games. Volume One: Making the Games*, 238–51, London: Routledge.

Tomlinson, Alan, and Christopher Young (2006), *National Identity and Global Sports Events: Culture, Politics, and Spectacle in the Olympics and the Football World Cup*, New York: State University of New York Press.

Torfing, Jacob (1999), *New Theories of Discourse: Laclau, Mouffe, and Zizek*, Oxford: Blackwell.

Whittaker, Jason (2018), 'Blake and the New Jerusalem: Art and English Nationalism into the Twenty-First Century', *Visual Culture in Britain*, 19 (3): 393–405.

Wright, Patrick (1985), *On Living in an Old Country: The National Past in Contemporary Britain*, London: Verso.

8

'Why would you play a game like that?':
Community and the pandemic in
Kazuo Ishiguro's *Klara and the Sun*

Emily Horton

## Introduction

Over one year on from the first arrival of the Covid-19 virus, and with a 'third wave' now spreading across the globe, it may seem early to announce the beginnings of a new 'pandemic literature'. To be sure, popular cultural interest in pandemic-related fictions and films is readily visible across the internet (Doherty and Giordano 2020), and one recent publication even suggests that those individuals reading and watching such outputs may actually experience more psychological preparedness to face pandemic-related difficulties (Scrivner et al. 2021). Nevertheless, when it comes to literary fiction, authors and critics have been more reticent to position their work in this way, asserting instead the importance of time and retrospection as necessary conditions for critical and creative assessment. As Lily Meyer (2020) writes, 'No one has had time to truly refine their ideas about personal life in a state of widespread isolation and existential dread … and because no inner experience of the coronavirus pandemic could plausibly be described as complete, prose that renders it static and comprehensible rings false.' Likewise, Laura Spinney (2020) reflects that 'it's too early to know if we'll reap a crop of pandemic-themed novels in years to come', but for the moment, 'literary fiction that explores contagion is thin on the ground'.

Kazuo Ishiguro's eighth novel, *Klara and the Sun* (2021), which I want to position within this category in order to explore its critical representation of Covid-19 era loss, is not necessarily intended in response to the experience of the pandemic – indeed, considering its publication date in early March of

2021, it seems unlikely that Ishiguro would have had sufficient time to properly incorporate meaningful references to this event. His own pronouncements on the novel likewise reflect this. 'I had no premonition or anything of a pandemic,' Ishiguro insists. 'I just saw a society that was going to be more isolating and isolated' (James 2021). More properly, from interviews Ishiguro has given on the novel, it is intended as a comment on developments in genetic engineering and AI technology, suggesting worries over the emergence a new, 'quite savage' meritocracy based in genetic enhancement and the impact this might have on existing social communities (Knight 2021: n.p.). Ishiguro states,

> Our assumption about what a human individual is and what's inside each unique human individual – what makes them unique – these things are a little bit different because we live in a world where we see all these possibilities of being able to excavate and map out people's personalities. Is that going to change our feelings toward each other, particularly when we're under pressure? When you actually face the prospect of losing somebody you love, I think then you really, really start to ask that question, not just intellectually but emotionally. (Knight 2021: n.p.)

Here, the author emphasizes the affective and ethical questions raised by genetic engineering, underlining the potentially disastrous ramifications these technologies might have on human relations, especially where the threat of personal loss informs decision-making. As Clara Nguyen (2021) writes, the novel offers 'a heartfelt exploration of technology's potential to affect the way we love', one which 'shines direct light on the tenuous connections that sustain an increasingly isolated world'. In other words, it probes technology's impact on an escalating contemporary solitude, especially where these developments claim to offer hope through revolutionary innovation.

Nevertheless, in the context of Covid-19's relentless toll on human lives, which has also impacted on how we interact publicly, how we educate and socialize children and how we assess the very value of different human lives, similar questions are also clearly at stake: Who gets to live? Who gets to thrive? And on what grounds? Indeed, the radically world-changing dilemmas raised by the availability of new genetic and AI technologies in the novel might be seen as continuing an already prominent and Covid-19 pertinent debate around the category of the 'human', especially as this concept defines access to basic rights, including education, a living wage and healthcare. As Brenda Carr Vellino writes, 'the category of the "human"' functions to 'designate which human rights subjectivities are visible, legible, intelligible, and audible in aesthetic, legal, political and ethical contexts' (2016: 149). Likewise, as Simon Cohn and Rebecca Lynch reflect, this prioritization has also tended to define global public health debate, where those qualifying as humans are automatically accorded 'an exceptional status' (2017: 286), often with tragic consequences for those more disadvantaged. What I am concerned to examine in this chapter is how this debate connects to the novel's central depiction of a pandemic-era lost community, seeing Covid-19 as that which operates at the tension between state investment in personal health (the individual) and the meaning of this for local and national communities. In effect, I read the novel as suggesting that a humanist account of the subject, prizing rationality and uniqueness, obstructs a healthy understanding of community solidarity, standing in the way of a larger appreciation of social obligation.

To elaborate, if the novel is concerned about individuals and how they are affected within the pandemic context, and if it suggests (as I believe) that this representation is bound up with a certain idea of the human, nevertheless, this depiction clearly positions these individuals within a larger social collective, which in different ways comes under threat by humanist philosophy. We see this already in Ishiguro's earlier novel *Never Let Me Go* (2005), where a similar focus on post-human commonality overtly disrupts taken-for-granted assumptions regarding the priority of the individual, instead making clear what Shameem Black explains as humanism's violence: the 'fundamentally exploitative discourse of use value' implicit within the concept of the human 'soul' (2009: 785). Similarly, in *Klara and the Sun*, as I read it here, Ishiguro brings to bear a larger cultural and theoretical debate around the meaning of the human, which underpins the text's representation of community as fragile and under threat. I hope to better explain this here as I look more closely at the novel's pandemic-era panorama, considering how representations of the relationships between humans, robots and nature come to stand in for changing social understanding, though one too eager to exalt the rational individual over the iterated and vulnerable body.

## The human and the post-human

It is difficult to understate the centrality of humanism to contemporary life, a situation clearly reflected in the society of *Klara and the Sun*. Underlining the importance of the figure of the 'human' within modern history and culture, Peter Boxall reflects, 'one becomes a subject of a sovereign state, with the privileges and sanctions that such subjection entails, to the extent that one can prove oneself to be fully human' (2013: 85). Within this context, a subject's ability to situate itself as part of a larger national community emerges as decidedly contingent: 'the plight of those who have been denied certain rights under sovereign law … has thus been determined by the question of who "counts" as human' (85); those populations oppressed within modern society experience this oppression precisely on the basis of their supposed non-humanity. In the context of Covid-19, this might include unemployed individuals without access to privatized healthcare; those denied necessary information about the importance of shielding; those with unequal access to vaccines; or those left otherwise unprotected in order to assist a logic of 'herd immunity'. As Judith Butler and George Yancy (2020) write, 'Because "the vulnerable" are not deemed productive in the new quasi-Aryan community, they are not valued lives, and if they die, that is apparently acceptable, since they are not imagined as productive workers, but "drains" on the economy. Although the herd immunity argument may not make this claim explicitly, it is there.'

Despite the importance of the human to modern social and political relations, however, as Boxall also notes, the category has increasingly come into question over the past half century, thrown into 'crisis' as it is opened to 'those elements which it has sought to exclude' (2013: 86). More broadly, while the suffering of those whose rights have been refused them under sovereign law has thus far been determined by their failure to qualify as fully human (85), in this way limiting political sovereignty to the domain of the white, able-bodied, Western male subject, more recent challenges to this category across the late twentieth and early twenty-first centuries have seen it extended to encompass more identities and communities or, alternately, dismantled to reveal its elitist and discriminatory foundations. As Rosi Braidotti puts this, those left out by humanism include 'the sexualized, racialized and naturalised others, who are reduced to the less than human status of disposable bodies' (2015: 11). Postcolonial, feminist and Marxist theory has worked to articulate these subjects' experience of oppression and disenfranchisement, making it clear how 'these "others" raise issues of power and exclusion' (11).

Critical theory emerges, then, as one important challenge to humanist thinking, laying bare its tendency to exclude and omit those positioned on the margins. More recent technological developments have also contributed significantly to this debate, promoting in particular notions of the 'post-human' or 'transhuman' as salient alternatives, redefining the human in technologically informed, digitally cognizant ways. To be sure, these categories are subject to diverse interpretations, in some cases denoting an effort to ascend *beyond* humanity's physical limitations into the realm of digital abstraction or cybernetic purity. Invoking gene-editing technologies such as CRISPR, which allows scientists to change human genes in ways that are inheritable across generations, and the 'body-hacking movement', in which participants implant 'RFID microchips and magnets into their bodies to better take advantage of potentially life-enhancing technology', Christine Emba (2016) explains that transhumanism is, in this sense, 'dedicated to promoting the use of technological advancements to enhance our physical, intellectual and psychological capabilities, ultimately transcending the limitations of the human condition'.[1]

Nevertheless, in its most celebrated versions, post-humanism endeavours not to transcend the human, but rather, precisely, to *ground* this, *retaining* a concern with the subject's inescapable materiality, and therefore also her interconnection with non-human matter. As N. Katherine Hayles explains, 'the posthuman view ... thinks of the body as the original prosthesis we all learn to manipulate, so that extending or replacing the body with other prostheses becomes a continuation of a process that began before we were born' (1999: 2). Embodiment in this way emerges as theoretically crucial, offering, in Hayles's words, 'an opportunity to put back into the picture the flesh that continues to be erased in contemporary discussions about cybernetic subjects' (5). Similarly, Rosi Braidotti champions the post-human precisely for its challenge to 'the arrogance of anthropocentrism and the "exceptionalism" of the Human as a transcendental category' (2013: 66). In other words, this critical position authorizes a rebuttal of humanism's transcendental presumptions, instead favouring a reassertion of materialist thinking as a means of situating the subject historically and corporeally. As Pieter Vermeulen remarks, rather than denoting 'the successful transcendence of nonhuman constraints ... it [instead] declares the end of humanism by insisting that the discrete, disembodied entity of the human never existed' (2014: 122–3). This emphasis on the body functions to reinforce the ties between the subject and everything around it. In Brian Massumi's words, 'It is the limit-expression of *what the human shares with everything it is not*: a bringing out of its *inclusion* in matter' (2002: 128; qtd by Vermeulen 2014: 122, original emphases).

Regarding the topic of community, then, it is significant how this critical position reinforces the importance of the collective, reaffirming an underlying connectivity with the surrounding world. Importantly, this point is sometimes overlooked in post-humanism's emphasis on the subject *as body*, where this is perceived (by liberal humanism in particular) as a critical failure to take into account the individual's defining rationalism. As Elizabeth Anker explains,

> This classically Cartesian animus treats the body as a problem to be disciplined, integrated, conquered, and overcome, lest its inherent captivity and suffering jeopardize the liberal freedom and autonomy conferred by rights … To be reduced or beholden to the body is to be labelled subhuman, and that equation has and continues to support the subjugation of 'people' according to gender, race, religion, sexual orientation, class, and species membership. (2016: 42)

In other words, the body continues to be perceived as a burden to be borne, just in the same way that empire itself seeks 'to dominate and subdue nature' in the interest of power and profit (42). In its focus on the corporeal, by contrast, and on the lack of metaphysical surety available to non-transcendent subjects, post-humanism upends this liberal understanding, instead underlining physical embodiment as the subject's defining (and interlinking) condition. This makes it much more attentive to the body's own needs, and less focused on self-determination and control. Even so, post-humanism too relies on a notion of 'the subject' that in a sense mirrors the contemporary individual as its normative base. As Braidotti herself admits, 'One needs at least some subject position', however distanced from the 'unitary or exclusively anthropocentric' (2013: 102). In this way, it becomes imperative to underline the need to reinterrogate the relationship between the post-human and community, bringing these two discourses back into dialogue as mutually conversant.

One way of doing this is to emphasize the centrality of the relational within post-humanist thought, where this encompasses an understanding of mutual interdependency based on shared bodily vulnerability. As Amelia DeFalco explains, within post-humanism's care-centred affective economy, vulnerability emerges 'as the normative effect of post-human vital embodiment, as opposed to an anomalous state that can be overcome or corrected via neoliberal practice' (2020: 31). Here, while 'jettison[ing] the implied anthropocentrism of [an] ethics of care philosophy', this theory nevertheless 'retains care's foregrounding of entanglement, embodiment and obligation' (31). In this way it reinforces the importance of community to the conceptualization of the postmodern subject, as a larger body within which the subject remains inevitably entwined.

What's more, within post-humanism, the definition of community extends beyond an awareness of relationality between humans to encompass connections between people and their surroundings far more generally (that is, with the non-human). As Braidotti puts it, this theory 'indicates and actualizes the relational powers of a subject that is no longer cast in a dualist frame, but bears a privileged bond with multiple others and merges with one's technologically mediated planetary environment' (2013: 92).[2] Furthermore, as Cohn and Lynch explain, the potential of this approach with respect to questions of personal health and well-being is that here, these categories themselves are 'broadened and re-conceived as generalised and shared. Rather than a property of a body or entity, the meaning shifts to being a quality of relationships between humans, other living things, the environment and even material objects' (2017: 287). In this way, 'the focus of health research shift[s] from the human to being a more distributed quality across heterogeneous relationships' (287), extending out to encompass a larger community shared between both humans and non-humans.

Looking to Ishiguro's novel, this reading of the post-human speaks to the technological innovations the text addresses but also and more centrally to the challenge to humanism these bring with them. To quote Hayles again, 'the posthuman view configures the human being so that it can be seamlessly articulated with intelligent machines. In the posthuman, there are no essential differences … between bodily existence and computer simulation' (1999: 3). In effect, the post-human *is* Klara as Josie's mother understands her, especially as she promises a seemingly impossible 'continuation' of Josie. The novel's engagement with this technological miracle brings to the fore new existential questions raised by computer engineering, but perhaps even more pertinently the (aforementioned) Covid-19 related questions regarding the meaning and value of the human within a pandemic context.[3] With this in mind, it seems worth reinforcing the centrality of this categorical challenge within the novel, in particular, with a view to what I see as its post-Covid-19 outlook on twenty-first-century living.

## Interior landscapes and digitized vistas

In fact, the novel's interest in Covid-19's affective and material impact on contemporary life is arguably apparent from the start of the text, in the confined interior setting and limited physical viewpoint that the protagonist, Klara, has on the world around her. The text begins, 'When we were new, Rosa and I were mid-store, on the magazines table side, and could see through more than half of the window' (Ishiguro 2021: 1). Awaiting her purchase from this store, Klara treasures such scant viewing opportunities, her connection to the outside world restricted by her access to one of the shop's two windows. Within this context, the storefront position is prized as a 'special honor' (5), with each Artificial Friend (or AF) granted a week in the display, in a surprisingly democratic economy. When Klara's turn finally comes, she makes a point of expressing her contentment about this opportunity, noting how the attraction of the window for her exists beyond its advertising value, more centrally encompassing its access to sunlight and its panoramic view on the street outside. She stresses how 'I was free to see, close up and whole, so many things I'd seen before only as corners and edges' (6). This opportunity makes her 'so excited that for a moment', she says, 'I nearly forgot about the Sun and his kindness' (6), the joy of an unblocked view trumping even her more pious sensibilities, as it promises unselfconscious immersion in the world around her.

When Klara is later moved from the store to Josie's home, in this way seeing her surroundings altered and extended considerably, this textual interest in interiority, and in the limitations of an indoor perspective, persists nonetheless. Indeed, Klara's viewpoint itself is framed throughout the novel via a medium of (sometimes pixilating) screens, which remind the reader of the considerable restrictions of her non-sentient outlook. As Alex Preston (2021) describes, her access to her surroundings is occasionally subject to glitches, 'so that perspectives are skewed, everything given a migraine-ish slant'. Likewise, with minimal exceptions, the events of this novel take place indoors, within the confines of four walls – and where they do not, they are flagged explicitly as anomalies. Klara and Josie both ask permission even to venture as far as the neighbour's house, while any longer excursions (for example, to the waterfall or the city) merit special precaution. The reasons the reader is given for this interiority relate not only to Klara's status as an AF but also to the fact that *all* children in the novel are confined to their houses, attending classes on their 'oblongs' or (in Rick's case) devising inventions to pass the time. The introduction of AFs into this society emerges as a strategy to make this loneliness more bearable, providing companionship in the only form available to this generation. Likewise, the few social reunions or 'interaction meetings' (Ishiguro 2021: 64) the children attend are freighted with anxiety and tension. As Josie's mother puts it, they are part of the 'work' the children must do to succeed in college (63).

The vision of solitude this scenario invokes, all the more amplified by online learning, overtly references the pandemic experience as we currently live this, where 'isolation' and screens have become an everyday element of contemporary global experience, forcing us to weigh up the value of physical health against the quarantine's mental toll. Indeed, while on the one hand this solitude has in some ways reawakened our modern investment in community, forcing us to reconsider our connections, obligations and debts to one another, and perhaps to reach out to individuals otherwise forgotten (for example, the many local volunteer groups and communication campaigns that have emerged across the globe during the lockdown),[4] on the other hand, there is also a sense in which this community sentiment has ultimately not taken us as far as we might expect, leaving in place divisions of race and gender referenced above. As Ramgobin et al. make clear, for example, however active charity organizations in the United States may have been during the pandemic, and however nominally community-minded some state governments in managing the lockdown, those individuals and communities with lower socioeconomic status remain 'less likely to have health insurance and follow up with medical care due to out-of-pocket costs, which in turn leads to a higher case fatality rate due to Covid-19' (2021: 107).

Moreover, where a need to isolate has in some ways also offered opportunities for the development of a variety of new online communities and technologically mediated connections, for example, in virtual schooling programmes, support groups, social media fandom societies and political campaigns, on the other hand, it remains unclear to what extent such resources can provide a replacement for face-to-face encounters, and indeed to what extent involvement in such communities might actually increase a sense of loneliness and isolation. A recent article examining new Harvard research precisely around Covid-19's mental health impact explains this as especially relevant to teenagers and young adults:

> [This community] may be particularly susceptible [to feelings of social isolation] because they are often transitioning from their 'inherited families to their chosen families' … Students in college may be struggling to fit in and feel homesick, while those not in school can feel disconnected from important social groups or communities. (Walsh 2021: n.p.)

Both of these scenarios are directly referenced by Josie and Rick's perspectives in the novel, as the former struggles to find a grounding within her new college-bound community, while the latter is left apart from this coterie due specifically to his unaltered genetic make-up. As Josie comments, 'a lot of things come in the way of friendships' within this society (Ishiguro 2021: 61), here, in particular, new technologies: Rick expresses fury at Klara's arrival as a symbol of Josie's new artificial friend group (60), whereas Josie herself fails or refuses to appreciate Rick's reasons for social distrust. There is 'no reason Rick can't come', she protests, when her mother suggests he might not enjoy her 'interaction meeting', and moreover, she nags him about his supposed promise to come until he agrees (64). Likewise, Klara's *own* experience of 'choosing a family' in the text can also be connected to this social anxiety, as her memories of the store and the other AFs invest her life in Josie's house with a tangible sense of homesickness. She reflects, 'I realized how much I'd grown used to making observations and estimates in relation to those of other AFs around me, and here too was another adjustment I had to make' (48).

On one level, such sentiments are, perhaps, reflective of an aging process relevant to modern society more generally and, in this respect, implicit within the larger bildungsroman dimensions of the novel. As Joseph Slaughter writes, 'The *Bildungsroman* ... is equipped to normalise the conditions of inclusion in and exclusion from the public sphere' (2007: 157), and in this respect, all bildungsroman contemplate loneliness at least to some extent as a condition of seeking inclusion: the protagonist leaves behind her early existence in order to enter into the 'collective will' (159). It is notable here, however, that social *in*clusion itself, in this novel, might be read as inherently lonely and atomizing, where the massive shift in normative lifestyles brought on by new technology and illness is pictured as deeply isolating, separating each individual and household from the surrounding society. In effect, what Josie signs up for in being 'lifted' is a childhood defined by persisting solitude: she gives up sociability in order to be normatively social.

In the context of the Covid-19 pandemic, this act of risk assessment carries considerable resonance, particularly in debate regarding a post-pandemic shift to digitized education. Here, corporate celebrations of new classroom and home-schooling technologies tend to mask both their potentially negative impact on children's mental health and their socially divisive implications, instead championing (in the words of a position paper published by Microsoft) the 'unprecedented opportunity to transform education across whole systems' (Fullan et al. 2020). Nevertheless, as Stuart Rimmer (2020) notes, for certain student populations, especially those 'left behind by digital poverty', online learning has 'pushed them further into social isolation':

> Being out of direct physical contact [for those students] means support needs might be slower and disengagement increased. Some students report lacking structure and momentum being lost as routines, previously used as social and mental health anchors to guide the week and help regulation, are eroded with flexibility and choice becoming a tyranny.

Furthermore, such changes can also be connected to an increasing privatization of public schools, in this way undermining the current system of state provision. As Jen Persson explains, 'Once schools become dependent on the tech giants' systems for teaching in class, homework, management and communications, and once a certain threshold is reached in the number of schools they operate in, then the state delivery of education becomes entirely dependent on private companies' (qtd in Fleming 2021). With respect to *Klara and the Sun*, such concerns are registered overtly within the novel's dystopian vision of corporate hierarchy, where access to education and later 'high ranking' professional success (Ishiguro 2021: 22) is limited to those who have been 'lifted'.

## Pandemic-era exclusions

The competitive and exclusive mindset laid out in this narrative scenario again returns the novel to that central question of what makes us human. For the text's imagined society, the answer to this question involves an explicitly humanist thinking, wherein the supposedly successful subject transcends physical barriers in the pursuit of personal and social progress. Rights to a good life, including an education and well-paid profession, are seen to demand an ascension *beyond* corporeal obstacles; where this is not possible or where one opts out, this merits exclusion. As one mother puts it to Mrs Arthur, implicitly criticizing Rick's parents' choices, 'Did his folks just … decide not to go ahead? Lose their nerve? … You've been so courageous' (Ishiguro 2021: 68). The judgement here that Rick's parents were insufficiently brave in their decision *not* to genetically alter their son, and that, by contrast, Josie herself 'will be grateful to [her mother] one day' (68), reinforces the cruelly competitive dimension of this supposedly progressive outlook, where extra-bodily transcendence, in a perverse extension of humanist ideals, becomes an agreed parental aim and a condition for social and professional success.

Indeed, the problem for Rick as explained within the novel is not simply that he fails to access the genetic potential that Josie now possesses – he is described as having 'genuine ability' (230) and in his work with drones is clearly very clever. The problem is that, without genetic alteration, he cannot practically access the online tutoring that would allow him to enter college: as his mother explains, 'The long and short of it is that we can't find screen tutors for him. They're either members of the TWE, which forbids its members to take unlifted students, or else they're bandits demanding ridiculous fees, which of course we are in no position to offer' (147). It is notable here that while again Ishiguro probably was not thinking of the pandemic while writing the novel, this exclusive tutoring conglomerate open only to 'lifted' students might itself be easily read in relation to this context as an implicit reference to an increasingly inaccessible (because privatized) body of online learning technologies.

The text includes various historical markers that might also be tied overtly not only to the context of the virus more broadly but also to Donald Trump's administration and to policies set in place at the time of the virus's arrival in the United States. Klara's frequent mentions of the RPO building, for example, from the very first paragraph of the novel, might be read as an ironic allusion to Trump's endeavours to slow down postal services in the build-up to the (Covid-19 affected) 2020 election, the acronym referencing the United States' historical 'Railway Post Office', a nineteenth-century innovation meant to increase the speed of postal delivery. Equally centrally, the link between the character 'Housekeeper Melania' and the Slovene American first lady is hard to miss, the former applauded amongst the mothers in the novel as proof that 'the best housekeepers still come from Europe' (66), while the latter is known for being the first first lady with naturalized citizenship, having been born in Slovenia, and whose native language is not English (Gunter 2018: n.p.).

Indeed, given Melania Trump's general support of her husband's anti-immigrant politics throughout his presidency, perhaps best reflected by her decision to wear a jacket emblazoned with 'I don't really care, do u?' during her visit to a child migrant detention centre in October 2018 (BBC 2018: n.p.), the novel's positioning of the character Melania as an immigrant white European housekeeper, tasked in part with Josie's care, might itself be seen to comment on this right-wing outlook and on the racist double standard it involves. Here the novel suggests an awareness that the former president's decision to invoke a state of emergency based on the supposed threat to US security posed by migrants at the Mexican-American border overlooks his own wife's status as a recent immigrant. It also overlooks, of course, the real threat posed by Trump's 'zero tolerance' policy towards children detained and separated from their parents at the border – a threat only further amplified by the arrival of the virus to these border detention centres (Kneedler 2020). The novel's repeated emphasis on fences and drones (Ishiguro 2021: 151, 248), as well as on the precarious fate of those left outside its 'lifted' demographic, including a building filled with 'four hundred and twenty-three post-employed people

... eighty-six of them children' (240), reinforces this anxiety directly, where such individuals are forced to find a protective community who will assist and defend them or risk the threat of violence from increasingly fascist and racist social factions (232).

Commenting on this contemporary experience of precarity and vulnerability, both in relation to undocumented migrant populations and Covid-19 itself, Butler's writing offers an important insight on changing sociopolitical discourses, especially as these ignore an underlying (and increasingly visible) bodily interdependence specific to the post-human. Reflecting, alongside Gayatri Chakravorty Spivak, on the plight of those denied human rights on the basis of their non-citizenship, Butler notes how 'these spectral humans, deprived of ontological weight and failing the test of social intelligibility required for minimal recognition include those whose age, gender, race, nationality, and labor status not only disqualify them for citizenship but actively "qualify" them for statelessness' (2007: 15–16). In the context of Covid-19, this experience of disqualification from state protection is again extended to other minority communities, who lack the means to isolate and protect themselves and still retain their employment. As Butler and Yancy put it,

> On the one hand, the pandemic exposes a global vulnerability. Everyone is vulnerable to the virus because everyone is vulnerable to viral infection from surfaces or other human beings without establishing immunity ... On the other hand ... the pandemic exposes the heightened vulnerability to the illness of all those for whom health care is neither accessible nor affordable. Perhaps there are at least two lessons about vulnerability that follow: it describes a shared condition of social life, of interdependency, exposure and porosity; it names the greater likelihood of dying, understood as the fatal consequence of a pervasive social inequality. (2020: n.p.)

Klara's own particular relationship to this historical reality is notably ambiguous in the novel, as she stands in for a number of contrasting social discourses emergent within this pandemic experience. From one perspective, Klara's sensibilities, while in some ways notably empathetic to those around her (much more so, for example, than the B3 model which soon replaces her robot prototype (Ishiguro 2021: 35, 40)), are also distinctly racist: she repeatedly makes note of black skin, but never white (68, 245). Furthermore, while wanting to help Josie and Rick, she does little to question or challenge the societal hierarchy within which they operate. Indeed, when asked if she can 'continue' Josie, rather than trying to 'save' her, she agrees that 'perhaps this is the better way' (214), in this way effectively agreeing to allow Josie to die, so that she can take her place.

On the other hand, as becomes repeatedly clear throughout the novel, Klara is also herself an unmistakable figure of minority exclusion and disenfranchisement, at points compared to a vacuum cleaner and made to ride in the trunk of Josie's car (145, 174). In the scene in which Klara, Rick and his mother meet up with Mr Vance in front of the theatre, this prejudice becomes explicit, tied to a discourse of parasitic invasion commonly used in the popular right-wing media against migrant communities (see Musolff 2016; Arcimaviciene and Baglama 2018). As the woman outside the theatre puts this, 'These are sought-after seats … They shouldn't be taken by machines … First they take the jobs. Then they take the seats at the theatre' (Ishiguro 2021: 242). Here, Klara's status as a machine within this space is figured as an unlawful incursion on citizens' rights, these calculated precisely in relation to an agreed social prioritization of biological humanity.

The questions that Mrs Arthur poses to Klara regarding the meaning of the 'human heart' and whether it exists as something more than 'an organ', which 'makes each of us special and individual' (218), should in this context be read not simply in relation to Klara's position as robotic substitute for Josie but more centrally as a critical comment on poetic humanist understandings of the subject as fundamentally immaterial, their meaning located outside or beyond the body, in the realm of transcendental reason or spirit. Rather than endorsing such understandings, the novel instead affirms humanity's fundamental condition as embodied matter. It does this in three ways: firstly, by approaching subjectivity itself (and the narrative voice with it) through the position of a post-human robot; secondly, by drawing links between the robotic and the human (for example, Josie is said to have a 'complex' but ultimately 'limited' human heart (219)); and thirdly, by recognizing with the ending the inevitable erasure of this post-human voice through a process of material decomposition. In the novel's terms, Klara will experience a 'slow fade' (298) as she sits abandoned in the rubbish dump, her rusting hardware eventually obstructing her processing capacities. Recalling the emphasis within post-humanist theory on materiality precisely as a clue to the subject's fundamental interconnectedness, as the body (again) brings to bear '*what the human shares with everything it is not*: a bringing out of its *inclusion* in matter' (Massumi 2002: 128, original emphases), there is a sense here whereby this ending reinforces Klara's place within a larger post-Anthropocene ecosystem, binding the human, the robotic and nature as a complex community.

## Wasted lives and redundant communities

Zygmunt Bauman's writing on 'liquid modernity' helps to explain this representation's materialist conception, even as it also positions the novel in relation to a larger political economy of instantaneity and obsolescence. Thus, Klara's status as a post-human robot and the fact that she is left to run out of power in a forgotten scrapyard in both cases reinforces what Bauman sees as a 'great transformation' in the experience of contemporary life (2000: 121), one in which meaning becomes at once increasingly affective or sensational – measured in relation to momentary intensities and immediate sensations (124) – and at the same time transient and dispensable – indifferent to long-term durability or communal solidarity. As Bauman puts it, 'It is Bill Gates-style capacity to shorten the timespan of durability … to dispose of things lightly in order to clear the site for other things similarly transient and similarly meant to be instantly used up, that is nowadays the privilege of the top people and which makes them the top people they are' (126). In other words, for Bauman, modernity's 'liquidity' or 'instantaneity' sees it pursuing a politics of obsolescence, which involves readily dispensing with the old in favour of the new (125–9). In Bauman's 2003 publication *Wasted Lives*, he further expands on this understanding to consider its socio-economic implications for disenfranchised minority communities, noting how such populations themselves becomes the disposable objects of this society, 'used-up' as expendable labour in a 'disembodied' capitalist system (5–6; and Bauman 2000: 121). As he puts it,

> The production of 'human waste', or more correctly wasted humans (the 'excessive' and 'redundant', that is the population of those who either could not or were not wished to be recognized or allowed to stay), is an inevitable outcome of modernization, and an inseparable accompaniment of modernity. It is an inescapable side-effect of *order-building* … and of *economic progress*. (Bauman 2003: 5, original emphases)

In other words, within this liquid modern political-economic system, excess labour itself becomes the material 'waste' disqualified from recognized humanity, dispensed with precisely in the name of biopolitical efficiency.

Klara's final abandonment in the novel reaffirms this analysis in no uncertain terms, likewise positioning her ironically, as a defunct model easily replaced and forgotten. What is especially interesting about this positioning in light of the pandemic is how this reflects not only on Klara but also on Josie, herself a figure of pandemic-like near-death illness, but one for whom the nominal status of human allows her a gesture of pity and compassion denied to Klara by their larger society. Indeed, Josie is allowed to be seen differently both from Klara *and* Rick insofar as she is granted the status of being 'lifted', and it is this notional uniqueness which facilitates her special treatment as a focus of care and community support. Yet in situating her separately here – as socially superior and therefore more deserving of attention – the novel makes clear this society's negligence of its other minority populations, particularly in a time wherein sickness and unemployment have become ubiquitous social problems. Within this context, the novel suggests, to prize uniqueness is effectively to forget community and solidarity: in other words, to ignore larger caring responsibilities for society's most vulnerable.

Towards the start of the novel, Josie plays a game wherein 'the characters continually died in car accidents' (Ishiguro 2021: 91), which provokes an appalled reaction from her mother: 'Why would you play a game like that, Josie?' (91). Defending herself in response, Josie reflects, 'It's just the way the game is set up, Mom. You get more and more of your people in the superbus, but if you haven't figured out the routes, you can lose all your best people in a crash' (91). While this reflection is positioned merely as an aside in the novel, the game otherwise irrelevant to the plot and storyline, nevertheless the scenario described arguably articulates the text's final assessment of right-wing Covid-19 policies, wherein these too involve a game of risk without any determined safe route, a politics of chance which ignores any clear sense of social obligation. With Klara ultimately left aside to rust in the scrapyard, and Rick fending for himself in an increasingly fractured country, Josie's own elite flourishing appears here not as success but merely social disregard, an implicit condemnation of humanist thinking within a now post-human world.

The implications of this ending for the novel's larger post-pandemic vision suggest a nod to a still more precarious future soon to come, wherein, as the world gradually begins to exit lockdown and loosen existing safeguarding regulations, ideas of community continue to shift towards disregard and individualism. Indeed, rather than applauding the various social safety-nets set in place during the pandemic period, which might include government investments in vaccine trials, furlough programmes, stimulus packages, volunteering incentives and educational programmes, what lies at the heart of this novel is an attention to the failures within contemporary social and political thinking to take into account the well-being of disadvantaged populations at a more systemic level and the larger effect this has had on community experiences. While perhaps there is still hope present in the novel's vision of Josie's miraculous recovery, and indeed perhaps even in the fact that she no longer needs Klara to provide her company, when considered as a larger whole, the novel is despairing about the future that awaits us, where voices like that of Klara and Rick remain distinctly passed over. If things are to improve, the text suggests, the post-human will need more properly to come into our vision.

## Notes

1 The high cost of these technologies, and their consequent inaccessibility to all but the most elite, speaks of the novel's anxieties regarding socio-economic division. As Emba reflects, 'If the benefits of human enhancement accrue only to the upper classes, it seems likely that inequality will be entrenched in ways deeper than just wealth, fundamentally challenging our egalitarian ideals' (2016: n.p.). Certainly, such fears are apparent in the wealth distinctions the novel draws between Josie and Rick, where the former's 'lifted' status emerges as aligned to her relative socio-economic privilege.
2 It bears noting how Jean-Luc Nancy's critical reinterpretation of Heidegger's existentialism to focus on the concept of *mitsein* (being-with) can also be placed in dialogue with the post-human here as foregrounding the constitutive role of relationality. As Marie-Eve Morin explains, 'For Nancy … Being is always already the plurality of articulated beings, which already themselves make sense, and which can, only because of this original and intrinsic articulation, come to be signified' (2009: 44). Indeed, 'for Nancy, singular being is always a corporeal being, a place of existence … A body is impenetrable, but it is not isolated or absolved' (45). In this way, Nancy's *mitsein* shares with post-humanism a similar focus on embodiment and interdependency, likewise seemingly underpinning Klara's distinctly relational approach to community. A special thanks to Peter Ely for drawing my attention to this.
3 It is worth recognizing how the questions the novel raises both about AI technologies and pandemic-era community are brought together through recent innovations around robot technology similar to those imagined in the novel, designed precisely as a way of mitigating loneliness during Covid-19. See Odekerken-Schröder et al. (2020) and DeFalco (2020).
4 For some analyses of these types of campaigns, see Buckland (2020); Carlsen, Toubøl and Brincker (2021); Lachance (2021); Mudera et al. (2021); Trautwein, Liberatore and Lindenmeier (2020).

# References

Anker, Elizabeth S. (2016) '"Commonly Human": Embodied Self-Possession and Human Rights in Jamaica Kincaid's *The Autobiography of My Mother*', in Sophia A. McClennen and Alexandra Schultheis Moore (eds), *The Routledge Companion to Literature and Human Rights*, 37–45, London: Routledge.

Arcimaviciene, Liudmila, and Sercan Hamza Baglama (2018), 'Migration, Metaphor and Myth in Media Representations: The Ideological Dichotomy of "Them" and "Us"', *Sage Open*, 8 (2), https://journals.sagepub.com/doi/10.1177/2158244018768657.

Bauman, Zygmunt (2000), *Liquid Modernity*, Cambridge: Polity.

Bauman, Zygmunt (2003), *Wasted Lives: Modernity and Its Outcasts*, Oxford: Wiley.

BBC (2018, October 14), 'Melania Trump Says "Don't Care" Jacket Was a Message', BBC News. https://www.bbc.co.uk/news/world-us-canada-45853364.

Black, Shameem (2009), 'Ishiguro's Inhuman Aesthetics', *Modern Fiction Studies*, 55 (4): 785–807.

Boxall, Peter (2013), *Twenty-First Century Fiction: A Critical Introduction*, Cambridge: Cambridge University Press.

Braidotti, Rosi (2013), *The Posthuman*, Cambridge: Polity.

Braidotti, Rosi (2015), 'Yes, There Is No Crisis: Working towards the Posthumanities', *DiGeSt. Journal of Diversity and Gender Studies*, 2 (1–2): 9–20.

Buckland, Rosalyn (2020), 'Medical Student Volunteering during Covid-19: Lessons for Future Interprofessional Practice', *Journal of Interprofessional Care*, 34 (5): 679–81.

Butler, Judith, and Gayatri Chakravorty Spivak (2007), *Who Sings the Nation-State?*, London: Seagull.

Butler, Judith, and George Yancy (2020), 'Judith Butler: Mourning Is a Political Act Amid the Pandemic and Its Disparities, *Truthout*, 30 April, https://truthout.org/articles/judith-butler-mourning-is-a-political-act-amid-the-pandemic-and-its-disparities/.

Carlsen, Hjalmar Bang, Jonas Toubøl and Benedikte Brincker (2021), 'On Solidarity and Volunteering during the COVID-19 Crisis in Denmark: The Impact of Social Networks and Social Media Groups on the Distribution of Support', *European Societies*, 23 (1): S122–40.

Cohn, Simon, and Rebecca Lynch (2017), 'Posthuman Perspectives: Relevance for a Global Public Health', *Critical Public Health*, 27 (3): 285–92.

Crawley, Ester, Maria Loades, Gene Feder, Stuart Logan, Sabi Redwood and John Macleod (2020), 'Wider Collateral Damage to Children in the UK because of the Social Distancing Measures Designed to Reduce the Impact of COVID-19 in Adults', *BMJ Paediatrics Open*, 4 May: 1–4.

DeFalco, Amelia (2020), 'Towards a Theory of Posthuman Care: Real Humans and Caring Robots', *Body and Society*, 26 (3): 31–60.

Doherty, Jane, and James Giordano (2020), 'What We May Learn – and Need – from Pandemic Fiction', *Philosophy, Ethics, and Humanities in Medicine*, 15 (4), https://peh-med.biomedcentral.com/articles/10.1186/s13010-020-00089-0.

Emba, Christine (2016), 'Opinion: Will Technology Allow Us to Transcend the Human Condition', *Washington Post*, 16 May, https://www.washingtonpost.com/news/in-theory/wp/2016/05/16/will-technology-allow-us-to-transcend-the-human-condition/.

Flannery, Halina, Sara Portnoy, Xeni Daniildi, Chandrika Kambakara Gedara, Gina Korchak, Danielle Lambert, James McParland, Lara Payne, Tania Salvo, Charlotte Valentino and Deborah Christie (2021), 'Keeping Young People Connected during COVID-19: the Role of Online Groups', *Archives of Disease in Childhood*, 17 February, https://adc.bmj.com/content/early/2021/02/17/archdischild-2020-320222.

Fleming, Nic (2021), 'After Covid, Will Digital Learning Be the New Normal?' *Guardian*, 23 January, https://www.theguardian.com/education/2021/jan/23/after-covid-will-digital-learning-be-the-new-normal.

Fullan, Michael, Joanne Quinn, Max Drummy and Mag Gardner (2020), 'Education Reimagined: The Future of Learning', http://aka.ms/HybridLearningPaper.

Gunter, Joel (2018), 'What Is the Einstein Visa and How Did Melania Trump Get One?', *BBC News*, 2 March, https://www.bbc.co.uk/news/world-us-canada-43256318.

Hayles, N. Katherine (1999), *How We Became Posthuman: Virtual Bodies in Cybernetics, Literature, and Informatics*, Chicago: University of Chicago Press.

Ishiguro, Kazuo (2021), *Klara and the Sun*, London: Faber and Faber.

James, Caryn (2021), 'Kazuo Ishiguro Returns to Literary Sci-Fi with "Klara and the Sun"', *Wall Street Journal Magazine*, 2 March, https://www.wsj.com/articles/kazuo-ishiguro-klara-and-the-sun-new-book-interview-11614692315.

Kneedler, Jennie (2020), 'Impact of Covid-19 on the Immigration System', *American Bar Association*, 7 December, https://www.americanbar.org/groups/public_interest/immigration/immigration-updates/impact-of-covid-19-on-the-immigration-system/.

Knight, Will (2021), 'Klara and the Sun Imagines a Social Scheme Driven by AI', *Wired*, 8 March, https://www.wired.com/story/kazuo-ishiguro-interview/.

Lachance, Erik (2021), 'COVID-19 and its Impact on Volunteering: Moving towards Virtual Volunteering', *Leisure Sciences*, 43 (1–2): 104–10.

Massumi, Brian (2002), *Parables for the Virtual: Movement, Affect, Sensation*, Durham, NC: Duke University Press.

Meyer, Lily (2020), 'The Literature of the Pandemic Is Already Here', *Atlantic*, 22 July, https://www.theatlantic.com/culture/archive/2020/07/zadie-smith-decameron-project-pandemic-literature/614458/.

Morin, Marie-Eve (2009), 'Thinking Things: Heidegger, Sartre, Nancy', *Sartre Studies International*, 15 (2): 35–53.

Mudera, Cariappa P., Rohit D. Bavdekar, Narinder Kumar, Aravind Veiraiah and Ranjith K. Nair (2021), 'Reaching Out to the Millions: A 5 Key Messages Rapid IEC Campaign during the COVID-19 Pandemic'. *International Quarterly of Community Health Education*, 16 March.

Musolff, Andreas (2016), *Political Metaphor Analysis: Discourse and Scenarios*, London: Bloomsbury.

Nguyen, Clara V. (2021), '"Klara and the Sun" Review: Kazuo Ishiguro's Shining Ode to Love', *Harvard Crimson*, 16 March, https://www.thecrimson.com/article/2021/3/16/klara-and-the-sun-science-fiction-novel-review-kazuo-ishiguro/.

Odekerken-Schröder, Gaby, Christina Mele, Tiziana Russo-Spena, Dominik Mahr and Andrea Ruggiero (2020), 'Mitigating Loneliness with Companion Robots in the COVID-19 Pandemic and Beyond: An Integrative Framework and Research Agenda', *Journal of Service Management*, 31 (6): 1149–62.

Preston, Alex (2021), 'Klara and the Sun by Kazuo Ishiguro Review – Another Masterpiece', *Observer*, 1 March, https://www.theguardian.com/books/2021/mar/01/klara-and-the-sun-by-kazuo-ishiguro-review-another-masterpiece.

Ramgobin, Devyani, Brendan McClafferty, Courtney Kramer, Reshma Golamari, Brian McGillen and Rohit Jain (2021), 'Papering Over the Cracks: COVID-19's Amplification of the Failures of Employer-based Health Insurance Coverage', *Journal of Community Hospital Internal Medicine Perspectives*, 11 (1): 107–10.

Rimmer, Stuart (2020), 'Exploring Online Learning and Student Mental Health', *Association of Colleges*, November, https://www.aoc.co.uk/exploring-online-learning-and-student-mental-health.

Scrivner, Coltan, John A. Johnson, Jens Kjeldgaard-Christiansen and Mathias Clasen (2021), 'Pandemic Practice: Horror Fans and Morbidly Curious Individuals Are More Psychologically Resilient During the COVID-19 Pandemic', *Personality and Individual Differences*, 168: 1–6.

Slaughter, Joseph (2007), *Human Rights, Inc*, New York: Fordham University Press.

Spinney, Laura (2020), 'The Covid Novels Are Arriving: And They'll Be a Warning to Future Generations', *Guardian*, 7 August, https://www.theguardian.com/commentisfree/2020/aug/07/covid-novels-warning-future-generations-first-world-war-spanish-flu-1918.

Trautwein, Stefan, Florian Liberatore and Jörg Lindenmeier (2020), 'Satisfaction with Informal Volunteering During the COVID-19 Crisis: An Empirical Study Considering a Swiss Online Volunteering Platform', *Nonprofit and Voluntary Sector Quarterly*, 49 (6): 1142–51.

Vellino, Brenda Carr (2016), 'Beyond the Trauma Aesthetic: The Cultural Work of Human Rights Witness Poetries', in Sophia McClennen and Alexandra Schultheis Moore (eds), *The Routledge Companion to Literature and Human Rights*, 148–58, London: Routledge.

Vermeulen, Peter (2014), 'Posthuman Affect', *EJES: European Journal of English Studies*, 18 (2): 121–34.

Walsh, Colleen (2021), 'Young Adults Hardest Hit by Loneliness during Pandemic', *Harvard Gazette*, 17 February, https://news.harvard.edu/gazette/story/2021/02/young-adults-teens-loneliness-mental-health-coronavirus-covid-pandemic/.

Wind, Tim R., Marleen Rijkeboer, Gerhard Andersson and Heleen Riper (2020), 'The COVID-19 Pandemic: The "Black Swan" for Mental Health Care and a Turning Point for E-health', *Internet Interv*, 20 April, https://www.ncbi.nlm.nih.gov/pmc/articles/PMC7104190/.

# 9

# Even the ghosts: Community in the wake

## Sara Upstone

At the beginning of summer my daughter plants a sunflower seed. There is an old bomb shelter in the garden, a relic from a war that neither of us can remember, and we place it expectantly atop the concrete structure. The summer is wet, and a thin spread of green moss grows over the earth. Each morning, we venture into the garden. A row of roses by the fence erupts into bloom. The earth in the newly planted pot remains unbroken.

It has been the longest year. My chronically ill body has encased me within the walls of our home, and everything is smaller. It is hard to remember what came before this now, what thought occupied the empty space before the incessant attention to staying alive.

When I try to locate myself, I find that I am no longer intelligible. Each weightless drop of a mask or breaking of a social distance slides my relation into an atmospheric perspective, my colours cooled, my sharp lines of selfhood troubled in a blurred and quiet hue.

I look for the words to write this down, amidst *ecriture feminine* and nation language, but I know no form for my broken-bodied unintelligible subject. Instead, without speaking, I invite the others I cannot see:

In a story called *Lanny*, a young boy, lost far from home.

In a book called *Broken Ghosts*, Emma, and Cowley, and Adam: three strangers, standing on a Welsh mountain after a drug-fuelled evening, watching strange lights in the sky – a single mother, a Scotsman and a recovering drug addict trying to stay clean.

In the pages of *Even the Dogs*, Robert, an alcoholic on the autopsy table, and his friends: some named, some nameless, some homeless.[1]

There are more, of course, that I have forgotten here.

I am reminded of how, in her book *In the Wake: On Blackness and Being* (2016), Christina Sharpe writes of living with the inheritance of horrors our ancestors have seen, and how an ethics of care can evolve by inhabiting the trauma of this past and recognizing its echoes in the present and its capacities for the future. To inhabit this precarity, the unsettling heirloom of trauma, I think, is to come with arms outstretched towards a community of care in which no one is forgotten. To reach in the heaviness of a wake that goes back further than can be remembered, to a haunting of this moment with the ripples resonant of those that have preceded us. In the echoes comes the lesson of a bequest, to know how it is that those who once were all flesh and feeling have become invisible. But also to feel the breath of a whisper of a promise.

To look forward into history and to find an encounter there with a spectre and a secret from which things could begin again in a slow dance of responsibility.

I turn to something I have written, something on a new kind of fiction, a writing that is *transglossic* (Shaw and Upstone 2021). An envelopment of voices. A removal of the singular. How would a criticism like this look, I ask myself? What does it mean to write a community of criticism? To be gently with the others. The author, the character, the narrator, and the critic; these trestled singings that are never separate, but from which the last – the critic – is often stood apart.

We write this down.

There is a rhythm to objects, Henri Lefebvre and Catherine Régulier (2003) write, those things that surround the body which as much as the body itself are a tremble of atoms. The words which come defy the pace of a typewriter, quavers and crochets, the Morse code clicking of keys. Slow, languorous semibreves typed in early mornings, the keyboard a pen, the screen as paper. Words waiting, in fragments, for answers.

* * *

One day we come into the garden and a stem has grown overnight, as if some magical feeding has taken place. The stalk is crooked, turned to the east, an invisible flower orienting itself towards the sun. From the front window of the house we can see across the street, a neat line of tall, triumphant yellow flowers standing proudly, erect, in a neighbour's garden.

We are waiting for the world to begin again.

Roland is also waiting. It helps to think of him as Roland in this moment, not as Barthes – not as the philosopher – but as the man, waiting for a rendezvous. He is waiting for a lover to arrive. '[a]m I in love? – Yes, since I'm waiting' (Barthes 1978: 39–40), he writes. As he waits, Roland perhaps cannot help but make his personal encounter a little more. It is just the way his mind works, the event pushing against its singularity:

> I depend on a presence which is shared and requires time be bestowed-as if were a question of lowering my desire, lessening my need. *To make someone wait*: the constant prerogative of all power. (40, original emphasis)

In knowledge of this power game, Roland tries to take the other's place: '[i] try to busy myself elsewhere, to arrive late; but I always lose at this game: whatever I do, I find myself there, with nothing to do, punctual even ahead of time. The lover's fatal identity is precisely: *I am the one who waits*' (39–40, original emphasis).

We know that Barthes is correct. It is fatal, this waiting. A fatal identity that places us always in a place of precarity: '*[t]o make someone wait*: the constant prerogative of all power'.

McGregor's chorus of homeless voices repeats this 'waiting', the word resonant as a refrain for page after page in lyrical prose. It is part of a 'vulnerable form' (Ganteau 2013: para 6), the performance of an ethical gesture that puts the words in harmony with those it aims to describe. In every basic function this waiting determines the place of the homeless: waiting for help, for a drink, a hit; the wait for a hostel, for a place in rehab, for benefits. And finally just '[w]aiting for what' (*ETD*: 69), the emptiness of experience captured in the unfinished sentence and the absence of an event.

Emma, Cowley and Adam – 'a slapper an-a nutter an-a ex-junkie' (*BG*: 17) – are also waiting. Waiting for their vision to be believed, waiting for recognition. Waiting, in a town that is a 'dome of scorched and seething need' (168), for something to still their restlessness – for Cowley, a job; for Adam, a new start; and for Emma, some beauty she can feel when 'in my heart, in the bit where it counts, there's nothing' (150).

Trapped in the storm drain, Lanny is waiting too.

Community, Jean-Luc Nancy tells us, is 'being-in-common', the understanding of a coexistence that is more than shared space or time, that is the recognition of our being in the world as always in the play between the individual and all others, 'the *in* that divides and joins at the same time' (1991: 8, original emphasis). Yet as we wait, it is impossible to be in a community with those who make us wait. Though we share a space with the woman who 'didn't even look' (*ETD*: 22) and those who 'turn away' (23), with the bearded poets or the university students, the 'pampered bastards' who will 'never burn inside' (249), yet we are no more than 'with' them. There will be no 'in' because 'it's still you and them. And it always fuckin will be' (65). We might invoke Emmanuel Levinas here, too. We might speak of the community as that which is only possible when the face of the other is seen – not to look out together on a shared landscape, 'a collectivity that is not a communion' (Levinas [1947] 1987: 94), but rather to face each other. For McGregor's voices say it plainly: 'They don't see us' (*ETD*: 4).

In this invisibility, we have already been put to death. It therefore matters little whether Emma, Cowley and Adam are alive or dead when the police break up the commune, or that Lanny is rescued after the village consider him to be dead. It is not unsurprising that both Robert's friends and Papa Toothwort may tell a story or save a boy, that as ghosts they are as alive and capable of agency as those who breathe.

There is no contradiction, either, between the acceptance of these deaths and a certain kind of community, much unlike Nancy's. Or rather we should say, our deaths are that upon which a certain kind of community relies. While Roland waits, Derrida (and it is helpful here not to think of him as Jacques) writes about us in *The Gift of Death* ([1999] 2008). He tells the biblical story of Abraham, the prophet who climbs a mountain to sacrifice his son, and asks, 'is not the spectacle of this murder, which seems untenable in the dense and rhythmic briefness of its theatrical moment, at the same time the most common event in the world?' (85):

> Everything is organized to insure this man would be condemned by any civilized society ... On the other hand, the smooth functioning of such a society, the monotonous complacency [*ronronnement*] of its discourses on morality, politics, and the law, and the very exercise of its rights (whether public, private, national, or international) are in no way perturbed by the fact that, because of the structure of the laws of the market that society has instituted and controls, because of the mechanisms of external debt and other comparable inequalities, that same 'society' *puts to* death or (but failing to help someone in distress accounts for only a minor difference) *allows to die* of hunger and disease tens of millions of children (those relatives or fellow humans that ethics or the discourse of the rights of man refer to) without any moral or legal tribunal ever being considered competent to judge such a sacrifice, the sacrifice of the other to avoid being sacrificed oneself. (86, original emphases)

We draw particular attention to 'because of the structure of the laws of the market ... the sacrifice of the other to avoid being sacrificed oneself"' (86), a certain kind of imperative that one can only call 'political'.

In the British press, every report on the spread of the lethal virus reassures the political community that the dead have underlying conditions. The government has produced clear guidelines to manage such loss, for it accepts that 'not only does such a society participate in this incalculable sacrifice, it actually organizes it' (86).

The disproportionate deaths of care home residents in their place of abode is in these circumstances unfortunate, the government declares, but it is now time to *get back to normal.*

Or, in other words, we must not confuse a temporary interruption with a waiting.

Papa Toothwort awakens wearing a mask (*Lanny*: 3), and this ancient spirit costumed for today is a prescient reminder that being in the wake is always a connection to something with roots, to the slow drip of time which feeds the watershed. So, far before this moment, Robert's friends tell us that it is when we have 'a turned ankle or a cracked skull or a diabetic epileptic fit' that we are 'most invisible at all … Like they'll leave you there for days, Like they'll leave you there as long it takes' (*ETD*: 58). When even some of us are named, it is those whose bodies are broken who come without recognition; it is the old man in the wheelchair of whom we must declare, 'we know him but we don't know his name', must admit that '[h]e's not even that old' but 'it's something to call him' (*ETD*: 2). Adam, too, has seen it. He remembers his trip to the Cwm Rheidol butterfly house. Remembers needing 'nothing more, in that time and in that place' (225). He remembers a man arriving with his family and going into the café and asking for a bucket of water to clean his car while his family go in to the view the 'stunning things' (226). And 'somehow it is linked, this is what he wants to say', his memory of the beauty of the flower and a world in which the car is everything, in which 'the car has to shine' (227). It is this experience which tells him that he has been released clean into a world 'governed by an infatuation with money, obsessed with money to the point that people with money enough to support them through a thousand generations are encouraged to make more, always more', 'so obsessed that they will kill to make more, lay cities desolate' (*BG*: 55).

Far away, in another timeline, Adolf Hitler signs on personal stationery an order for the 'mercy killing' of the incurably ill. This includes those with epilepsy, schizophrenia, general paralysis, Huntington's disease and other neurological conditions. The main criterion for inclusion is if the subject is 'not employable in institutional work beyond doing purely mechanical tasks' (Rotzoll et al. 2006: 20).

We watch this from the wake. We watch, and count: the 70,273 of 1939–41 (Rotzoll et al. 2006: 22) and the 80,000 and growing of 2019–21.[2] And we are reminded of what Derrida says: 'failing to help someone in distress accounts for *only a minor difference*' ([1999] 2008: 86, my italics).

And what is the story of *Even the Dogs* if not an ethnic cleansing, if not precisely this kind of murder. The title of the book brings us to this realization: a town in war-torn Bosnia on which a policeman declares '[t]here is nothing for you there. There, even the dogs are dead' (113). We know that this is as bad as it gets. When we find Robert's body, his dog Penny is dead beside him. Inhabiting this place, this Britain, where even the dogs are dead.

Waiting for some money, waiting to score, Danny sits his dog Einstein next to him because he knows that the passers-by who cannot see him will turn and drop their heads in compassion to the animal at his feet.

It is, then, a matter of life and death, this community. It is a matter of justice, for the courts are 'another place where we know how to sit and wait' (*ETD*: 85). We sit, waiting, without knowing that justice is that which 'must not wait' (Derrida 1992a: 26). As we wait, we are in the service of this politics which must discriminate in the name of the market, which means we are 'completely powerless to induce the slightest effective change', because we cannot 'assign the least responsibility' (Derrida [1999] 2008: 86). When the moment of revelation comes, the judgement against Emma, Cowley and Adam is clear – 'a slut, and a junkie and a thug ... Our innocent peasants? I do not think so' (*BG*: 294), say the journalists. We go with Danny's friend, Charmaine, to the housing office and watch as she tells the story of her mum's boyfriend threatening to hit her baby, who 'told them all this down the Housing but all they heard her say was I left home', meaning intentionally homeless (*ETD*: 27). And we see Heather, who loses custody of her child and asks the courts to wait for her to sort herself out, who promises to get it together, who testifies but is told 'it's not a question of waiting. This is a permanent order' (104). And, finally, we are there with the body of Robert himself. Silent, but failing to be credible. His bruises discounted because it is a tendency of alcoholics to frequently fall. When only a bullet hole, the detective declares, will be seen as proof of crime.

In such moments we are always in the wake; we are not even an 'ex-junkie' anymore. This is what Miranda Fricker calls 'testimonial injustice', a 'prejudice in the economy of credibility' (2007: 1) that can only be seen in the 'socially situated conception' (4). Lanny's mum says she cannot draw, and Pete knows 'someone must have said something' to turn that into truth because his own mum never sang, someone telling her when she was young that she could not hold a tune (*Lanny*: 15). But the individual here is just an unconscious conduit; for testimonial injustice is socially and structurally embedded, a stereotype formed in the 'social imagination' (Fricker 2007: 4) that says *you are not credible to be believed*.

Or, in short, it is a community that makes us wait. This community that Fricker calls the 'community of epistemic trust' (45).

We see the woman in the court follow her explanation to Heather by asking 'do you understand what that means?' (*ETD*: 104). She recognizes that though we are perhaps the most intelligent, the knowledge to make sense of our own inequality has been secreted away from us, that we cannot communicate what it is the system has denied, for that power is itself a function of the deprivation. In this sense, we are subject to what Fricker calls a 'situated hermeneutical inequality' (2007: 7), which is to say we have been refused the acquaintance to understand the othering, the starvation of our discursive empowerment which means we are barred from membership of a communal structure, 'a gap in collective interpretive resources ... an unfair disadvantage when it comes to making sense of their social experiences' (1).

This is the difference between Adam and Cowley – Adam, who is full of knowledge, brimming with it; who knows the politicians, listing them by name, and the policy; and who leads a diatribe against the 'enforced sameness ... a widespread attitude ... government enforced' where 'people are killing themselves, in this isolated, inward-looking, mean country that its populace voted for it to become' (*BG*: 74–5); and Cowley, who only knows his injustice, and who then sees only an imagined Europe as the answer to his suffering, who thinks that Brexit will not make a difference but who also thinks maybe it is worth it if it means the waiting might stop. There is, here, what Robert Eaglestone (2018) calls a cruel nostalgia, but there is more than that, too. For it is hard in such moments not to imagine something better, to remember a past he cannot possibly recall, when the Romans and the English came, and the Welsh climbed the hills where 'we'd build our own places ... little towns all a-way up' (*BG*: 134).

And there is, as we turn backwards in the wake, some connection here between our living death and that other demise, the loss of our collective international selves. There is some assemblage we want to speak of, although it is not as straightforward as we might like, not as simple as saying that loving one's European neighbour is the same as rescuing one's vulnerable compatriots. For Derrida points to the 'non-neighbor not as private enemy but as foreigner' ([1999] 2008: 104). Yet he also says that Europe is that which has neglected its responsibility to the other, asking 'why does it suffer from ignorance of its history, from a failure to assume its responsibility, that is, the memory of its history *as* history of responsibility?' (6). So though we want to say that these situations are the same, want to ask how it is possible to make a community across nations if you cannot protect the stranger, yet we cannot. There is no easy way to find a place in our conversation for the old lady who Lanny's mum approaches when he goes missing, who calls the boy a 'moping little gypsy' whose mother 'may as well be a foreigner' and mourns 'the real community … a community that is dead and gone thanks to people like her, buying up houses' (*Lanny*: 114–15). For, if, in the denial of our identity, we become closer to the stereotype, then that is to be expected – it is, indeed, part of how the system secures itself, 'identity power's ability to shape the people it cramps' (Fricker 2007: 56).

We were the softest, once, but our words have ossified with the prohibition of our tears.

As the masks slip, and the restrictions ease, we cannot name our mistreatment. There has been no conscious raising, no groups organized, no education programmes to tell us how to mobilize our thoughts. We are unintelligible to ourselves. The only protection of one's identity there can be in such moments is to gather closer together with those for whom trust remains, to find the 'solidarity and shared resources' (54) of those who share the same injustice as yourself.

And it would be an answer certainly. It would be the best answer for everyone to say that this were a community; that we, in our waiting, are a community for ourselves. And indeed some might call us that, even if that community is a 'community of the bereft' (Ganteau 2013: para 7). But as Fricker explains, 'The mere fact that one might live around other individuals in the same predicament is insufficient for affiliation to a community' (2007: 55).

And we know this. The voices say that Robert 'had all of us' (*ETD*: 30), but he dies alone. He lives around many others, but he dies in the stillness of his own breathing slowing, the shock of his own steady rhythm turned to a gasp and nothing else, each of us who speaks of him isolated by our own suffering, addiction or pain. When Robert's daughter Laura comes to visit, it is a moment of 'all the waiting come to an end' (99), and we want to believe that this will be the moment, that this will be the instant when it comes. But there is no peace that follows, the cliché and the reality butted up against each other in the taste of salt on skin: 'his tears all wiped away or something more or less like that' (99).

Less like that.

\* \* \*

A bud appears, a cocoon of petals birthed from the sunlight and the rain.

The world decides it is time to go out.

Roland admits that 'Sometimes I want to play the part of the one who doesn't wait' (Barthes 1978: 39–40).

We are surprised to find that Derrida has offered a reply. For our murder, he reminds us, is 'not even invisible'; for despite our othering 'a few voices are raised to bring it all to our attention' (Derrida [1999] 2008: 86).

What if we begin community here, we ask, in this wake where we are seen? To ask, as Derrida does, '[w]hat would responsibility be if it were motivated, conditioned, made possible by a history?' (7). To ask, as Sharpe does, 'what would justice mean?' if we accepted the legacy of exclusions upon which it rests. For Sharpe, writing on race, to think, '[w]hat happens when we proceed as if we *know* this, antiblackness, to be the ground on which we stand, the ground from which we attempt to speak, for instance, an "I" or a "we" who know, an "I" or a "we" who care?' (2016: 7).

In the stories, we ask these questions. While in this place the answers are absent, in the rhythm of the book, in the forward and backward turn of paper and the broken time of reading, something else takes place. From the space of exclusion, from the site of unintelligibility, a fracture of light opens. Into the political community comes through the backward glance of the wake the possibility of something other, something transcendent. It is what we might call an 'ethical community'. For it is ethics, and not politics, that it at stake in epistemic injustice (Fricker 2007: 2), Ethics here that 'remains on the side of the transcendent, the infinite or the unconditional', where 'what opposes this realm is named politics' (Fagan 2013: 131).

As we see Robert cut open on the autopsy table, his name unknown, a plural voice recounts the rituals of remembrance he should have had. All bound in sacrament, we find the verbal construction of a sacred space in which Robert's dead body is given its weight; it is the recognition of a community in which he was valued and irreplaceable, a non-monetary value of selfhood distinct from the imperatives of the political, a Viking burial of 'all his family and friends' (*ETD*: 40), or 'another place or time' with 'crowds, and carriages' (55).

After the mountain, too, Emma posts her story on social media and what happens is proof that '[o]nce I speak, I am never and no longer myself, alone and unique' (Derrida [1999] 2008: 61). People begin to gather where she, Adam and Cowley saw the lights in the sky. Against all of Cowley's brash noise, against the pub with its rowdy conversation, there is a new prose for what happens on the top of the mountain:

Under circling satellites whose lights like that of the stars wink out with the returning day yet whose clicks and pulses continue to relay data through airless wastes at last it is noiselessly broken into nothing at the eastern shore of Llyn

Syfydrin where, in the reeds, a sign of slat on slat has been erected and which on the cross-beam reads:

*Llyn y welediageth*

*croeso pawb*. (*BG*: 114)

The words which make an explicit promise: '**lake vision,** *everyone* **welcome**'.

This space, enshrined not by law, or by boundary, is one in which all who come are 'citizens' (327). Europeans and the clinically vulnerable are welcome here; there are babies, and those too old to walk – 'even some in wheelchairs … A huge EU flag flaps against the sky' (310). This cacophony, this conterminous everything, is not Europe as it is, but as it might be, the concept of Europe that for Derrida is a *democracy to come* which has always rather been a 'concept to come of democracy' (2005: 8), the promise of a future term which signifies both equality and freedom. We watch the act of Emma making biscuits for her son and find a metaphor for this community, the young boy unable to understand how a collection of such diverse elements can make the whole:

– How'd you make these biscuits?
  I tell him and he looks puzzled – But all that stuff's wet, he says.
– Ey?
– The eggs and the milk. All that stuff's wet.
– Aye, so?
– Well, how come these are crunchy and nice?
– The heat in the oven does that.
– How, tho?
– Magic. (*BG*: 46)

We see here in hands wet with batter, in the rise of heat, in these slides of matter, a metaphor of defiance against hermeneutics and its inequalities. A realization of what Fred Moten and Stefano Harney call the 'undercommons', an implicitly Nancian 'way of being with others' (2013: 112), a space where shared action creates a collective thinking (or 'study'), an anarchic community without definition that resists global capital and its organizing structures and a defiant claim for being in the world, joyfully and centrally. The mountain is loud, and vociferous, and frequently filled with the voices of the abject and the impure. It is, in many ways, intolerable. Which is another way of saying that it is a space of pure, unconditional hospitality, a movement beyond 'what I know, control, predict, can limit or decide on' which it is not to be confused with hospitality's opposite: the conditional safety of tolerance (Fagan 2013: 84).

The voices against this community call it a 'commune'; they talk of illegal immigrants, and of the trespass of private land, and of law:

> *Society, to function properly, needs structure. It needs the rules of social contract, mutually beneficial to all involved. This, ah, this gathering; well, this kind of thing, if left unchecked, could usher in the very breakdown of that. We will have a dispersal, make no mistake about that.* (*BG*: 261, original emphasis)

In the rule of law, the idea of 'mutually beneficial to all' (261) somehow leads to a dispersal, which means an 'all' that is not everyone. It is an irony that is not lost on us that this dispersal is to be carried out in the name of a Criminal Justice Act (275).

In the stories, however, the laws can be broken. Elsewhere, we see Pete let Lanny into his home. Pete who opens the door with hospitality and calls Lanny 'my friend' (*Lanny*: 24). This man and boy who see each other and disrupt Pete's language of '*my* kitchen' and '*my* paper' (*Lanny*: 19, my italics) with a shared inhabitancy. A man and boy who break the rules of the village, which looks at them with suspicious eyes, a nameless collective reporting on the events.

It breaks the laws, this friendship. Like Nancy's community it relies upon no shared framework, this old man and this young boy. It breaks the laws, this friendship, and opens the space for the decision upon which responsibility relies; for 'wherever I have at my disposable a determinable rule ... there is no longer any place for justice or responsibility (Derrida 2005: 83). Which is why when Lanny goes missing, Pete is there too – not just the parents, doing what parents should, but Pete, too, doing what he chooses. This responsibility, this decision, is for a new kind of community forged in a different kind of waiting: Lanny, who asks, 'Which do you think is more patient, an idea or a hope?' (*Lanny*: 41); Lanny who cries because of the boy in the water charity leaflet, who when his mum says they cannot get their wasted water to him looks at her like she has 'said the most grotesque thing ever uttered' (71). This radical empathy.

To choose a child for this relation is to point to the possibility of the universal. For it is the child, Fricker tells us, who shows the most hope of epistemic justice (2007: 94), existing in a liminal space between observation and socialization. It is the student, the amateur, Moten and Harney declare, whose 'not being-ready, is also kind of an openness to being affected by others' (2013: 116). It is therefore no surprise that Lanny has 'an innate gift for social cohesion' (*Lanny*: 12) that the art project he builds with Pete is not for one other person, but 'for everyone ... to make them fall in love with everything' (58).

In this 'everything' we are brought to a promise, a whispered prayer for a community of justice, a 'hermeneutical micro-climate shared by hearer and speaker' (Fricker 2007: 174) in which the possibility of meaningful testimony arises. And though the child is privileged, others find this too. Near the end, before it all breaks apart, we go with Emma to the mountain as she meets the wayward father of her son. She has been a body 'without territory', driven by 'a wildness inside you to which you must dig down' (*BG*: 39), saying yes to every man or woman who finds her sexually attractive. But here, amongst others, when the long-lost boyfriend tries to kiss her stretch marks, she says, '[n]ot yet … *not yet*' (344, original emphasis). She becomes, then, for the first time, the one who makes another wait. And Adam is here too, overhearing an articulate rendering of his own unheard testimony by a man quite unlike himself but speaking with the same fire as his own (335). In the hermeneutical micro-climate, he and the speaker are part of what Moten prefers to call a 'coalition': 'the recognition that it's fucked up for you, in the same way that it's fucked up for us. I don't need your help. I just need you to recognize that this shit is killing you, too, however much more softly, you stupid motherfucker, you know?' (Moten and Harney 2013: 140–1).

That we are all waiting. All waiting to be rescued.

These communities are not operative, but inoperative. They are communities without product that sparkle against the dull sheen of their unravelling in the 'real world'. What emerges on the mountain is what Adam has already found in the second stage house that he visits after his release from prison. But the second stage house has its funding withdrawn even though it is a success. Sal, who runs the centre, speculates on Brexit, the promised 350 million returned to the NHS and the 'lying fuckers' who promised it (*BG*: 58) – a promise that has not redeemed itself in community, but unravelled it. It is a place of genuine transcendence, where there is no 'rehab' because it is 'not relearning' but 'learning, for the first time' (72), that happens there. And what happens is Derridean 'responsibility and accountability' (64), an ethics constructed through the other as Adam stops seeing people as objects, and instead see them as people, 'so very different and so very the same' (68), but also a space where there is bread on the table and flowers in a vase.

Are there sunflowers growing there, we wonder?

It is not the individuals in relation to each other but the being-in-common that matters here, the 'in' that is the moment of our collective presence. For as Nancy defines it, 'singularity is relationship; it is plural in its very concept' (Fagan 2013: 103); or, in Moten and Harney's words, it is the possibility that comes when 'authoritative speech is detached from the notion of a univocal speaker' (2013: 135). In this model of relation being-in-common implies no commonality in terms of outlook, implies no shared identity; indeed, it is rather the very being-in-common that forms commonality.

In *Even the Dogs* it is always a 'we' that speaks for Robert, always a collective first-person plural. As Halberstam writes that Moten and Harney's use of homelessness is neither a metaphor nor an idealization (2013: 11), the neurotic is recuperated (138) and the collective voice of Robert's friends speaks as a singularity of Harney and Moten's prophets, 'the one who tells the brutal truth, who has the capacity to see the absolute brutality of the already-existing and to point it out and to tell that truth, but also to see the other way, to see what it could be' (131). In Lanny's village, the voices that Papa Toothwort hears, swirling across the novel's pages in unattributed fragments, the curved lines like waves, merge from separate thoughts into later graphics intersecting. Likewise, their voices held in separate chapters, Emma, Cowley and Adam finally come together at the novel's ending. In the trepidatious moment of possibility, just before we watch as the police break it all apart, Adam sees them all in the halo of a helicopter light, and they are 'everyone in its too-bright light looking all exactly the same … I can't make out any individual face at all' (*BG*: 337).

There is bread on the table and flowers in a vase.

\* \* \*

At the end of August the weather settles into its own waiting, for a new season. We clear away the last of the summer vegetables and the paddling pool. We leave the sunflower out on the roof of the bomb shelter, the bud still closed.

We return from stories to find the government declares it is no longer a matter of law but of personal responsibility. In the stores, the legal requirement to wear masks is replaced by a recommendation. The concept of clinical vulnerability is abolished. It is, the popular press declares, 'a freedom day'. We get tape and pins and put the sign back on our front door which reads 'Please leave deliveries on the porch'.

A community, Derrida writes, is a matter of the common – 'the sharing of the incommensurable freedom or equality of each and every one' (2005: 56). And the warfare between these terms, between freedom *or* equality, is a biological warfare of an '*auto-co-immunity*' that attacks itself (35, original emphasis).

We see a slow trickle into the silence, only punctuated by media reports of sickened celebrities, and children, and are reminded of Danny's dog, of a long history of compassion fatigue in which there is an 'unwillingness to give in proportion to demands except when these demands take a spectacular form' (Taithe 2007: 135).

We are reminded of Derrida's words, of the operable community, and the impossible nature of unconditional hospitality. And the hurried, repeated threat of T. S. Eliot's (1922: n.p.) famous verse: 'HURRY UP PLEASE IT'S TIME'.

For its own repeated call Derrida reminds us: 'because of the structure of the laws of the market … the sacrifice of the other to avoid being sacrificed oneself' ([1999] 2008: 86).

Waiting, we understand that the living have given us up for dead.

But we have on our side the intimate touch of voices that haunt the wake – the Viking burials, the ancient villages and the children of folklore – and we are not so easily silenced. In fact, we are not silent at all. Papa Toothwort turns from a tree to a child, becomes himself the agent of hermeneutical justice, drawing Lanny's mother to the drain in the wood where he is trapped. And there is not death, but life. At the inquest into Robert's death, caught in the double meanings of language, a court case ends and the dead are resurrected: 'We rise. What else can we do, we fucking rise' (*ETD*: 195). And as the batons come down on those in the mountain community, even though it is 'all over. Ended', still, 'behind the rocky ridge a sun burns brightly and waits to rise again' (*BG*: 356).

If you do not recognize these resurrections, if they do not seem real, it is because the renaissance moves further and further away. The writers and the critics are aware of this. Even before this pandemic, Alison Donnell speaks of the country's racial politics and writes that 'what may have seemed "optimistically probable" in terms of transforming national culture in the 1990s when Gilroy and Hall published many of their seminal essays on conceptualizing black identity, has now been relegated to the realms of the "hopefully possible"' (2006: 198). Blake Morrison (2019), too, believes '[i]t's dispiriting to think that things have got worse since the years of my adolescence, that the dreams we had of global harmony and understanding, a world purged of racism and xenophobia, now look deeply naive'. The magic of the resurrection holds this fact. The miracle defies the comfort of the happy ending and reminds us of what is only possible within the realms of future hope. These 'alternative topographies of possibility' (Edwards 2019: 2–3) are what Caroline Edwards calls fictions of the 'not yet' (23).

We want to make of this more than a utopia. We ask, instead, for a critical commentary on the present, a transformation into what we once called a utopian realism 'that could be possible as much as impossible' (Upstone 2016: 6).

In the wake, we know that this ambition can only come from a haunting: that it is the view from history that transforms the no place of utopia into here and now. A ghost arrives, a visitation that is proven to be nothing – just a brocken spectre, they say – yet in the envelopment of a transglossic moment is simultaneously everything. We imagine it like the corona of light of St Elmo's Fire warning sailors of their doom, a ship haloed by the electric field of a lightning strike. Yet here, on the mountain, it is the past we see illuminated in the glow of light, the ending we witness also a tether between the world and the fragile ether of our anticipation. And we know from this that it is the past that serves as prototype – that makes the dream into a plan for a potential future. Or what, if we were designers of a new world, we might choose to call a 'design fiction' (Levine 2016).

In the design fiction of the new world, it is a mistake to see these resurrections as a statement of life and to forget what is revealed in the promise of death, in the space of an encounter with what Derrida calls 'the different figures of the gift of death' ([1999] 2008: 12). For in the resurrection, it is always a transaction with the death that is being announced. And so we ask you to consider that we have, perhaps, not been brought back to life but rather back to a spectre of death, to the secret place where we are breathing but always dying:

A slut.
A junkie.
A thug.
Pre-existing conditions.
Useless eaters.

We would like to show you that it is here, in this death both literal and figurative (for there is no difference between the two), that the political community might cede to the ethical community of care. For the encounter with death is an encounter with responsibility. Before his resurrection, Adam has been treated with a 'reality therapy'. What comes from this is an alternative schooling of '[t]hree R's ... realism, responsibility, and right-and-wrong' (*BG*: 77). It is an education in knowing '[i]t is all Real': that 'it was too easy to label people as mentally sick and that problems of behaviour had a deep social component' (78).

Or, in other words, an education in the ethical commitment to those who wait.

Derrida knows that it is in turning to death that we understand such responsibility. For in death, Derrida tells us, we assume something that can neither be given by someone else or taken, that must be taken on by the individual alone, and 'therein lies freedom and responsibility' ([1999] 2008: 45). Abraham walks up the mountain, alone and silent. He walks to his son's death and 'assumes the responsibility that consists in always being alone … retrenched in one's only singularity at the moment of decision' (60). Seeing the face of God, Derrida offers 'a scandal and a paradox', inspired by Levinas, in Abraham's lonely but never alone journey. It is through this encounter with death, then, responsibility as envelopment, both an account of oneself and a simultaneous refusal to speak, that the individual creates what is needed to take responsibility for the other. Not the death of 'simple annihilation' in Heidegger's *Dasein* but a death that is '*of* the other or *for* the other' (48, original emphases). This place, this realization, which is 'the ethical dimension of sacrifice' (48).

The encounter with death, in the wake, that is the ultimate example of what Michael Naas calls Derrida's *example* (1992: xvi), the sample of an event which serves not as representation of a politics but as grounds for its invention.

In a hospital, a previously healthy, unvaccinated man declares his regret at his foolishness. He has seen death. He declares the political community and its economics to be bereft.

Those who have never, prior to the loss of a vote, committed themselves to Europe trace their ancestry and apply for citizenship and a European passport.

We invite you here to this quiet place. To where Robert is dissected on the table and we ask, 'what if they paid this much attention to us all' (*ETD*: 133). To this death that requires, finally, to step inside the other, to in the face of death carry the other and the weight of our broken body. To know, intimately, Levinas's words that 'only a being whose solitude has reached a crispation through suffering, and in relation with death, takes its place on a ground where the relationship with the other becomes possible' ([1947] 1987: 76). To hear that it is only in death that somebody says, '[y]es, that's him' (*ETD*: 161). It is only when Lanny is 'dead', lost and beyond hope to all but his parents, that the community re-enchants itself, 'as if to accept that he is just another missing child is to do a disservice to the place, this charming village, this extra-special place' (*Lanny*: 157).

And we invite you as Emma's old man gives her the meaning of 'bridge' in her vision, as he leans over from its scaffold and lets himself fall, his suicide a resistance: to say, '[d]on't let me fade completely' (*BG*: 120); to say, 'let see them issue a final demand *now*' (121, original emphasis). To this visibility which reminds us that responsibility for the other comes not in the denial of the inevitability of death but in taking no part in its emergence. To a reminder that it is the other who commands not to be killed (Michaelson 2015: 50), who waiting already for death requires that its demise not be precipitated, even if already determined, already inevitable. Who demands that there be no power over its undecided yet inevitable fate.

It is in such a clamour for life that this death, we suggest, is therefore also a refusal to wait. Roland conjures this with the story of a departure:

> A mandarin fell in love with a courtesan. 'I shall be yours,' she told him, 'when you have spent a hundred nights waiting for me, sitting on a stool, in my garden, beneath my window.' But on the ninety-ninth night, the mandarin stood up, put his stool under his arm, and went away. (Barthes 1978: 40)

When Robert's friends rise, when the sun rises at the end of *Broken Ghosts*, when Lanny lives, our encounters with death are also a resistance to those who decide who waits. We are inhabitants, here, in a site of non-being, or what Sharpe calls 'the orthography of the wake', for blackness enshrined in the hold of the slave ship – where to be in the wake is 'to think the ways the hold cannot and does not hold even as the hold remains' (2016: 20–1).

Our death holds us. Yet it does not hold. It is what Halberstam (2011) calls failure's radical possibility. There is no resolution to our stories. Lanny, rescued, becomes but an ordinary boy, huddled behind the bus shelter smoking with his friends. Alive, 'he knows people were cheated of the story they expected. Or wanted' (*Lanny*: 208). He has tried to 'lose the memory of Dead Papa Toothwort' (208), a symbol of this failure of remembrance, this forgetting, that for Halberstam is part of the quiet of death, its failure to completely signify (2011: 86).

We claim it now, this failure, in which we stumble towards the future. We claim it not as the opening of hope to a new way of seeing, but as the design fiction in the wake, as a breath taken in the process of time, a littering in the organization of space and a fucked-up inability to make a successful meaning. To 'work toward the whimper rather than the bang … because "bang" narratives are almost always … "to the speaker's benefit"' (150). To know, as Derrida does, that to be European, one 'must not be European through and through' (1992b: 82), for if one does not fail, then one has closed the door to the other that makes the paradox imaginable.

The dead keep speaking, asking '[f]or how else, but through the morally exceptional discursive moves of the few, is a community able to come to see things differently as a matter of routine?' (Fricker 2007: 107).

Or, in other words, it is death that makes us all, together, possible.

*   *   *

In the third week of September, we go into the garden to clear away the summer.

Image credit: Sara Upstone.

## Notes

My thanks to Kristian Shaw for his comments on an early draft of this chapter, and permission to invoke our joint concept of the transglossic.

1 These texts will be cited in the chapter by abbreviations: *BG* for *Broken Ghosts*; *Lanny* for *Lanny*; and *ED* for *Even the Dogs*.
2 On 13 October 2021, there had been 138,000 deaths in the UK from Covid-19. Figures across the pandemic have consistently put the percentage of disabled deaths at between 58 and 60 per cent (see Bosworth et al. 2021)

## References

Barthes, Roland (1978), *A Lover's Discourse*, trans. Richard Wagner, New York: Hill and Wang.
Bosworth, Matthew, Daniel Ayoubkhani, Vahé Nafilyan, Josephine Foubert, Myer Glickman, Calum Davey and Hannah Kuper (2021), 'Deaths Involving COVID-19 by Self-Reported Disability Status during the First Two Waves of the COVID-19 Pandemic in England: A Retrospective, Population-Based Cohort Study', *Lancet*, 6 October, https://www.thelancet.com/journals/lanpub/article/PIIS2 468-2667(21)00206-1/fulltext.
Derrida, Jacques (1992a), 'Force of Law: The Mystical Foundation of Authority', in Drucilla Cornell, Michel Rosenfeld and David Gray Carlson (eds), *Deconstruction and the Possibility of Justice*, 3–67, New York: Routledge.
Derrida, Jacques (1992b), *The Other Heading: Reflection on Today's Europe*, Bloomington: Indiana University Press.
Derrida, Jacques ([1999] 2008), *The Gift of Death*, 2nd ed., trans. David Wills, Chicago: University of Chicago Press.
Derrida, Jacques (2005), *Rogues: Two Essays on Reason*, Stanford: Stanford University Press.
Donnell, Alison (2006), 'Afterword: In Praise of a Black British Canon and the Possibilities of Representing the Nation "Otherwise"', in Gail Low and Marion Wynne-Davies (eds), *A Black British Canon*, 189–204, Basingstoke: Palgrave Macmillan.
Eaglestone, Robert (2018), 'Cruel Nostalgia and the Memory of the Second World War', in Robert Eaglestone (ed.), *Brexit and Literature: Critical and Cultural Responses*, 92–104, London: Routledge.
Edwards, Caroline (2019), *Utopia and the Contemporary British Novel*, Cambridge: Cambridge University Press.
Eliot, T. S. (1922), *The Waste Land*, https://www.poetryfoundation.org/poems/47311/the-waste-land.

Fagan, Madeline (2013), *Ethics and Politics after Poststructuralism: Levinas, Derrida and Nancy*, Edinburgh: Edinburgh University Press.
Fricker, Miranda (2007), *Epistemic Justice: Power and the Ethics of Knowing*, Oxford: Oxford University Press.
Ganteau, Jean-Michel (2013), 'Trauma and the Ethics of Vulnerability: Jon McGregor's *Even the Dogs*', *Études Britanniques Contemporaines*, 45, http://journals.openedition.org/ebc/940.
Griffiths, Niall (2019), *Broken Ghosts*, London: Jonathan Cape.
Halberstam, Judith (2011), *The Queer Art of Failure*, Durham, NC: Duke University Press.
Lefebvre, Henri and Catherine Régulier (2003), 'The Rhythmanalytical Project', in Imogen Forster (trans.), *Rhythmanalysis: Space, Time and Everyday Life*, 71–84, London: Continuum.
Levinas, Emmanuel ([1947] 1987), 'Time and the Other', in Michael A. Cohen (trans.), *Time and the Other and Additional Essays*, 29–94, Pittsburgh: Duquesne University Press.
Levine, Davis (2016), 'Design Fiction', *Medium*, 13 March, https://medium.com/digital-experience-design/design-fiction-32094e035cd7.
McGregor, Jon (2010), *Even the Dogs*, London: Bloomsbury.
Michaelsen, Cathrine Bjornholt (2015), 'Tracing a Traumatic Temporality: Levinas and Derrida on Trauma and Responsibility', *Levinas Studies*, 10: 43–77.
Morrison, Blake (2019), '"Call Yourself English?', *New Internationalist*, 2 October, https://newint.org/features/2019/08/14/long-read-call-yourself-english.
Moten, Fred and Stefano Harney (2013), *The Undercommons: Fugitive Planning and Black Study*, Oakland: AK.
Naas, Michael (1992), 'Introduction: For Example', in Jacques Derrida (ed.), *The Other Heading: Reflection on Today's Europe*, vii–lix, Bloomington: Indiana University Press.
Nancy, Jean-Luc (1991), 'Of Being-in-Common', in Miami Collective (ed.), *Community at Loose Ends*, 1–12, Minnesota: University of Minnesota Press.
Porter, Max (2019), *Lanny*, London: Faber and Faber.
Rotzoll, Maike, Paul Richter, Petra Fuchs, Annette Hinz-Wessels, Sasha Topp and Gerrit Hohendorf (2006), 'The First National Socialist Extermination Crime: The T4 Program and Its Victims', *International Journal of Mental Health*, 35 (3): 17–29.
Sharpe, Christina (2016), *In the Wake: On Blackness and Being*, Durham, NC: Duke University Press.

Shaw, Kristian and Sara Upstone (2021), 'The Transglossic: Contemporary Fiction and the Limitations of the Modern', *English Studies*, 102 (5): 573–600.
Taithe, Bertrand (2007), 'Horror, Abjection and Compassion: From Dunant to Compassion Fatigue', *New Formations*, 62: 123–36.
Upstone, Sara (2016), *Rethinking Race and Identity in Contemporary British Fiction*, London: Routledge.

# Index

Aboulela, Leila
   *Bird Summons* 82
   *Elsewhere, Home* 17, 69–70, 75–9, 81–2
Afghanistan War 4, 94
Allende, Madame 99–100, 107
Anderson, Benedict 8, 14, 59, 63 n.4, 96
Anker, Elizabeth 182
Applebaum, Anne 12, 42
Arendt, Hannah 12, 25, 30
   *The Origins of Totalitarianism* 30–3, 42
austerity 3, 5, 9, 155

Barthes, Roland 73, 200–1, 206, 215
Bataille, Georges 18, 102
Bauman, Zygmunt 12, 112–13, 123, 191
Benthien, Claudia 135, 137, 139, 148
Berlant, Lauren 54, 62,
Berlant, Lauren, and Warner, Michael 101, 107
Bhabha, Homi 137
Big Society 4, 6
*Bildungsroman* 186
Black Marxism 98–9
Black radical tradition 90, 98, 107
Blair, Tony (*see* The Labour Party)
Blake, William 111–12, 114–17, 158, 172 n.1
Blanchot, Maurice 18, 102
Boxall, Peter 10, 179–80
Boyle, Danny 157–63, 165–8, 171
Bradford Riots 3
Braidotti, Rosi 76, 180–3
Brexit 4–6, 8–9, 11–13, 16–17, 19, 25–8, 32–3, 39, 41, 52–3, 69, 80, 91–3, 155, 157, 161, 163–71, 172 nn.1, 6, 173 n.7, 205, 210
*Brexitland* (Soboloewska and Ford) 25–8, 33, 41
Brexlit 9, 19, 35, 171, 172 n.6
Britain (*see* nation/country)

British Asians 3, 69, 131–6, 140, 142–6, 148–9, 164
Burns, Anne 48
Butler, Judith 180, 189

Cameron, David 4, 91, 171
capitalism 2, 8, 10, 18, 29, 32, 38–9, 90, 92–6, 98, 107, 113–14, 118–20, 122–3, 125, 191, 208
   *Capitalist Realism* (Fisher) 115, 126
Carson, Jan 45–7
   *Children's Children* 45–6, 49–55, 57, 58, 62
   *The Last Resort* 80
Cartwright, Anthony 35
class politics 2, 5, 31, 34, 36, 38–9, 41–2, 53, 56, 76–8, 89, 94–5, 98–9, 113–14, 117, 126 n.1, 127 n.5, 137–41, 160, 165, 168–9, 193 n.1
Codell, Julie F. and MacLeod, Dianne Sachko 136, 139–41
Coe, Jonathan
   *Middle England* 19, 26, 35, 41, 157–72
   *Number 11*, 112, 127 n.6
colonialism 5, 8, 16, 46–7, 49–50, 53, 62–3 n.2, 68–9, 76, 95, 98–9, 107, 133, 135–44, 148–9
anti-colonialism 99–100, 107
post-colonialism 6, 17, 46–7, 53–4, 63 n.1, 75, 90, 131, 134, 140, 162–3, 180
communism 27, 96, 100, 126, 127 n.4
community 1–13, 67–8, 73, 77, 81, 83, 89, 111–14, 116, 123–5, 179–85, 193 n.2, 200–4, 207–9, 211–14
closed community 11, 102–4
*communitas* 125
community cohesion 3, 112–14
counter-community 90, 97, 100–2, 106–7

ethnic/religious community 3–9,
  16–18, 27, 40–1, 47–8, 50–1, 53, 56,
  62, 70, 76–7, 89, 95–7, 131–9, 141–9
global/planetary community 1–11, 15,
  32–3, 75, 92–3, 113–14, 123, 156,
  164–6, 170, 183–4, 189
local/regional community 2–3, 6–7, 9,
  11–12, 37–8, 41, 68–75, 76–9, 81–2,
  113–14, 123–4, 179, 206, 212
national community 5, 8, 16–17,
  25–32, 41–2, 45–8, 67–70, 82–3,
  89–96, 101, 106–7, 108 n.2, 156–60,
  164–5, 167, 170, 180
precarious community 18–19, 37, 48,
  71–4, 81–3, 118, 155–6, 179, 188,
  192, 200
urban community 18, 112–13,
  119–23, 142
Conservative Party 4, 8, 32, 91, 171
conviviality 17, 38, 54, 58, 62
Cornwell, Bernard 34, 39, 41
Coronavirus (*see* Covid-19)
cosmopolitanism 8, 17, 54, 70, 92, 156–7,
  162, 165, 168–9
Covid-19 7, 9, 12–14, 19, 25, 161, 171,
  177–83, 185–9, 192, 193 n.3, 212,
  217 n.2
Cox, Jo 13, 29, 168
Cracknell, Linda 17, 70–2, 74–5, 77, 81
culture wars 27, 30, 165
Cunningham, Michael 8

Davies, Eli 53, 60–2
Delanty, Gerard 113–14, 123, 125
*Demos* 2, 92, 95
Derrida, Jacques 10, 12, 14, 58, 202–5,
  207–9, 211–15
devolution 27, 29–30, 70, 155, 164
Di Masso, Andrés 113, 119–20, 122

England (*see* nation/country)
*Englishness* (Henderson and Jones)
  28–9, 40–1
ethnocentrism 16, 25–30, 32–3, 40–1
European Union 5, 91, 155

Fagan, Madeline 207–8, 210
Fanon, Frantz 136, 138–9, 144–7
Farmer, Barney 34, 37–9, 42

far-right extremism/fascism 7, 27, 30, 189
feminism 90, 93–4, 100, 180
Fisher, Mark (*see* Capitalist Realism)
Floyd, George 13
Fricker, Miranda 204–7, 209–10, 215

Ganteau, Jean-Michel 201, 206
gentrification 113–14, 119–20, 122, 124,
  126, 126 n.1, 127 n.4
ghosts (and haunting) 36, 38, 47, 54–8,
  126, 200, 202, 212–13
Gilbert, Jeremy 2, 5, 89, 93
Gillian Rose 2
Gilroy, Paul 12, 17, 54, 62, 70, 75, 132,
  163, 212
globalization (*see* global community *and*
  capitalism)
Gopal, Priyamvada 99
Gray, Alasdair 69–70
Grenfell Fire 13
Griffiths, Niall 19, 172 n.6, 199, 201,
  203–5, 208–14, 217 n.1

Halberstam, J. 211, 215
Hall, Stuart 12, 92, 134–5, 141–4, 148,
  163, 212
Hand, Felicity 131, 133–4
Harvey, David 115–16, 118, 127 n.2
Hayles, Katherine 181, 183
Hertz, Noreena 29, 41
Hobsbawm, Eric 8, 96, 159
humanism/posthumanism/
  transhumanism 19, 179–83, 187,
  190, 192, 193 n.2
hybridity 2, 11, 14, 46, 62, 75, 89–90, 95,
  97, 133

identity 2, 6, 11, 17, 27–30, 58–9, 70, 73,
  75, 91, 93, 95–6, 101–6, 108 n.4, 114,
  119, 131–2, 134–8, 142–8, 156, 159,
  162–6, 169, 171, 201, 206, 211–12
  (*see also* national community)
incomers 17, 70–2, 74–5, 81
independence movements 6, 17, 27–8,
  67–70, 73, 155
individualism 1–2, 5, 7, 19, 31, 73–5, 77,
  79, 81–2, 89, 96, 111–12, 114–19,
  124–6, 143, 178–9, 182, 185–6, 190,
  192, 201, 204, 206, 210, 213–14

internationalism 90, 98–100, 107
Iraq War 4, 94
Ireland (Republic of) (*see* nation/country)
Ishiguro, Kazuo
  *Klara and the Sun* 19, 177–9, 183–93
  *Never Let Me Go* 179

Johnson, Boris 32, 157, 171

Kay, Jackie 89–92, 96–100, 106–7
  *The Adoption Papers* 98
  *Bantam* 99–100
  *Trumpet* 17–18, 90, 1017
kinship 77, 90, 97, 101–7, 132, 170
Kunzru, Hari 8

Labour Party 1–4, 17, 28, 89, 92–6, 155
Lacan, Jacques 137, 144, 148
Levinas, Emmanuel 14, 201–2, 214
liberalism 7, 27–8, 30, 41, 56, 89,
  92, 98, 134, 145, 155, 160,
  165–6, 182
Loick, Daniel 90, 97, 100–2, 105, 107
loneliness 5, 16, 25, 29–31, 33–4, 38–42,
  115, 122, 184–6, 193 n.3, 214

Magennis, Caroline 47, 51, 54–5, 57,
  61, 63 n.5
magic realism 16, 45–50, 53–5, 57–8, 60,
  62, 126
Malone, Patricia 48–50, 52
Marxism 1, 18, 31, 94, 98–100, 107, 120,
  127 n.4, 180
Massumi, Brian 181, 190
Mbue, Imbolo 15
McEwan, Ian 9, 112
McGill, Bernie 47, 55–8, 60, 62
McGrath, John 99
McGregor, Jon 19, 201–2
McIntyre, Alasdair 116
McLeod, John 97–8, 131
metamodernism 9, 13
migration 5, 8, 27, 29–30, 51–2, 68–70,
  75, 94–5, 121, 168–70
Mitchell, David 8
modernity/modernism 8, 10, 31, 37,
  113, 166, 169, 179–80, 185–6, 191
Modood, Tariq 18, 134, 149
Monbiot, George 115–16

Moss, Sarah
  *Ghost Wall* 33–4, 41, 172 n.6
  *Summerwater* 17, 70, 75, 78, 80–3
Mozley, Fiona 18, 112–13, 118, 120, 125,
  127 n.2
multiculturalism 3–5, 8, 17–18, 36, 54,
  75, 89–99, 101, 105–6, 120, 131–6,
  140, 143, 145, 149, 156, 162–4, 166,
  168–9, 171
Mundair, Raman 18, 132–3, 136, 147–9
Muñoz, José Esteban 104–5

Nancy, Jean-Luc 10, 12, 14, 67, 90, 96, 193
  n.2, 201–2, 209–10
  *Inoperative Community* 10, 81, 90,
  96, 101–2
nation/country
  Britain 5–6, 13, 16–17, 26–32, 46, 48,
    50, 52–3, 70, 89–92, 95, 107, 115,
    131–6, 140, 148–9, 155–72, 172
    nn.2, 6, 204
  England 6, 9, 16, 25–34, 40–1, 69–70,
    99, 138–9, 158, 163–6, 172 n.4
  Ireland (Republic of) 11, 46, 55, 62
    n.2, 63 n.3
  Northern Ireland 5–6, 16, 45–53, 55,
    60, 63 n.3, 80, 156, 158
  Scotland 5–6, 17, 67–71, 75–83, 99,
    101, 158
nationalism (*see* national community)
neoliberalism 2–5, 7, 13, 18, 29–30,
  38–9, 89–90, 92–3, 100, 106, 108
  nn.1, 2, 111–20, 124–5, 127 n.2, 133,
  170, 182
New Labour (*see* Labour Party)
new Scots 67–69, 75–6
nomadism 17, 67, 70, 76
Northern Ireland (*see* nation/country)
nostalgia 5, 8, 11, 15–16, 29, 33, 41–2, 68,
  71, 114, 132, 164, 166–9, 171, 205

O'Donnell, Róisín 47, 55, 58–62

Porter, Max 19, 199, 201–6, 209, 211–12,
  214–15, 217 n.1
postmodernism 10–11, 131, 134, 182
post-postmodernism 9–11
Powers, Richard 15
Preston, Alex 111, 184

Procter, James 131, 138
Prosser, Jay 105

queer politics 11, 17–18, 81, 90, 95, 97–8, 100–2, 104, 107

race (and racism) 2, 11, 28, 30, 33, 40, 54, 89, 95–8, 105–6, 132, 136, 182, 185, 189, 207
Rancière, Jacques 73, 77
Randhawa, Ravinder 18, 132–6, 142–3, 145–6, 149
realism 16, 49, 126, 212–13
Ricoeur, Paul 133
Robeson, Paul 100, 107
Rushdie, Salman 53

Salamon, Gayle 104–5
Scotland (*see* nation/country)
Sharpe, Christina 200, 207, 215
Silk, Michael 12, 156, 160, 162–4
Smith, Ali 9, 13–15, 173 n.7
Smith, Zadie 8, 18, 112, 132–4, 136, 140–1, 143, 145, 149
social media 6, 69, 185, 207
socialism 1, 100
Spivak, Gayatri Chakravorty 189
state-of-the-nation 41, 157
Summer Olympics 2012 19, 155–62, 164, 167–71, 173 n.7

Syal, Meera 18, 132–4, 136–9, 149

Tallack, Malachy 17, 67, 70–5, 77, 79, 81–2
Tempest, Kae 18, 111–12, 114–18, 121, 126, 127 n.3
Thatcherism 1–4, 8, 94, 113, 163, 167
*The Undercommons* (Moten and Harney) 208–11
totalitarianism 30, 33, 38
trans politics 17, 90, 101–5, 107
transglossic literature 9, 13, 19, 200, 213, 217
Trump, Donald 8, 13, 188
Turner, Victor 125

utopianism 67, 103, 105, 107, 168, 212

Valluvan, Sivamohan and Kalra, Virinder 5, 89, 91, 93
Van Gennep, Arnold 125
Varty, Anne 91, 97
Verhaeghe, Paul 116, 119

Williams, Raymond 25
World Trade Center 4

Yanagihara, Hanya 15
Yancy, George 180, 189
Yeats, William Butler 51, 54

www.ingramcontent.com/pod-product-compliance
Lightning Source LLC
Chambersburg PA
CBHW062216300426
44115CB00012BA/2095